BROTHERS MINOR: LANCASHIRE'S LOST FRANCISCANS
INVESTIGATIONS AT PRESTON FRIARY, 1991 AND 2007

Jeremy Bradley and Stephen Rowland

Contributions by
Enid Allison, Andrew Bates, Fiona Brock, Christopher Bronk Ramsey,
Gordon Cook, Mark Gibson, Christine Howard-Davis, Elizabeth Huckerby, Louise Loe,
Roişin McCarthy, Peter Marshall, Jennie Stopford, Ian Tyers, and Helen Webb

Illustrations by
Marie Rowland and Anne Stewardson

2020

Published by
Oxford Archaeology North
Mill 3
Moor Lane Mills
Moor Lane
Lancaster
LA1 1QD
(*Phone:* 01524 541000)
(*website:* http://thehumanjourney.net)

Distributed by
Oxbow Books Ltd
10 Hythe Bridge Street
Oxford
OX1 2EW
(*Phone:* 01865 241249; *Fax:* 01865 794449)

Printed by
Print2Demand, 17 Burgess Road, Hastings, East Sussex, TN35 4NR

ISBN 978-1-907686-35-1
ISSN 1345-5205

Series editor
Rachel Newman
Indexer
Marie Rowland
Design, layout, and formatting
Marie Rowland

Front cover: Preston, on Henry Teesdale's publication of Hennet's *Map of Lancashire* 1830 (with permission from Digital Archives Association); line illustration of Brunel Court tiles

Rear Cover: Excavating the north-west corner of the chapel (top); one of the medieval graves within the chapel (middle); the site facing south-east, with the external graves in the foreground and the chapel behind (bottom)

LANCASTER IMPRINTS   Lancaster Imprints is the publication series of Oxford Archaeology North. The series covers work on major excavations and surveys of all periods undertaken by the organisation and associated bodies.

Contents

List of Illustrations

Figures

Plates

Tables

Abbreviations

AMS	Accelerator Mass Spectrometry
CO	Cribra Orbitalia
CPR	Crude Prevalence Rate
f	Forma: intraspecific rank in plants below variety, the smallest taxonomic category
LA	Lancashire Archives
OA	Osteoarthritis
OS	Ordnance Survey
Perthes' disease	Legg-Calve-Perthes' disease
PRN	Primary Record Number within the Lancashire Historic Environment Record
SD	Spondylosis deformans
SN	Schmorl's nodes
TPR	True Prevalence Rate

Contributors

Enid Allison
Canterbury Archaeological Trust Ltd, 92A Broad Street, Canterbury CT1 2LU

Andrew Bates
formerly of Oxford Archaeology North

Jeremy Bradley
formerly of Oxford Archaeology North

Fiona Brock
formerly of Oxford Radiocarbon Accelerator Unit, Research Laboratory for Archaeology

Christopher Bronk-Ramsey
Oxford Radiocarbon Accelerator Unit, Research Laboratory for Archaeology, Dyson Perrins Building, South Parks Road, Oxford OX1 3QY

Gordon Cook
Scottish Universities Environmental Research Centre, Rankine Avenue, Scottish Enterprise Technology Park, East Kilbride G75 0QF

Mark Gibson
Oxford Archaeology South, Janus House, Osney Mead, Oxford OX2 0ES

Christine Howard-Davis
formerly of Oxford Archaeology North

Elizabeth Huckerby
formerly of Oxford Archaeology North

Louise Loe
Oxford Archaeology South, Janus House, Osney Mead, Oxford OX2 0ES

Roişin McCarthy
formerly of Oxford Archaeology South

Peter Marshall
Historic England Scientific Dating Coordinator, 4th Floor, Cannon Bridge House, 25 Dowgate Hill, London, EC4R 2YA

Stephen Rowland
Oxford Archaeology North, Mill 3, Moor Lane Mills, Moor Lane, Lancaster LA1 1QD

Jennie Stopford
55 Alma Terrace, York YO10 4DL

Ian Tyers
Dendrochronological Consultancy Ltd, Lowfield House, Smeath Lane, Clarborough, Retford DN22 9JN

Helen Webb
Oxford Archaeology South, Janus House, Osney Mead, Oxford OX2 0ES

Summary

Preston, the administrative centre of modern Lancashire, was one of the most important medieval boroughs in the north-west of England. Increasing prosperity during the nineteenth century, however, meant that most of its early heritage was lost to redevelopment and, to date, it has yielded little archaeological evidence of its medieval past. However, in 1991 and 2007, development-led excavations just to the north-west of the historic town centre revealed significant medieval remains. Although badly damaged by later development, these included the foundations of a substantial stone building with evidence for several internal features. Evidence from associated finds, including painted window glass and line-impressed floor tiles, suggested that it was ecclesiastical in origin. The western part of the building was the best preserved, and excavation showed it to have accommodated at least four rows of east/west-aligned burials; several more were identified immediately outside the building, and two groups of cut features further to the east and west are probably the remnants of other graves, hinting at an extensive cemetery to the north of the building.

Analysis, funded by English Heritage (now Historic England), has allowed these truncated and fragmentary remains to be identified as the last remnant of Preston's Franciscan friary, which was founded on the outskirts of Preston in *c* 1260, and remained in use until it was closed in 1539, during the Dissolution of the Monasteries by Henry VIII. If the building was part of the friary church, then it is likely that the burials are those of wealthy patrons, who had been interred in a side chapel or transept, appended to its north side. This work has also allowed other, less coherent, structural evidence, identified in 1991, to be interpreted as elements of the church, parts of the cloister or claustral ranges, or perhaps service buildings, lying to the south, thus permitting the full size of the friary precinct to be better understood.

The well-preserved nature of many of the burials provided an unusual opportunity for scientific analysis, including radiocarbon dating of the human remains, dendrochronological dating of the coffins, and osteological analysis of the skeletons. Drawn together, these individual strands provided a rich picture of the lives and appearance of the friars and their patron families, throughout the life of the Friary.

Although no physical remains could be associated with the south range, cartographic and documentary evidence strongly suggest that, after the dissolution of the Friary, parts of it remained in use, first as a private house belonging to the Breres family, later (from *c* 1680 to 1789) used as a 'house of correction'. Much altered, it survived into the mid-nineteenth century, serving finally as part of the Canal Foundry, before being demolished, when its site was effectively lost.

Résumé

Preston, l'actuel centre administratif de la région du Lancashire moderne, était l'une des villes la plus importante du nord-ouest de l'Angleterre à l'époque médiévale. La prospérité croissante au XIXème siècle eut toutefois pour conséquence la perte de la majeure partie de son patrimoine primitif au profit du réaménagement et, à ce jour, elle n'a apporté que peu de preuves archéologiques de son passé médiéval. Cependant, en 1991 et 2007, des fouilles menées lors de l'aménagement d'une aire située juste au nord-ouest du centre-ville historique, ont révélé d'importants vestiges médiévaux. Bien que gravement endommagés par les développements ultérieurs, ceux-ci comprenaient les fondations d'un important bâtiment en pierre ainsi que plusieurs éléments de décoration internes distincts. Ces éléments décoratifs proviennent de découvertes associées, comprenant des vitraux et des carreaux de sol imprimés, provenant probablement d'un bâtiment ecclésiastique. La partie ouest du bâtiment était la mieux conservée et les fouilles ont montré qu'elle avait hébergé au moins quatre rangées de sépultures alignées est / ouest ; plusieurs autres ont été identifiés immédiatement à l'extérieur du bâtiment, et deux groupes de vestiges archéologiques creusés en profondeur plus à l'est et à l'ouest sont vraisemblablement les restes de sépultures, suggérant un vaste cimetière au nord du bâtiment.

L'étude, financée par English Heritage (actuelle Historic England), a permis à ces restes tronqués et fragmentaires d'être identifiés comme le dernier vestige du couvent franciscain de Preston. Le couvent a été fondé à la périphérie de Preston en 1260, et est resté en usage jusqu'à ce qu'il soit fermé en 1539, lors de la dissolution des monastères par Henri VIII. Si le bâtiment faisait partie de l'église du couvent, il est probable que les sépultures soient celles de riches patrons, qui avaient été enterrés dans une chapelle latérale ou un transept, annexé à son côté nord. Ces travaux ont également permis d'interpréter d'autres éléments structurels moins cohérents, identifiés en 1991, comme des éléments de l'église, des parties du cloître ou des rangées claustrales, ou peut-être des bâtiments de service, situés au sud, ce qui permet de mieux comprendre le quartier du couvent.

La bonne conservation de bon nombre des sépultures a fourni une opportunité inhabituelle pour l'analyse scientifique, notamment la datation au radiocarbone des restes humains, la datation dendrochronologique des cercueils et l'analyse ostéologique des squelettes. L'ensemble de ces différents résultats ont fourni une image riche du quotidien et de l'apparence des moines, ainsi que de leurs familles patronnesses, au sein de la vie du couvent.

Malgré qu'aucun vestige physique ne puisse être associé à la partie sud, des preuves cartographiques et des preuves documentaires suggèrent fortement que, après la dissolution du couvent, certaines parties de celui-ci sont restées en usage, d'abord comme maison privée appartenant à la famille Breres, puis, plus tard (de 1666 à 1789) utilisée comme une «maison de correction». Bien qu'ayant subi d'importantes altérations, elle a néanmoins survécu jusqu'au milieu du XIXème siècle, devenant finalement partie intégrante de la fonderie du Canal, avant d'être démolie, lorsque son site a été effectivement abandonné.

Zusammenfassung

Die Stadt Preston, die heute der Verwaltungssitz der modernen Grafschaft Lancashire ist, war im Mittelalter eine der wichtigsten Stadtgemeinden in Nordwestengland. Im Verlaufe des 19. Jahrhunderts und mit zunehmendem industriellen Wohlstand verlor die Stadt jedoch fast all ihr mittelalterliches Erbe durch rigorosen Um- oder Neubau. Das führte letzendlich dazu, dass es bisher kaum archäologische Funde aus Prestons mittelalterlicher Stadtgeschichte gab. Das änderte sich mit den kommerziell durchgeführten Grabungsarbeiten in den Jahren 1991 und 2007, die wichtige Hinweise auf Prestons mittelalterlichen Stadtkern zu Tage brachten. Obwohl die architektonischen Überreste durch spätere Neubauten stark beschädigt worden waren, konnten die Archäologen die Fundamente eines beträchtlichen Steingebäudes nachweisen, welches außerdem Hinweise auf interne Mauern und andere Baumerkmale aufzeigte. Unter seinen Kleinfunden befanden sich Buntglasscherben und ornamentierte mittelalterliche Bodenfliesen, die auf eine kirchliche Nutzung des Gebäudes hinwiesen. Der westliche Teil des Gebäudes war am besten erhalten und die Grabungen ergaben, dass dieser Teil mindestens vier Reihen von Ost-West ausgerichteten Gräbern enthielt; weitere Gräber konnten direkt auf der anderen, der Aussen-, Seite des Gebäudes nachgewiesen werden. Zwei Gruppen von sehr tiefliegenden Schnitten östlich und westlich waren wahrscheinlich Überreste weiterer Gräber, welche auf das Vorhandensein eines ausgedehnten Friedhofes nördlich des Gebäudes deuteten.

Durch eine Analyse, die durch English Heritage (heute Historic England) gefördert wurde, konnten die Steinfundamente und diese durch moderne Bauarbeiten gestörten Befunde als die letzten Überreste von Prestons Franziskaner-Kloster identifiziert werden, welches in einem Außenbezirk Prestons in den Jahren um AD1260 gegründet und bis zu seiner Schliessung AD1539 im Rahmen der Klosterauflösungen unter Heinrich VIII von Mönchen bewohnt und genutzt worden war. Falls die gegrabenen Fundamente Teil der Klosterkirche waren, dann ist es sehr wahrscheinlich dass es sich bei den Gräbern im Inneren um diejenigen reicher Schirmherren und Geldspender handelte, welche in einer der sich an der Nordseite anschließenden Seitenkapelle oder dem Transept beerdigt worden waren. Die modernen Untersuchen haben bei der Identifizierung und Deutung der Funde von 1991 enorm geholfen, und erlauben uns heute, die Fundamente als Teil der Kirche, des Kreuzgangs, des Claustrums, oder aber als Gebäude der Bediensteten zu verstehen, da sie südlich des Hauptgebäudes lagen. Durch die Analysen kann nun die Größe und Ausrichtung der gesamten Klosteranlage besser verstanden werden.

Viele der Bestattungen waren sehr gut erhalten und boten die seltene Gelegenheit, weitere wissenschaftliche Untersuchung durchzuführen, unter anderem die C14 Datierung der menschlichen Überreste, dendrochronologische Untersuchungen der Särge und Knochenanalysen der Skelette. Zusammengenommen ergaben all diese Analysen ein ungewöhnlich klares Bild vom Leben und Aussehen sowohl der hier lebenden Mönche als auch der Familien ihrer Gönner und Schutzherren durch die Jahrhunderte hinweg, in denen das Kloster Bestand hatte.

Obwohl keine Bauelemente der südlichen Klosteranlage geborgen werden konnten, wissen wir aus mittelalterlichen Urkunden und Landkarten, dass nach der Auflösung des Klosters ein Teil der Anlage weiterbenutzt wurde, erst als Privathaus der Familie Breres und später (von AD1680-1789) als „Bewährungshaus" (engl. „House of Correction", nach den Armutgesetzen Elizabeths I von AD1601). Obwohl durch viele Umbauten verändert, überlebte das Gebäude bis in die Mitte des 19. Jahrhunderts, als letztes als Gießerei am Kanal („Canal Foundry" auf alten Karten), bevor es vollkommen demoliert wurde und die restlichen Überbleibsel der Klosterfundamente dem Erdboden gleichgemacht wurden.

Acknowledgements

Many people contributed to the project, which was undertaken in three distinct stages. The first, the evaluation and watching brief undertaken in 1991 in association with the construction of the A59 Ringway, was undertaken by Patrick Tostevin, Deirdre Winstanley, and Peter Iles, all formerly of the Lancaster University Archaeological Unit (now Oxford Archaeology (OA) North). Those works were funded by Lancashire County Council.

The watching brief and subsequent rescue excavation, carried out by OA North at Brunel Court in 2007, was undertaken on behalf of BPS Developments, and particular gratitude is offered to Eric and David Mahoney. The excavation was directed by Richard Lee, with assistance from Alexander Beben, Caroline Bulcock, Vickie Bullock, Steve Clarke, Pascal Eloy, Joanne Hawkins, Pip Haworth, and Caroline Raynor.

Not only did Doug Moir and Peter Iles, both of Lancashire County Archaeological Service, provide monitoring and vital support during the fieldwork at Brunel Court, but they were instrumental in gaining the involvement of English Heritage (now Historic England). Doug Moir also very kindly organised liaison with members of the Franciscan Order, and special gratitude is owed to Father James McCurry for his assistance, and to Father Michael Robson, for his valuable information concerning his doctoral research on the history of the Franciscan Order in England.

Elements of the post-excavation programme of assessment and analysis were undertaken by Kathryn Blythe, Sandra Bonsall, Tim Christian, Joanne Levey, and Christina Robinson. The project was managed by Stephen Rowland, and quality assured by Rachel Newman, who also managed the 1991 excavations. The post-excavation programme, from the compilation of a project design, through assessment and analysis, to the production of this publication, has been generously funded by Historic England. Mark Bowden, Kath Buxton, and Barney Sloane are thanked for their work in the initiation of the project, and particularly Helen Keeley, Project Assurance Officer, who monitored the project throughout this work. The summary was translated into French by OA East's Séverine Bézie. The German translation was by Dr Dot Boughton.

Extracts from the maps of Kuerden (Fig 5), Lang and Porter (Figs 2, 30), Lieutenant-General Carpenter and Major-General Wills (Fig 6), Shakeshaft, Baines, Myers (Fig 7), and the Ordnance Survey maps of 1849 (Figs 7, 34), and 1893 (Fig 4) were accessed from, and are used with the permission of, Lancashire Archives, Preston. Neil Spurr, of Digital Archives Association (https://digitalarchives.co.uk), kindly gave us permission to use an extract of Henry Teesdale's publication of Hennet's *Map of Lancashire* 1830 for the cover image. Bill Shannon kindly provided the extract from the Buck Brothers' *Southern Prospect of Preston* (Pl 2), and Plate 15 was reproduced from Fishwick's *The History of the Parish of Preston in Amounderness in the County of Lancashire* (1900).

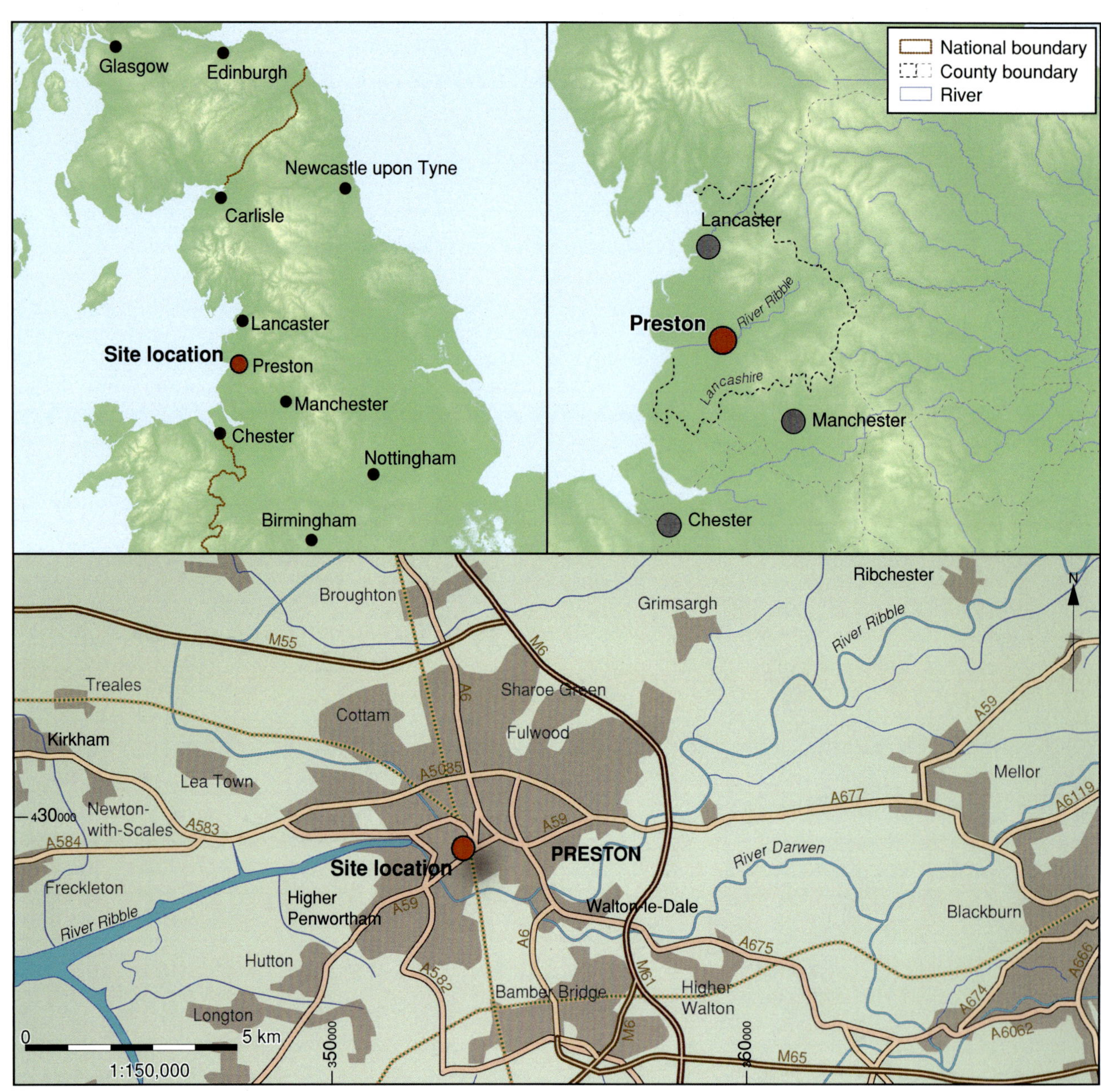

Figure 1: The location of the excavations (Contains OS data © Crown copyright and database right (2017))

1

INTRODUCTION

Development in Preston in 1991 and 2007 provided a rare opportunity to investigate part of the medieval town that hitherto had not been subject to any substantial archaeological investigation. Both projects offered an opportunity to examine the putative site of Preston's Franciscan friary, the last vestiges of which had been destroyed in the nineteenth century, in the course of the construction of the Lancaster Canal and later railway. Both interventions were prompted by development: in 1991 by the creation of the A59 Ringway (Tostevin and Iles 1992), and in 2007 by the erection of an hotel, in what is now Brunel Court.

Location

Preston, a medieval town, and a city since 2002, has long been one of the most important settlements in Lancashire, and is now the administrative centre of the modern county (Fig 1). Its historic centre overlooks the north bank of the River Ribble, which, rising at Ribblehead in North Yorkshire, flows into the Irish Sea at Lytham, some 12 miles (19.3 km) to the west of Preston. The city stands within one of the river's lowest meanders, being, together with Penwortham on the south bank, at the lowest bridging point on the natural main communication corridor along the western edge of the Pennines (Clemesha 1912, 1-2; Lancashire County Council (LCC) and Egerton Lea 2006). These two settlements lie close to the upper limit of tidal influence, and, immediately to their west, the Ribble estuary opens out, separating the coastal wetlands of south-west Lancashire from those of the Fylde, to the north (Middleton *et al* 2013; 1995).

Most of the lower Ribble Valley lies on Permian and Triassic sandstone (Old and New Red Sandstone; British Geological Survey (BGS) 1979; 2008), overlain by boulder clays and glacial moraine, and masked, in the Ribble Valley, by alluvium. Preston itself occupies a low plateau of glacial sand and gravel (Clemesha 1912; Lawes Agricultural Trust 1983). The city is now within a generally mixed agricultural landscape, with the fertile Lancashire Plain to the north, stretching *c* 20 miles (32.2 km), as far as Lancaster. The Fylde, to the north-west of Preston, is today a low-lying, and generally flat, agricultural landscape, although as late as the eighteenth century it was largely wetland (Middleton *et al* 1995). Small-scale drainage of the area had begun in the Middle Ages, growing considerably in scope from the eighteenth century onwards, and ultimately the Fylde peatlands became some of the better arable land in the region (Cunliffe Shaw 1956, 296) or served as rich pasture.

The putative site of Preston's Franciscan friary (centred on NGR SD 5310 2990) forms a discrete area within the town (Pl 1), bounded to the east and west by Ladywell Street and the railway respectively, to the south by the

Plate 1: Aerial view of modern Preston, with Fishergate/Church Street and Friargate (in white), Marsh Lane and Ladywell Street (in blue), and the excavation area (in orange) highlighted (Imagery © 2017 Google; Map data © 2017 Google)

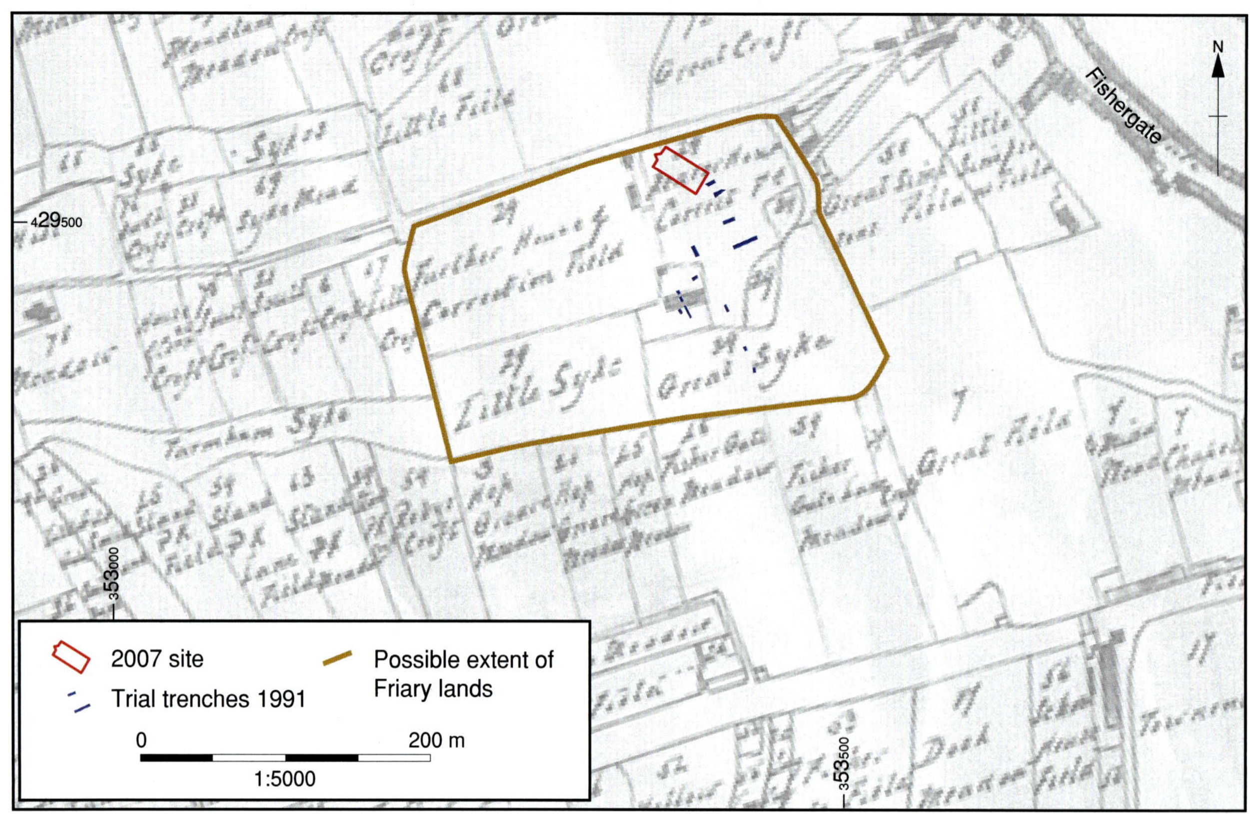

Figure 2: Lang and Porter's map of Preston, 1774, with the excavation areas superimposed

A59 Ringway, and the north by Marsh Lane, the latter being the only thoroughfare of proven antiquity. Although it occupies a central location within the modern city, prior to the nineteenth century it lay well away from the principal medieval streets of Fishergate, Church Street, and Friargate (*p 7*), in a semi-rural situation. Map regression places the investigations mainly within the area of *Nearer House of Correction Field*, and of the House of Correction itself, as depicted on Lang and Porter's map of 1774 (Fig 2).

The 1991 Evaluation

The 1991 project was carried out in advance of the construction of the A59 Ringway (the Penwortham Bypass; LUAU 1991a; 1991b; Tostevin and Iles 1992). A major urban infrastructure project, the new road cut a swathe from Marsh Lane to Corporation Street and beyond, passing beneath the main railway line and demolishing Cable Street, Barracks Street, and the Dock Street railway sidings, whilst skirting what is now Brunel Court to the north-west (Fig 3). The archaeological work comprised small-scale evaluation (12 machine-cut trenches in total) in advance of the groundworks, followed by an intermittent watching brief (undertaken on three separate days over the course of the summer) as these progressed.

The archaeological evaluation was carried out in two phases. The first (Trenches 1-8) focused on the site of the friary as shown on the 1849 Ordnance Survey (OS) map (an area now buried by the southern lane of the Ringway), some railway sidings, and a landscaped slope between the two. The second (Trenches 9-12) examined the proposed northern easement of the upgraded A59, which was roughly midway between Ladywell Street and the former line of Barracks Street, an area that now falls within Brunel Court, and is just to the south-east of the area investigated in 2007. All the machine-cut trenches were between 2 m and 3.5 m deep, and were excavated through deep post-medieval horizons. In some trenches, however, a possible medieval horizon and a wall were identified, some 1.25 m beneath the ground surface.

The three occasions when a watching brief was undertaken during construction of the bypass, being somewhat restricted in nature, provided little extra information. Two visits were made to a site '…located in the vicinity of Marsh Lane and Barracks Street, immediately opposite Ladywell House and Ladywell Street' (LUAU 1991b, 6). The first recorded near-completed earthworks associated with a 6 m-wide easement (between 0.5 m and 2 m deep) and a central drainage trench (up to 2 m deep), which together ran the length of the centre of the Ringway. Recording was significantly impeded by the depth of the excavations, which were either dangerously unstable, or had been box-shored by the developer, obscuring the trench sections. The second visit was approximately eight weeks later,

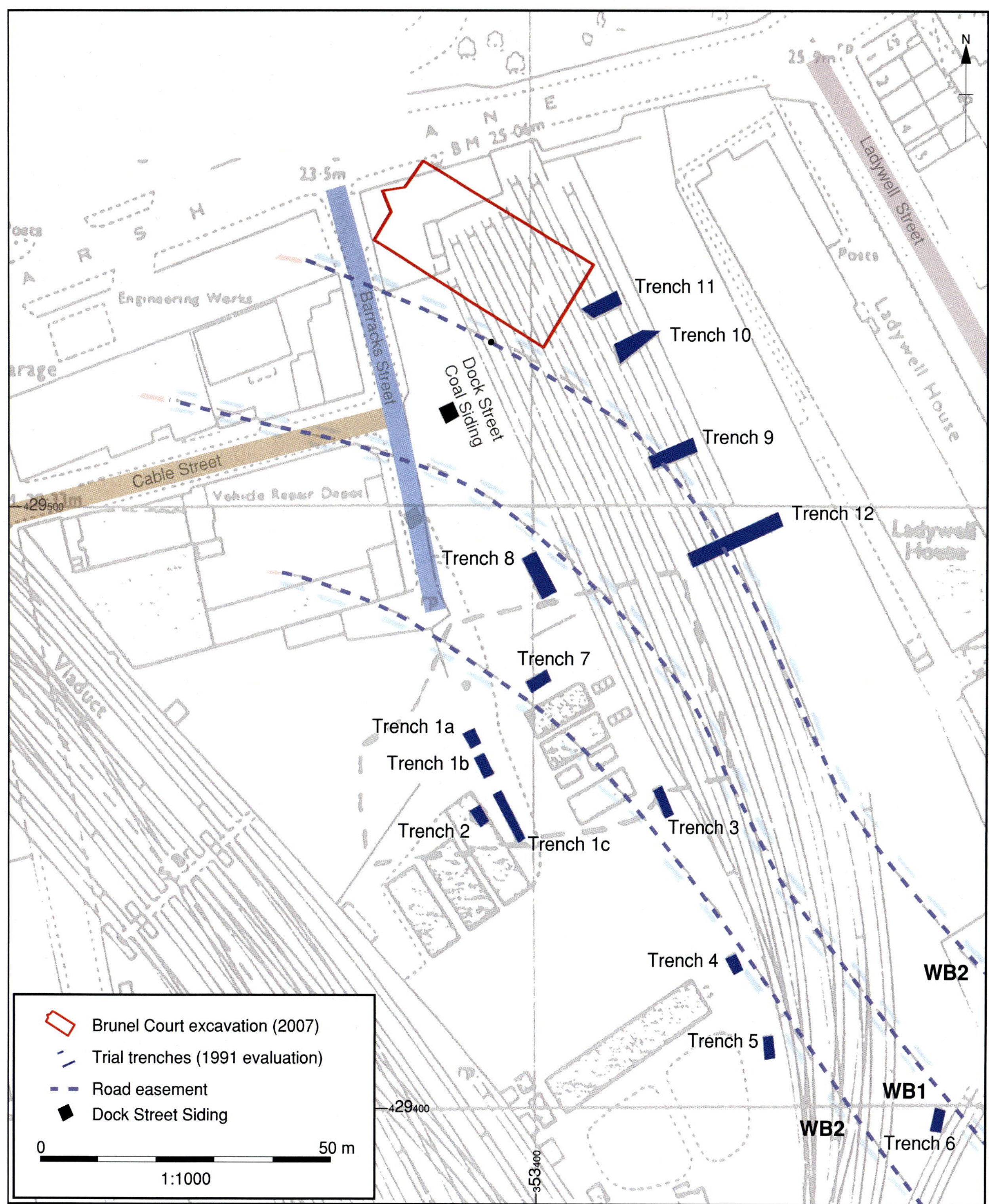

Figure 3: The positions of the 1991 and 2007 archaeological works, superimposed on the 1983 Ordnance Survey map

after a considerable amount of landscaping had been undertaken. Little was visible, with the exception of a cutting in the area formerly occupied by Barracks Street. Extensive made-ground deposits were encountered there and, whilst these sealed a cobbled surface, this in turn sealed a layer containing bricks and other demolition debris. A third visit, some four weeks later, was made after the majority of works were completed.

The 2007 Excavation

No further archaeological work was undertaken in the area until 2007, when groundworks for the basement of an hotel at Brunel Court, on the Marsh Lane street frontage (Fig 4), were monitored. In the course of these

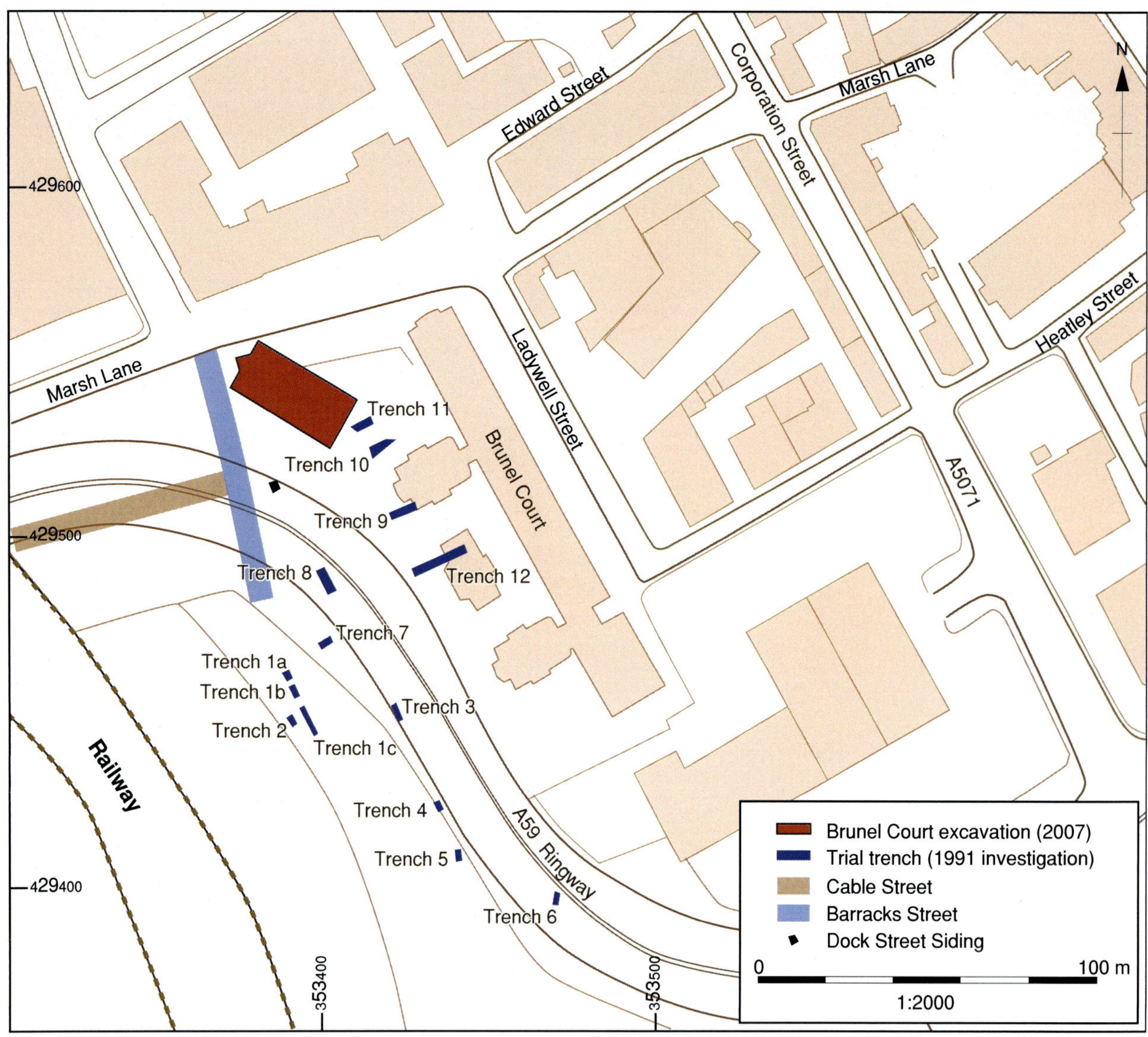

Figure 4: The Ladywell area of Preston, showing the position of the archaeological works of 1991 and 2007

works, the ground level was reduced substantially, to provide a basement and secure footings for the new structures. As a result, late, undifferentiated, deposits were removed by machine to a depth of *c* 2 m across a roughly rectangular area, 41 m north-west/south-east by 17 m north-east/south-west. After manual cleaning, natural geological deposits were identified some 2.2 m below the modern ground level, and although they had been peppered with clusters of concrete piles, deeply buried, but highly truncated, archaeological remains were also revealed, comprising rectilinear stone structures, numerous graves, and a ditch. In addition, wooden objects, such as coffins and stakes, had been preserved by the anaerobic conditions. These features, being recognised as archaeologically significant, were excavated by hand, and recorded in detail, over the course of three weeks in March 2007, and a programme of palaeoenvironmental sampling was initiated.

It was soon apparent that many of the remains encountered were of medieval date, and that the most significant were of ecclesiastical origin. Controlled archaeological investigation of such deposits is rare in the North West, especially in an urban context (Newman and Newman 2007, 105), and effectively unique in Preston. Due to the circumstances, and significance, of the discovery, and through the facilitation of the Lancashire County Archaeology Service, English Heritage (now Historic England) funded the programme of archive completion, post-excavation assessment, analysis, and publication (OA North 2007; 2008; 2010; 2011).

Post-excavation Programme

The post-excavation programme followed English Heritage (now Historic England) guidelines (English Heritage 1991; Historic England 2015a). Given the significance of the discoveries made in 2007, the subsequent analysis was also undertaken with due consideration of national and regional research frameworks, and the agenda laid out in these (English Heritage 2003; 2005; Hinton 1987; Greene 1992; Medieval Pottery Research Group 1994; Newman 2006; Newman and Newman 2007; McNeil and Newman 2006; Newman and McNeil 2007). These all stress the importance of multi-disciplinary approaches to the study of medieval religious houses, particularly in urban contexts, and their communities, and these informed the programme of post-excavation analysis developed for the project.

The predominantly funerary character of much of the evidence recovered in 2007 was regarded as highly significant: in the North West, such osteological remains are generally badly preserved and as a result poorly understood. It was also considered important to view any monastic site within its religious and socio-economic context, especially in terms of relationships with the urban hinterland and its population. Thus, not only did the investigation seek to examine aspects of the demography, palaeoepidemiology, and palaeopathology through the study of the skeletal remains, but also to integrate those data with other information, such as the mode and locus of burial, to look at the socio-economic status, living environment, occupations, and lifestyles of those excavated.

Data obtained from the 2007 excavations are significantly more coherent than those from the more limited works undertaken in 1991. Accordingly, the results of the former provide a framework into which the earlier findings have been placed, thereby allowing scope for confirmation, or reinterpretation, of some of the earlier conclusions (Tostevin and Iles 1992).

Dating Programme

The highly disturbed nature of the site meant that little reliable dating was available from items of material culture, for instance pottery and floor tile. However, the unusually good levels of preservation of organic materials, principally wood and human bone, enabled the development of a programme of scientific dating, utilising both dendrochronology (tree-ring dating) and radiocarbon dating. Within the tables, the radiocarbon results are presented as conventional radiocarbon ages (Stuiver and Polach 1977), and are quoted in accordance with the international standard known as the Trondheim convention (Stuiver and Kra 1986). The results of these programmes of work were further enhanced using Bayesian chronological modelling. This provides a probabilistic method for combining different sorts of evidence (such as radiocarbon and tree-ring dates, archaeological stratigraphy, *etc*) to estimate the dates of events that happened in the past, and for quantifying the uncertainties of these estimates. The results are known as posterial density outputs (*Ch 4*). These probability distributions can be expressed as ranges and are shown in italics to distinguish them clearly from date estimates that have not been produced by modelling.

Structure of the Report

This report merges and synthesises the analyses of the archaeological data from the 1991 and 2007 interventions, although, inevitably, it is dominated by the evidence from 2007, and focuses on the building, and its associated burials, found then. *Chapter 1* serves not only to introduce the project, but also presents an outline account of the general development of Preston from the post-Roman period to the nineteenth century, providing a socio-political context for the Franciscan foundation whilst in use, and for the post-dissolution survival and later uses of the friary buildings, until their demolition and effective loss in the nineteenth century. *Chapter 2* presents a narrative interpretation of the structural evidence, and *Chapter 3* reports on the skeletal assemblage, whilst *Chapter 4* details the material culture, environmental evidence, and various forms of dating. The volume culminates with an interpretative synthesis of the evidence (*Ch 5*).

Project Archive

The project archive includes all the data and appropriate material (excluding human bone and unconserved wood) gathered during the course of the 1991 evaluation and the 2007 excavation. The human remains have been reburied and the completed archive deposited with the Harris Museum, Preston.

Archaeological and Historical Context

Although there are numerous prehistoric (particularly Bronze Age) sites and artefact findspots associated with the course of the Ribble in and around Preston (LCC and Egerton Lea 2006), there is little evidence that the area of the modern city formed a particular focus for prehistoric activity, or that their presence had any particular influence on the development of the town. Similarly, although there was a significant Roman presence at Walton-le-Dale, on the south bank of the river, marking an important bridging point (Gibbons *et al* in prep), there is little to suggest a Roman origin for Preston itself. It is possible, however, that elements of the Roman road network, namely King Street (Margary 1957, 100; road 70c/70d), linking Wigan and Lancaster, and road 703 (*op cit*, 106), on the north side of the Ribble, linking Kirkham to Ribchester, and eastwards to a Pennine crossing, may well have had some indirect influence on the early development of the town.

Archaeological remains from the early medieval period (*c* 410-*c* 1066), particularly any relating to the five centuries following the end of Roman administration, are extremely rare in Lancashire. The few extant contemporary documents provide a veneer of political history, indicating that, during the seventh century, the region came within the Anglian kingdom of Northumbria, but almost nothing is known of secular settlement (Newman 1996, 93). Whilst several sites along the river Lune, to the north, have produced ecclesiastical sculpture dated to the eighth to eleventh centuries (Bailey 2010), in the Ribble Valley only Whalley has produced similar evidence, although a putative early Anglo-Saxon burial site has been suggested at Ribchester (*op cit*, 102; Kenyon 1991, 80).

The complexity of the situation and the linguistic, perhaps ethnic, diversity of the region is indicated by place-names that variously contain British, Old English, or Scandinavian elements, sometimes in combination (Ekwall 1922, 146; Kenyon 1991; Higham 2004, 32-4). As a result, even where early medieval dispersed settlement has been identified in the Ribble Valley, for instance the probable ninth-century farmstead at Ribblehead in North Yorkshire, the identity of the inhabitants remains hard to define (Batey 1995, 71-6).

The internationally significant Cuerdale hoard, a huge collection of silver coins, ingots, jewellery, and hacksilver, was found near Walton-le-Dale in 1840 (Graham-Campbell 2011). Individual items originate from across Europe and Asia, and demonstrate that it was deposited some time around 905 (Archibald 1992, 20; Kershaw 2014), being interpreted as a political payment, or perhaps the war chest of a Viking army seeking to reassert dominance over the area around the Irish Sea after their expulsion from Dublin in 902. From the amount of freshly minted coins in the hoard, the depositors seemingly relied upon considerable financial support from the Kingdom of York, within which Lancashire seems to have been incorporated from the later ninth century (Graham-Campbell 1992, 107; Newman 1996, 103; Higham 2004, 34).

It has been suggested that a *burh* was established at Penwortham by Edward the Elder, the first king of Wessex to be titled King of the English, in *c* 920 (Higham 2004). The Ribble would then have marked the border between his expanding kingdom to the south, and the Viking-controlled lands to the north, once parts of the former Anglian kingdom of Northumbria (Kenyon 1991). Less than a decade later, Edward's son and successor, Aethelstan, had reasserted English hegemony as far north as the River Eamont and Stainmore (in Cumbria) or even beyond (Swanton 2000). Actual evidence of the putative *burh* has proved elusive, but it is clear that some form of settlement had been established before the Norman Conquest in 1066, at both Preston and Penwortham (Newman 1996, 97). Thus it seems that the Ribble Valley remained important, as both a communication route to eastern England, via the Pennines, and, at times, as a boundary between territories, until and beyond the Norman Conquest (Higham 1992, 21; 2004, 32).

Preston itself (the name meaning Priest's homestead; Clemesha 1912) is first mentioned in 1086, listed in the Domesday Book as *Prestune*, and it would appear to have been the principal manor of Amounderness (Faull and Stinson 1986). Often referred to, in later post-Conquest sources, as a hundred (an administrative sub-division of a county in early medieval England; Higham 2004, 36), the name Amounderness is of Scandinavian origin, incorporating a personal name, *Agmundrholdr*, and 'ness', meaning headland (Ekwall 1922, 139). The first reliable record of the name is in 934, when the territory was granted to the Archbishop of York by King Aethelstan. Historically, it lay between the rivers Cocker and Ribble, to the north and south, and extended westward from the Bowland Fells on the western flank of the Pennines, to the Irish Sea (Cunliffe Shaw 1956, 7-8). Between 1055 and 1065, Amounderness was held by Tosti Godwinson, brother of the last Anglo-Saxon king, Harold II, as part of the Earldom of Northumbria (Walker 1997, 105-13). In 1086, the area north of the Ribble fell within the Diocese of York, and the county of Yorkshire (Faull and Stinson 1986; Higham 2004, 36), that to the south forming part of the nascent county of Cheshire.

The manor of Preston was therefore clearly extant from at least the eleventh century, if not before. Indeed, some have suggested that it originated as early as the seventh century (Hunt 2009, 12-13), Preston's patron saint being Wilfrid, a seventh-century Northumbrian abbot of Ripon, and subsequently Bishop of York. The town's church, standing on Church Street, was dedicated to him by 1094 (Williams and Martin 2002, 795-6), although now its dedication is to St John (LCC and Egerton Lea 2006). Wilfrid's early eighth-century hagiography, the *Vita Wilfridi*, records that, in *c* 670, some land next to the Ribble was among several *Regiones* given to the church (and perhaps, to Wilfrid himself; Charles-Edwards 2013, 405), perhaps providing the impetus for the foundation of the settlement (Hunt 2009, 13).

Given the vagueness of the location, however, this interpretation of the passage is not universally accepted.

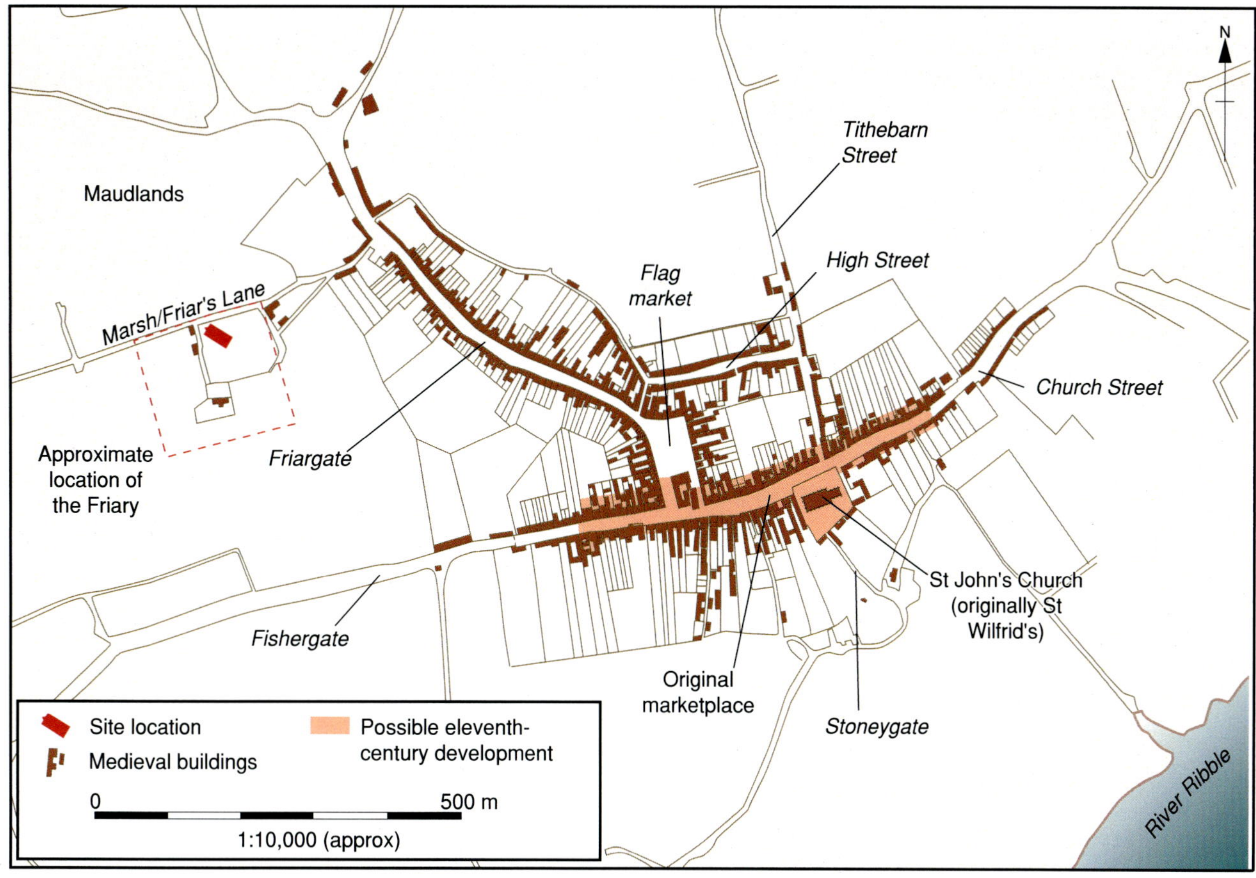

Figure 5: Kuerden's map of Preston c 1680, with possible eleventh-century development highlighted

Indeed, it could imply that the land granted to Bishop Wilfrid already contained churches, from which heretical British clergymen had been chased with 'the sharp edge of a hostile sword' (Colgrave 1927, 114). The weapons were presumably wielded by adherents of the Roman church, whose beliefs, through the representation of Wilfrid, had won the favour of King Oswy of Northumbria at the Synod of Whitby in 664 (Colgrave and Mynors 1969). Were this the case, Preston could already have been the central *villa* or *tun* of an estate, collecting renders and services from a wider group of settlements (Charles-Edwards 2013, 405-6).

Following the Norman Conquest, the settlement had developed along the east/west axis formed by the still-extant Church Street and Fishergate, and around its crossroads with Friargate (Millward 1955, 71; Fig 5). These streets occupy the ridge that forms the spine of the modern city. Irrespective of the foundation date, the church seems to have stood at the heart of the earliest settlement, straddling Stoneygate, the road which may originally have led to the Ribble crossing at Walton-le-Dale (Hunt 2009, 19-20).

The post-Conquest borough

After the Norman Conquest, Domesday Book records that Preston was one of the many holdings granted by William I to Roger de Poitou, a Norman knight

and key supporter of the king. It appears that none of Preston's 61 townships generated sufficient revenue to be worth mentioning by the Domesday assessors (Williams and Martin 2002, 795-6; Clemesha 1912, 8), and only 16 were populated, albeit rather sparsely, the rest being described as 'waste' (*ibid*). Whilst William I's 'Harrying of the North' in 1069/70 is perhaps the most likely explanation for this desolation, it is possible that the area had not recovered from Norse raids in 1058 (Walker 1997, 104). Alternatively, it is possible that the limited record for the region simply indicates that the area had not been fully integrated into Yorkshire's administrative system (Edmonds 2009, 8) and that the assessors had made use of earlier information rather than making a full visitation in 1086 (R M Newman *pers comm*).

Reference to the borough, or, rather, more accurately, the burgesses, of Preston, is first made in 1179 (Farrer and Brownbill 1912), but the town clearly enjoyed borough status before that date. From a legal perspective, boroughs were settlements which had been granted special privileges, the nature of which varied from place to place, but which allowed the burgesses (those inhabitants who had paid to occupy a plot of land within the town) greater corporate autonomy and a less onerous relationship with their lord (Beresford 1967). In return, the lord hoped to gain financially from the increased economic activity encouraged within the borough. The characteristics were a settlement that was populous, that counted tradesmen and those involved in industries amongst its inhabitants, and had a market and a court; moreover, the inhabitants held their tenements (building plots and associated land) in free burgage, and were thus able to buy, sell, or exchange those plots as and when they saw fit (Platt 1979, 151). It has been suggested that Roger de Poitou, influenced by the creation of boroughs in his family's French holdings, may have granted such rights (referred to as the *Ordinances of Breteuil*) to Preston soon after he acquired it in the eleventh century (Clemesha 1912, 10). Such an early date would, however, be unusual, as most documented borough charters date to the later twelfth and early thirteenth centuries (Beresford 1967).

Following the death of William I in 1087, Roger de Poitou supported his successor, William II ('Rufus'), whose reign was beset by intrigue, rebellion, and internecine conflicts with his brothers and his barons (Cassady 1986; Barlow 1999). William sought to expand his kingdom into the lands north of Lancaster, and captured Carlisle in 1092 (Swanton 2000), when Roger's loyalty was rewarded with widespread grants of land, much of which lay in the historic county of Lancashire, a tract that became known as the Honour of Lancaster. William II died in 1100, and as soon as 1102, Roger had fallen from favour with the new king, Henry I, losing his position and his English lands (Clemesha 1912, 11), possibly because he had supported the claims of William the Conqueror's eldest son, Robert Curthose, Duke of Normandy, as William II's successor, over those of Henry (Greenwood and Bolton 1955, 8; Barlow 1999, 140).

Roger was exiled to France, but his loss was essentially Preston's gain, as the Honour of Lancaster, including Preston, passed into hands that were, at various times, royal, or at the very least, those of powerful magnates. In 1179, Henry II granted (or rather, sold) a Royal charter to the town. It cost the burgesses a collective sum of 100 marks (*c* £67) but, henceforth, they were allowed to trade toll-free across the country, to regulate their own trade affairs, and to retain many of the fines levied in their own courts (Clemesha 1912; Hunt 2009, 22). More Royal charters were granted by John (1199), Henry III (1227), and Edward III (1328 and 1352), permitting further rights, including allowing the burgesses to hold fairs to encourage trade from yet further afield (*ibid*). With such support, Preston became the region's dominant urban centre by the thirteenth century (White 1996, 129).

The appearance and character of the medieval town was as much a reflection of its socio-economic role as it was an artefact of its geography. At that time, the medieval thoroughfares of Fishergate and Churchgate (Old Norse *–gate*, now anglicised to Church Street) still formed the principal east/west axis of the town (Fig 5). The parish church, on the south side of Church Street, straddled the crossroads, the southern arm of which comprised Stoneygate, and, to the north, St John's Lane (now Tithebarn Street). The medieval market, so important to the town's economic success, may originally have been held just to the west of the church, where Kuerden (*c* 1685; regressed by Conzen 1968) depicts the street as being notably wide (Conzen 1968; Hunt 2009). Lying at right-angles to the main streets were long narrow burgage plots, a minimum of 12 feet (3.6 m) wide at the street frontage (Hunt 2009, 25), where they were occupied by houses and other buildings. These plots, so characteristic of medieval settlements, were traditionally used for a wide range of activities, including horticulture and small-scale animal husbandry, as well as a variety of industries and crafts. Preston's commercial and physical expansion led to the development of several new streets, the most substantial of which is now known as Friargate, tracing a somewhat sinuous north-westerly route from Fishergate. The junction of these streets with Churchgate became the Flag Market (Hunt 2009, 20-1).

The burgesses were not restricted to practising agriculture on their own property, but also had rights to plant and graze the fields that surrounded the town. Although Lang and Porter's map of 1774 (Fig 2) depicts the fields around Preston after they had been enclosed, the extent of the original medieval fields can be seen by the large number of boundaries that preserve the aratral (S-shaped) earthworks created by ploughs pulled by slow-turning oxen (Eyre 1955). Particularly on the west side of town, many of the fields shown by Lang and Porter are broken into blocks by narrow, sinuous fields on an east/west alignment. Many of these are named *Syke*, meaning a small stream, rivulet, or ditch (Armstrong *et al* 1952, 490), and it is possible that they reflect the pattern of natural or man-made drainage within this fairly damp area bounded by the lowest meander of the Ribble.

The interests of the Lords of the Honour of Lancaster were not restricted merely to commercial development in Preston and its surroundings, and due attention was also paid to matters spiritual. In 1124, Stephen of Blois, who would ascend the throne of England in 1135, granted land at Tulketh to a group of Savigniac monks so that they could build an abbey (Farrer and Brownbill 1908). The exact site is uncertain, but it is likely to have lain well to the north-west of the medieval centre. The Savigniacs lent their name to the nearby Savick Brook, but they were clearly not happy at Tulketh; after just three years they moved to the Furness Peninsula, where Stephen had gifted them a substantial estate.

The site at Tulketh may have been reoccupied by the late twelfth century, by the leper hospital of St Mary Magdalen, which was furnished with a free chapel under the patronage of the Lords of Lancaster (Farrer and Brownbill 1908, 163). Its lands lay within the area now known as Maudlands (derived from the name of the hospital's patron saint; Clemesha 1912, 12), on the north side of Marsh Lane (Fig 5), and west of Friargate (LCC and Egerton Lea 2006, 20). By 1465, the hospital itself was no longer occupied and, although the chapel seems to have remained in use into the mid-sixteenth century, it may not have retained its original function throughout that time (Farrer and Brownbill 1908, 163).

The Franciscan friary

The area between Friargate, Church Street, and Marsh Lane (formerly Friar's Lane; Hewitson 1883, 281), and opposite Maudlands, was occupied by Preston's third (and seemingly only other) major medieval religious institution, the Franciscan friary of St Clare. The Franciscans, more properly the Order of Friars Minor (literally: 'lesser brothers'), was a monastic movement that followed the Rule St Francis of Assisi (died 1226; Robinson 1913a), which emphasised poverty, obedience, and loyalty to the Catholic Church. It quickly found Papal support, and advocates, including one of his earliest acolytes, St Clare, soon spread the teaching more widely. In 1224, at the behest of Francis himself, the order was brought to England by Agnellus of Pisa, and it spread rapidly through the country from its beginnings in Canterbury, London, and Oxford (Robson 2006). The charismatic Agnellus became both an advisor and a friend to Henry III, an important supporter, if not the founder, of Preston friary (*p 8*).

As a mendicant order, the Franciscans, or Greyfriars, were restricted by their vows of poverty (although the definitions and depths of that poverty were the subject of much debate and division within the order; Robinson 1913b), and were not allowed to own anything that could not be gained from begging, or which could not be used immediately, such as their eponymous grey habits. Accordingly, the order was dependent on the generosity of benefactors to fund the purchase of the land on which their institutions stood, and the materials from which they were constructed (Greene 1992, 167).

The poverty required of the Greyfriars led to the practice, and physical expression, of a form of monasticism very different from that of other orders, such as the Cistercians, who sought rural seclusion and acquired vast tracts of land and associated wealth (Newman 2006). The need to beg pushed the mendicant friars into more populous areas, with orders such as the Franciscans and the Dominicans deliberately seeking urban sites in order to preach to a large audience and dispense charity (including education and the care of the sick). Indeed, it is likely that this interaction was key to their support, both by secular benefactors and by the Papacy, and to their proliferation, with each of the five great mendicant orders: Franciscans; Dominicans; Carmelites; Augustinian or Austin Friars; and Servites (the latter made little impact in England) originating in the earlier thirteenth century and expanding rapidly from their Mediterranean roots (Oliger 1910). As many as 189 mendicant houses were founded in England (Knowles and Hadcock 1953), with most larger towns hosting at least one, and sometimes more, friaries from the four principal orders in England.

One of the few surviving documents relating to the medieval origins and history of Preston friary is a grant by Henry III, dated 25 October 1260. This gifted five oak trees, from the local Forest of Sydwood, for building (Farrer and Brownbill 1908, 162), and suggests that the friary was probably founded around that time. Henry III's younger son, Edmund ('Crouchback'), who was created the first Earl of Lancaster in 1267, also granted gifts towards the erection of the house (Baines 1870, 442; Clemesha 1912; Knowles and Hadcock 1953), and has been credited with its foundation (Farrer and Brownbill 1908). There is a possibility, however, that the site may have been founded by the Prestons of Preston, at a slightly earlier date (Clemesha 1912, 18-19). That family may well have provided the land on which the friary stood, as, later in the Middle Ages, they are recorded as owning adjacent plots (Farrer and Brownbill 1908, 162). Their association with the site may have led Leland, writing in the reign of Henry VIII, to link the original foundation to a Viscount Gurmaston (or Lord Gormanston), who was an Irish representative of the family recorded in 1390 (Baines 1870, 442; Farrer and Brownbill 1908, 162).

Little is known about the physical form of the friary, either the composition or the placement of its constituent buildings. Typically, however, Franciscan houses would contain the same suite of buildings as other monasteries, essentially comprising a church and ancillary buildings, many of which would have surrounded a cloister. They would include a chapter house, dormitory, refectory, infirmary, kitchen, and a library, as well as gardens, a graveyard, and, sometimes, granaries and a school of theology (Robson 2006, 177). The friary at Preston is thought to have consisted of a small quadrangle with cloisters and a chapel/church (Knowles and Hadcock 1953; Tostevin and Iles 1992, 62). Among the few relevant documents that survive are various bequests for masses, which might suggest that it was also equipped with one or more chantry chapels (Fishwick 1900, 198).

Together with the houses at Coventry, Lichfield, Stafford, Shrewsbury, Chester, Llanfaes, and Bridgnorth, Preston fell within the Custody of Worcester (founded 1225-30), one of the seven *custodia* through which the Franciscans administered their English and Welsh houses

(Willis-Bund and Page 1971). The North West was not particularly well-served with friaries, perhaps reflecting the fact that much of the region was economically under-developed, and largely occupied by dispersed, rather than nucleated, settlements (Newman 2006). Indeed, the friary at Preston is the only confidently identified Franciscan institution between Chester and Carlisle (cities which also had Dominican houses and also, in the case of Chester, Carmelites). Friaries are only known from four other north-western towns: Augustinian houses in Warrington and Penrith; Dominicans at Lancaster; and Carmelites at Appleby in Cumbria (*ibid*).

As beggars, and late arrivals to many towns, friars are unlikely to have had much choice in the positioning of their houses (Greene 1992, 167). The centres of many towns had already witnessed several centuries of development, and it was thus not unusual for such religious orders to acquire vacant, and often less desirable, land in the more peripheral or undeveloped parts of medieval towns. In Newcastle, all four mendicant orders were granted marginal sites (Harbottle 1968; 1976), as were the Greyfriars at Lewes (Gardiner *et al* 1996, 100) and Carmarthen (James 1997, 102), whilst at Leicester, the Dominican and Austin Friars were each given sites on the damp western side of the town (Greene 1992, 168). The position of Preston's friary, approximately 200 m from the main thoroughfares of Friargate and Fishergate (Lang and Porter 1774; Fig 5), is similar to that granted to the Franciscan friars of Beverley (Armstrong and Tomlinson 1987, 50, 51, fig 28). Indeed, the relatively rural location of the institution is highlighted by an account of a minor disturbance in 1338, when a group of armed rioters, including John, Nicholas, and William Deuyas, hid in the fields near the Greyfriars' house. There, they set an ambush, and drove one Thomas Starkie and his fellows into the friary church (Farrer and Brownbill 1912, 73).

The friary's peripheral location need not have been a disadvantage, however, not least because it allowed the institution to utilise the natural and agrarian resources that such a site could provide. This aspect is perhaps highlighted by the disputes over fields recorded between the Preston friars and those who rented land at Maudlands (Farrer and Brownbill 1908). Certainly, the friary avoided some of the less salubrious positions tolerated by other mendicant houses, such as that of the Exeter Greyfriars, whose first site was so unpleasant that it was to prove fatal to nine brethren in the space of two years (Foreman 1996, 233).

Preston friary in the post-medieval period

A few sources provide some sparse information about the friary around the time of its dissolution in 1539 (Farrer and Brownbill 1908, 162-3; Fishwick 1900, 200). One records that, not long before, parts had been leased to one Thomas Breres, probably the brother of its subsequent owner, Oliver Breres (Fishwick 1900, 325).

After the dissolution of the house, the site was sold by the Crown, on 18 June 1540, to Thomas Holcroft for £126 10s (Farrer and Brownbill 1908, 162-3), as were the Augustinian and Dominican Friaries at Warrington and Lancaster. Holcroft, of minor Lancashire gentry stock, was a careful politician and an astute speculator, whose many roles included that of King's Commissioner. In this capacity, he was responsible for dissolving at least nine monastic houses in the North West, and gradually acquired their lands for himself (*op cit*, 107-11).

As at his other sites, Holcroft may originally have intended to demolish the friary church and use it as a stone quarry. It is perhaps less likely that he considered building himself a house from the recycled stone, as he had done at the former Cistercian monastery of Vale Royal in 1544 (Robinson 1998, 193). Whether he undertook much demolition is also unclear, for once he had made his acquisition, he '…shortly afterwards conveyed the same to Oliver Breres' (Fishwick 1900, 200). Moreover, Holcroft may have been aware of Sir Thomas Langton's claim that the wall stone of the friary had actually been sold to him by the King (*ibid*). Langton sought to help himself to the stone in 1545, when parts of the friary were sacked by 'ryottous' persons, 'provokers of the Kyng's peas' [*sic*] who, with 'swords, bylls, and long pyked staves', entered the site and took away 1000 'wayne loods of stone' (*ibid*). Fishwick thought a considerable part of the friary must have been demolished (1900, 203) and, although the duration of the trespass by these 'twelve or more' men (*op cit*, 200) is not recorded, it might be inferred that the stolen stone was from demolition stockpiles, rather than directly from the buildings themselves.

The surviving parts of the friary were subsequently used as a dwelling by Oliver Breres and his family (Baines 1870; Tostevin and Iles 1992, 62). He was recorded as Steward of Preston Guild in 1542, becoming an Alderman, and was elected mayor in 1558 (Fishwick 1900, 345). In 1553, his brother, Thomas, took up residence at the former friary, and the family's association with the site was of sufficient length and note for them to be known as the 'Breres of the Freres' (Clemesha 1912, 293). It is probable that the family occupied the site into the early seventeenth century, perhaps until 1616, when Thomas Breres died (Fishwick 1900, 346).

A year later, a meeting of the Justices of the Peace held at Lancaster resolved that £500 should be collected within the county for the construction of a house of correction at Preston (*op cit*, 202). It was no doubt considered more cost effective to utilise the former friary buildings (*ibid*), and this was presumably the gaol that Kuerden records at the site in *c* 1685 (Hardwick 1857, 115; Fishwick 1900, 202). This building would appear to be marked as a 'House of Correction' on Major-General Carpenter and Lieutenant-General Wills' map of 1715 (Fig 6), although,

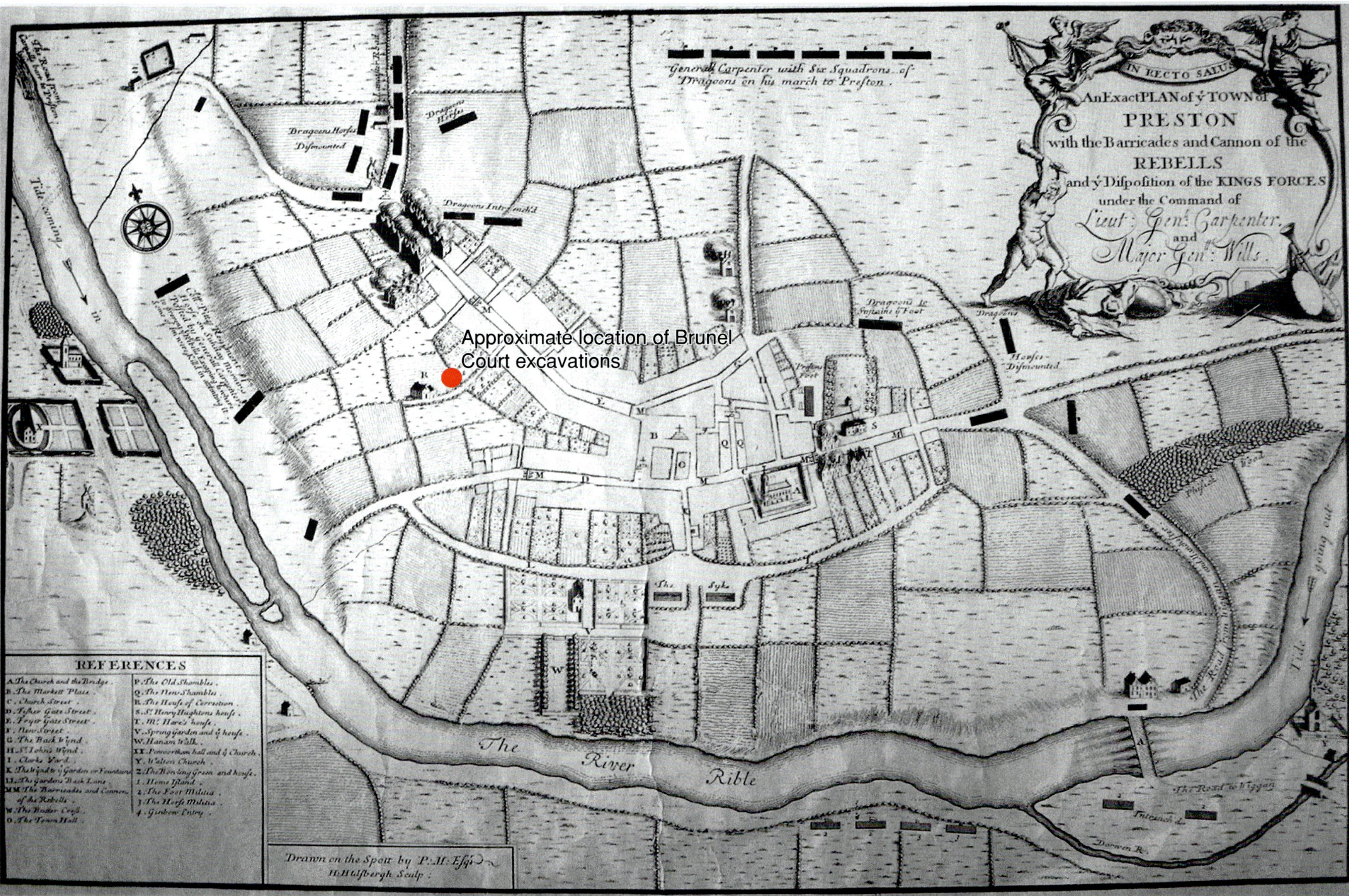

Figure 6: Lieutenant-General Carpenter and Major-General Wills' map of the Battle of Preston, 1715, showing the approximate site of the friary

Plate 2: Samuel and Nathaniel Buck's southern prospect of Preston, c 1728

due to the degree of stylisation, it is uncertain how accurate the representation of a single T-shaped structure is. A print of Preston by the Buck Brothers in *c* 1728 shows a very similar building (albeit with a central two-storey porch on its western, rather than eastern, face; Pl 2) within a neat square enclosure.

The area occupied by the friary appears on reconstructions of survey documents that are thought to have been made by Dr Richard Kuerden, sometime around 1685 (Smith nd), which together with Lang and Porter's map (1774; Fig 2) depict several buildings within this rural area. These include a small building (attributed to *Jno Singleton dy* [sic] *house*; Smith nd), which appears to stand at the junction of Marsh Lane and a small north/south-aligned lane. A little to the south is a second, larger, rectangular building, with its long edge on the western side of that lane, whilst further to the south still is an east/west-aligned building within an L-shaped enclosure. Its position suggests that this represents the House of Correction, whilst the documents attributed to Dr Kuerden record it as *ye fryers*, under the name of *Tho Anderton* (*ibid*).

Documentary and cartographic records relating to the fate of the friary in the later eighteenth and nineteenth centuries do not always agree. In 1789, surviving elements were being used as private cottages (Fishwick 1900, 202), perhaps including Lang and Porter's (1774) more northerly structures, which possibly explains his simpler configuration of the House of Correction. It is suggested that most of these buildings, including that formerly used as the gaol, were removed during landscaping associated with the construction of the Lancaster Canal at the end of the eighteenth century (PRN 1416). Others report that the cottages that succeeded the gaol occupied the shell of the 'old chapel,' and that these survived until the beginning of the nineteenth century, complete with three of the original lancet windows (Fishwick 1900, 202). Survival of elements of the friary into the nineteenth century might be inferred from the inclusion of medieval stonework in the walls of Barracks Street and Marsh (formerly Bridge) Lane (PRN 1416). The former had been set out by 1809, but neither thoroughfare seems to have been developed in the area of the friary until sometime between 1822 and 1836 (Shakeshaft 1809; Baines 1824; Myers 1836; Fig 7).

Shakeshaft's map of 1809 does not show Lang and Porter's more northerly structures, although he does depict a central rectangular building on the same alignment, and in a very similar position, to that shown by Lang and Porter, and which Baines (1824) annotates as 'Old Priory'. Whittle, writing in first half of the nineteenth century, reports that the old gaol was converted into a cotton factory (Whittle 1837; Hewitson 1883, 281, fn 3), although this may equally be represented by a complex of structures to the south of the rectangular building, first shown by Shakeshaft

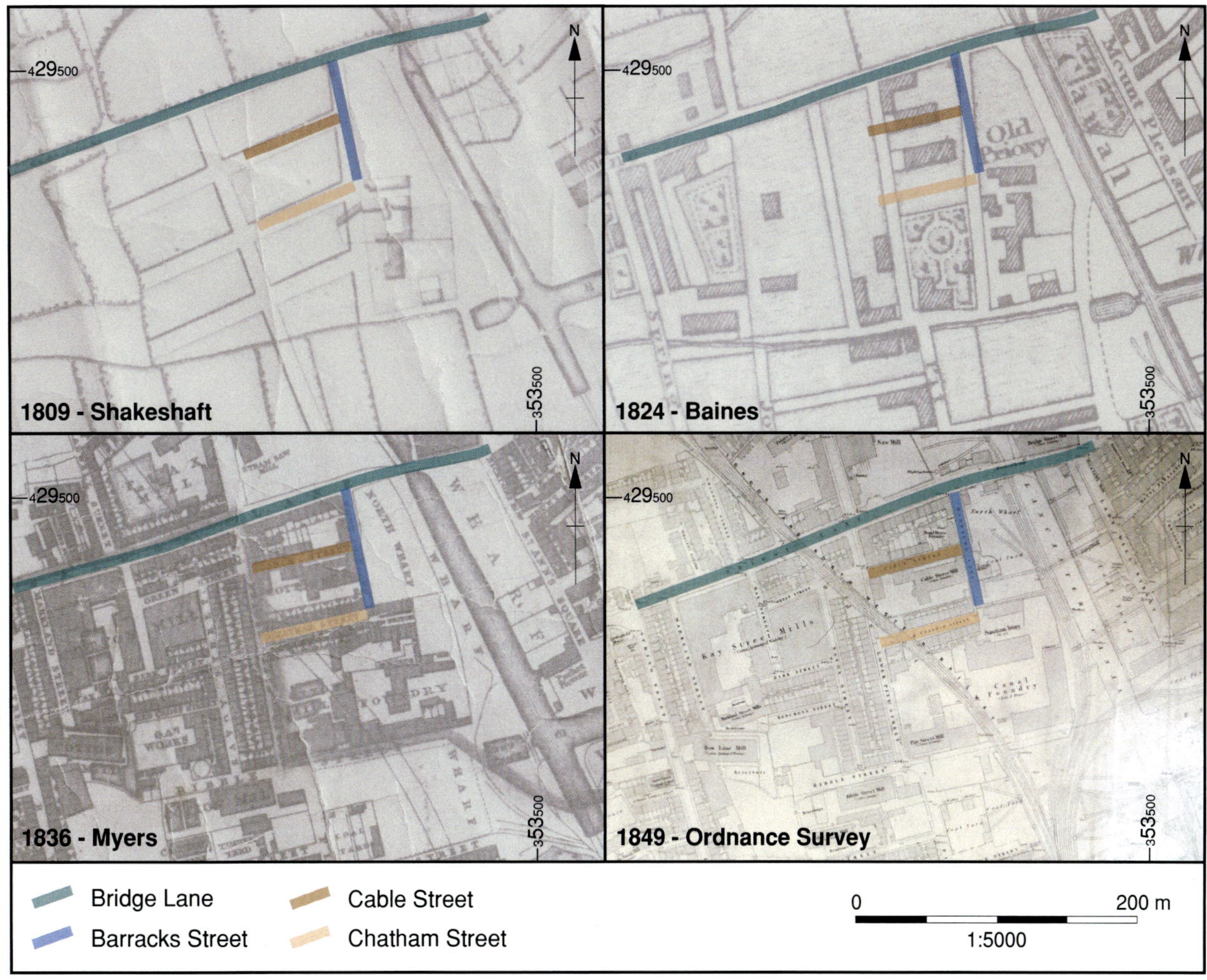

Figure 7: Shakeshaft's (1809), Baines' (1824), Myers' (1836) maps, and the first edition Ordnance Survey Town Plan (1849), showing the nineteenth-century development of Marsh Lane

in 1809 and labelled as a foundry by Myers in 1836. The maps also show the newly built canal, with wharves on either side.

Nineteenth-century development

The pace of nineteenth-century development in and around the former friary precinct was extremely rapid. Shakeshaft shows the new street grid, and, although Baines suggests that local development up to 1824 was largely concentrated along Fishergate to the south, Myers' map indicates that the entirety of the friary grounds and their immediate surroundings had become densely occupied by 1836. In the areas adjoining the canal, and to the east of Barracks Street, this development was largely industrial, with wharves, coalyards, and a foundry. However, there is some cartographic evidence to support assertions that, amidst the sweeping changes wrought by industrialisation, at least one structural element of the friary survived well into the nineteenth century (Hardwick 1857, 116; Baines 1870, 442). As late as the Ordnance Survey (OS) town plan of 1849, the most northerly structure belonging to the Canal Foundry displays a remarkably similar configuration to that shown in the locale by Shakeshaft (1809) and by Baines (1824).

In the mid-nineteenth and twentieth centuries, the construction of the railway and associated processes, just to the west of (the Pitt Street siding), and eventually over (the Dock Street siding), the line of the canal, is likely to have caused the destruction of further elements of the friary, although its site is annotated on both the 1849 and 1893 OS Town Plans. Nineteenth-century construction works seem regularly to have encountered archaeological remains, with coffins (including one of lead, discovered in 1841), human bones, and worked stone from the area between Cable Street, Chatham Street, and the former canal, in particular, from the Coalyard of Pearson and Coles (Hewitson 1883, 280). Amongst the artefacts recovered was an 'octagon-shaped stone', perhaps the 'holy water stoup' illustrated in Fishwick (1900, 202). In the later twentieth century, the heart of the friary precinct, largely between Barracks Street and the railway line, was removed by the new cutting for the A59 Ringway, whilst its eastern part was redeveloped as halls of residence for the University of Central Lancashire.

Plate 3: The better-preserved north-western part of the building, from the south-west

2

THE ARCHAEOLOGICAL EVIDENCE

The *in situ* archaeological evidence was largely derived from the 2007 excavation, and consisted of a poorly preserved building associated with some 33 graves. There was clear evidence of some refurbishment to the building, and the graves proved to have been dug throughout the lifetime of the structure (*Ch 3*). This information has allowed features identified in the 1991 excavations to be reassessed, indicating that some can now be associated with this site.

The Friary Church?

The principal archaeological feature on the site was identified towards the centre of the area investigated, and has been interpreted as the partially destroyed remains of a rectangular stone structure, *c* 12 m east/ west by at least 6 m north/south (Pl 3; Fig 8). The extant

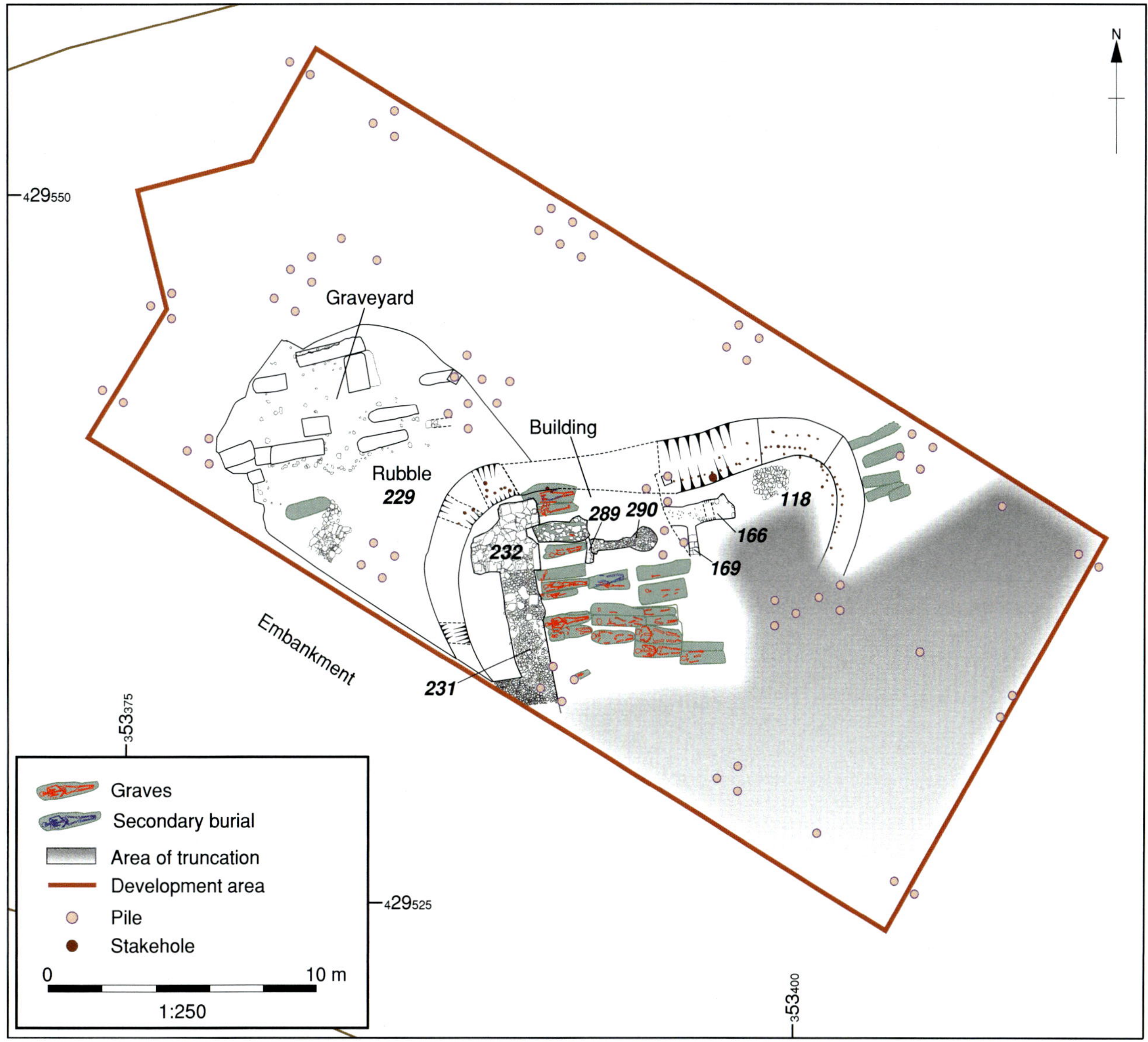

Figure 8: The 2007 excavation

15

remains comprised a series of cobble foundations bedded on the surface of the natural sandy clay. In places, for instance the west wall, *231*, these footings were 1.5 m wide, and a single course of dressed and rubble sandstone survived above them, being all that remained of the otherwise robbed-out walls. The north wall had not fared so well, surviving as several discrete, and variably preserved, elements. Its central part, *290*, comprised a much-damaged cobbled footing, whilst to the east, the wall was likely to have been completely robbed, leaving only shallow construction cut *166*, filled with sandy rubble *167*. Any relationship between these two features had been destroyed by piling, but their differing construction techniques, and the fact that they were not contiguous, might suggest that they represented different phases of construction and later modification.

There was evidence for a buttress at the north-west corner (*232*), and a roughly square patch of cobbles (*118*), at the eastern limit of the robbed-out section of the northern wall, probably indicated the position of a north-eastern buttress. There was no trace of any east wall, it probably having been completely removed by later disturbance. A narrow north/south section of wall (*169*), *c* 1 m in length, was found 2 m west of the putative north-east buttress, with another (*289*) in a similar position, near the western end of the building, where it was closely associated with cobble footing *290*. It is possible that these represented internal divisions, or supports for architectural elements, such as arches. To the north-west of this building, sandstone rubble layer *229* may represent an associated construction horizon.

Intramural burials

Twenty broadly east/west-aligned graves were identified in association with the building (Fig 9). They varied somewhat in their dimensions, with some (for instance G8 and G10) being atypically narrow, and several others were very neatly cut, with near-vertical sides and flat bases. It was clear that all of

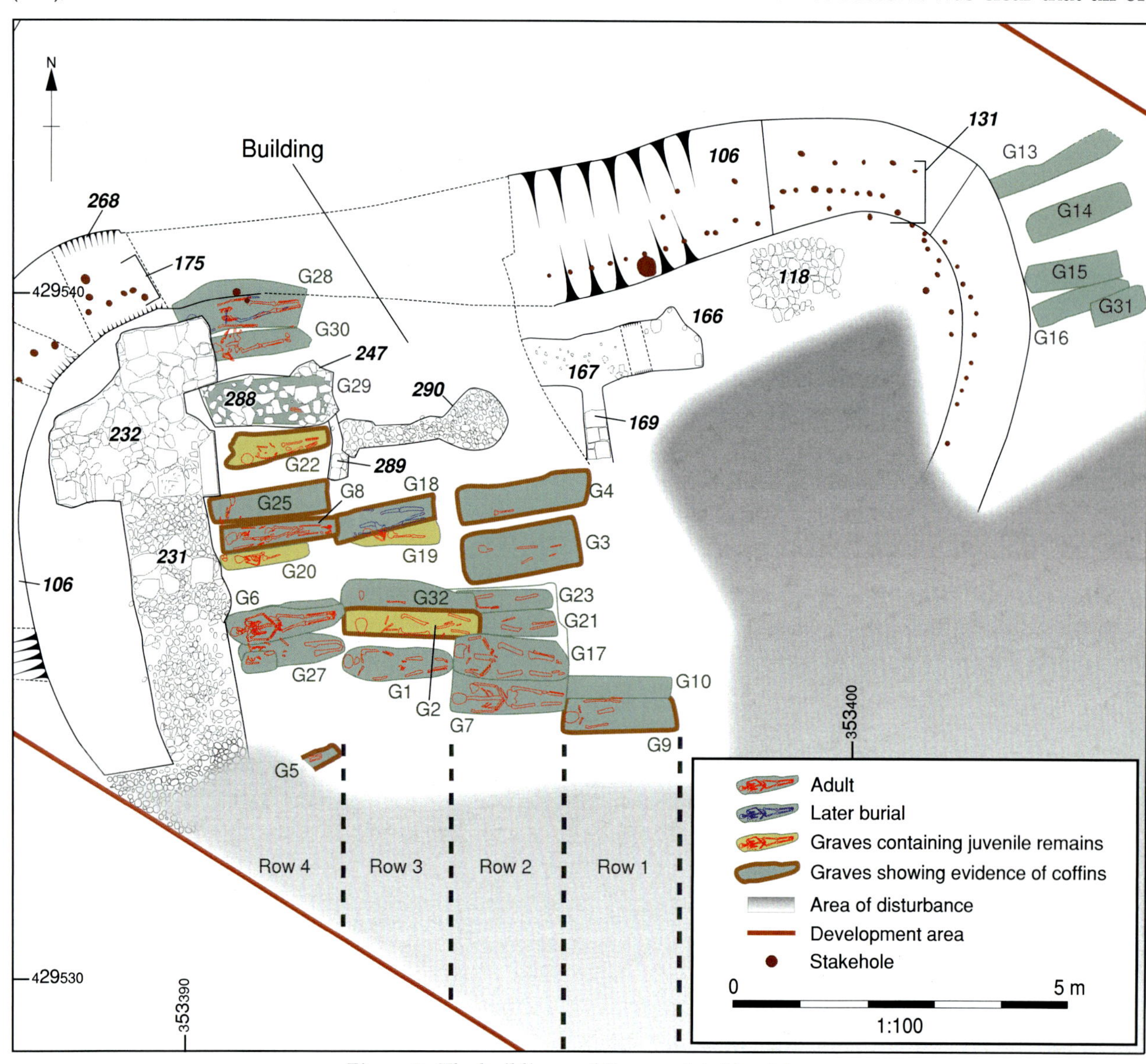

Figure 9: The building and its associated burials

16

the skeletons had their heads to the west and, where sufficiently complete for their positions to be defined, had been laid in a supine posture, generally with the hands folded over the loins.

There seems to have been a reasonable degree of organisation to the graves, as they formed four fairly well-defined rows (Rows 1-4). Despite this, there was some intercutting, both within the rows, and, in several instances, between them, with the heads of some skeletons damaged by the feet of later interments to the west. In addition, the sides of graves in the western and northern parts of the building seem to have been closely aligned with the northern wall. Other graves could well have been set out with reference to surviving internal features, as the graves in Rows 2 and 3 seem to have respected wall stubs *169* and *289*. More speculatively, it appears that some of the graves were aligned on lost features, for instance, a group of nine graves (G1-2, G7, G9-10, G17, G21, G23, and G32) in Rows 1-3 were angled very slightly to the south of their neighbours, suggesting that they had been aligned on a lost internal feature on the eastern side of the building.

Although it is now impossible to determine whether or not the graves had originally been marked in any way, it seems that specific spaces, if not necessarily exact graves, had seen successive reuse. For example, it is likely that the creation of grave 6 (Row 4) had almost entirely removed an earlier burial (Pl 4). Conversely, the three interments within grave 2 (Row 3) were likely to have been made within the same cut on at least two separate occasions, leading to the disturbance of the earlier burials. Considered together, this might suggest that particular locations had been sought for burial, and that space may have been at something of a premium.

The preservation, completeness, and even the physical presence of articulated human remains within the graves was rather variable, owing to the high degree of disturbance, which had reduced many of the graves to depths of only a few centimetres. Indeed, the most easterly row (Row 1) comprised only two graves (G9 and G10) at its southern end, of which grave 10 lacked any human remains. This would confirm the impression, given by the absence of structural remains, that local disturbance had been particularly severe in that part of the site.

Several graves (G2-5, G8, G9, and G18) contained fragmentary timbers, which have been interpreted as the remains of coffins (Pl 5), or grave linings, although differentiation between the two must remain largely subjective (*Ch 4, pp 48-9*). The latter may well have been the case with grave 3 (Row 2), however, which was notably wide, and contained very degraded fragments of boards some 50 mm thick; if these timbers had been used for a coffin, rather than a lining, it would

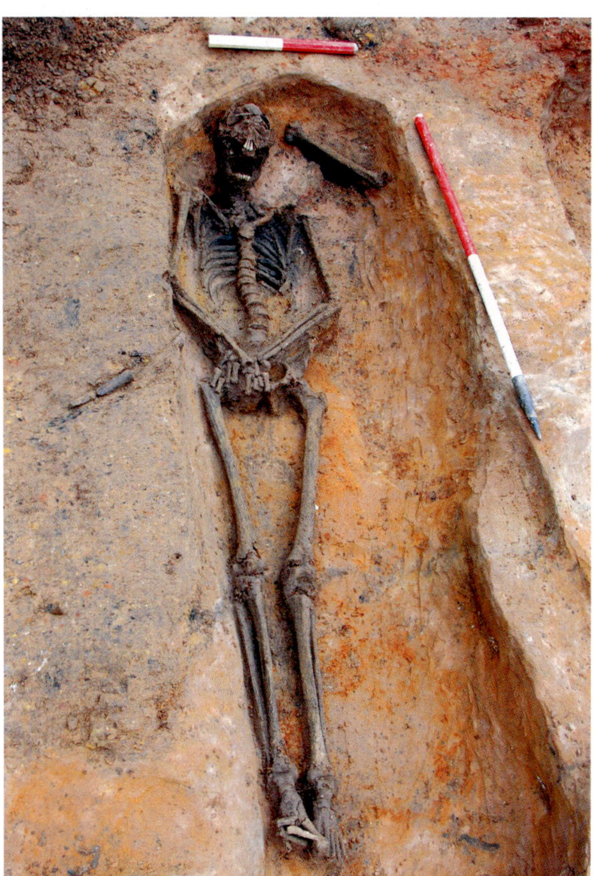

Plate 4: Grave 6, cutting a shallow earlier interment (top), from where the disarticulated upper arm bone may have originated

*Plate 5: Skeleton **158**, grave 8, on the base of a wooden coffin*

have been extremely heavy. Several graves (including G22 and G25 in Row 4) contained only a few pieces of corroded ironwork, which may well have been the remains of nails, but there were no other indications, such as soil stains, that others among the remaining better-preserved burials had originally included wooden elements.

Rows 1 and 2

Many of the graves lacked clear stratigraphic relationships with their neighbours, but there was some evidence, both from the stratigraphy and the scientific dating, that the earliest burials lay at the eastern end of the building (Row 1; Fig 10), with subsequent burials occupying more westerly positions (Rows 2-4). Timber from the most easterly, and stratigraphically earliest, grave (G9) was subject to dendrochronological analysis, and was found to derive from a tree that must have been felled no earlier than 1242 (*Ch 4, p 51*). Two of the skeletons in Row 2, those from graves 21 and 23, were radiocarbon dated. Because both graves shared

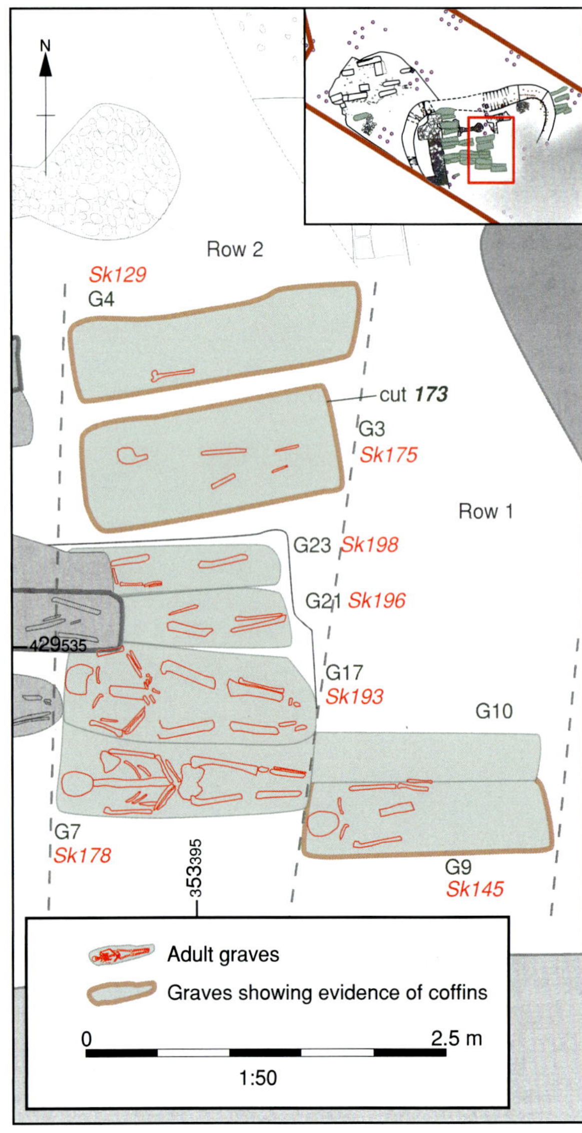

Figure 10: The graves within Rows 1 and 2

stratigraphic relationships with others containing bones also dated by radiocarbon assay, the skeletons in graves 21 and 23 were among several included in the Bayesian chronological modelling. In the case of Row 2, that modelling indicated that the person in grave 23 died in or after *cal AD 1280–1315*, whilst the person in grave 21 died some time in or after *cal AD 1320–1350* (Table 1). All of the skeletons were of adults in Rows 1 (G9) and 2 (from south to north, graves G7, G17, G21, G23, G3, and G4). Grave 23 contained the poorly preserved skeleton of a mature adult woman, whose head had subsequently been removed by burials to the west. The backfill (*199*) of her grave contained a fragment of twelfth- to thirteenth-century pottery (*Ch 4, p 44*), which was broadly contemporary with her demise.

Little remained of skeleton *196* within grave 21, other than an articulated left leg, the remainder of the skeleton having been removed by the subsequent excavation of grave 17, to the south. The occupants of graves 7 and 17 (male skeletons *178* and *193* respectively; *Ch 3*) were the most complete of any of the individuals in Row 2. They lay side-by-side, and it is possible that they were closely contemporary. The posterior density date calculated for the well-preserved older man in grave 17 suggested that he had died in or after *cal AD 1415–60* (Table 1), implying that he, at least, might have been a late insertion into a row of earlier graves, and perhaps had been placed among his ancestors. The bones of both were stained black, possibly through contact with an organic deposit that was identified across the surrounding graves, but, despite the squareness of their grave cuts, there was no evidence that either had been buried within a coffin.

At the northern end of the row, graves 3 and 4 were very slightly offset from their neighbours, and more widely spaced. Grave 3 was formed by an unusually wide rectangular cut (*173*), some 1.7 m long by 0.7 m across. Small fragments of timber at the northern edge suggested the presence of a coffin or timber lining. A single piece of fourteenth- to fifteenth-century decorated floor tile was recovered from the backfill (*Ch 4, p 46*), although its significance for dating the grave is debatable. The tile was probably incorporated into the grave fill after the deceased was interred, thus providing a *terminus post-quem* for that event; however, it is also possible that it entered the backfill as a result of later disturbance of the grave and any overlying surface, and could thus post-date the burial by a considerable period. Grave 4 also contained the remains of a coffin/timber lining, with a pair of boards, up to 1.7 m long, at its base. Rather less survived of the adult skeleton, *129*, contained within.

Row 3

Stratigraphic relationships and scientific dating indicated that most of the five graves in Row 3

Row	Grave	Material dated	Lab No	Dendrochronological date	Likely date rage	δ¹³C (‰)	Radiocarbon Age (BP)	Calibrated Date at 95% probability	*PDE Date at 95% probability*
1	9	Coffin *155*	-	After AD 1242	1260-1300	-	-	-	-
2	17	Skeleton *193*	OxA-26220	-	-	-19.8	459±25	cal AD 1410–1460	*cal AD 1415–1460*
2	21	Skeleton *196*	OxA-26219	-	-	-19.4	536±24	cal AD 1325–1435	*cal AD 1320–1350*
2	23	Skeleton *198*	OxA-26233 SUERC-39417	-	-	-19.2 -	662±26 700±30	cal AD 1275–1385	*cal AD 1280–1315*
3	2	Coffin *123*	-	After AD 1345	1350-1400	-	-	-	-
3	18	Coffin *184*	-	After AD 1312	1350-1400	-	-	-	-
4	8	Skeleton *158*	OxA-26224	-	-	-19.6	385±25	cal AD 1440–1630	*cal AD 1440–1495*
E-M	30	Skeleton *235*	OxA-26221 OxA-2622	- -	- -	-19.2 -19.3	679±25 625±25	cal AD 1280–1390	*cal AD 1280–1320 (81%) or 1355–1385 (14%)*

Note: E-M=extramural; *PDE=Posterior Density Estimate*

Table 1: Scientific dates from the burials

(graves G1, G2, G32, G19, and G18, from south to north; Fig 11) were later than those in Row 2. Graves 2 and 32 cut graves 21 and 23 to the east, and this, together with dendrochronological dating of timbers from graves 2 and 19, suggested that they were mid- to late fourteenth-century interments. Although the completeness and preservation of the skeletons in Row 3 were similar to those of Row 2, there were differences in the nature and demography of the burials. For example, there was evidence for reuse of several of the graves, with grave 19, which contained the skeleton (*181*) of a three- to four-year-old child, having been recut at a slight angle by well-defined rectangular grave 18, which contained the incomplete, but articulated, remains of a mature adult (*186a*), together with elements of a second adult (*186b*), who may conceivably have been the original occupant of the coffin. The surviving timbers in grave 18 indicated a trapezoidal coffin (*184*), some 1.85 m long, 0.55 m wide at the head, and 0.37 m at the foot.

Grave 2 was also rectangular, neatly cut, and contained oak coffin timbers that may have originally been nailed together and reinforced with one or more iron strap (*Ch 4*). They produced a dendrochronological date no earlier than AD 1345 (Table 1). Inside, the partial, articulated, skeleton of a mature woman (*124a*) was accompanied by the mostly disarticulated bones of second woman (*124b*), who presumably represented an earlier interment (*Ch 3*). Grave 2 also produced the disarticulated remains of a young child (*125*), although it is uncertain whether this individual had been disturbed by the subsequent burials, or by more

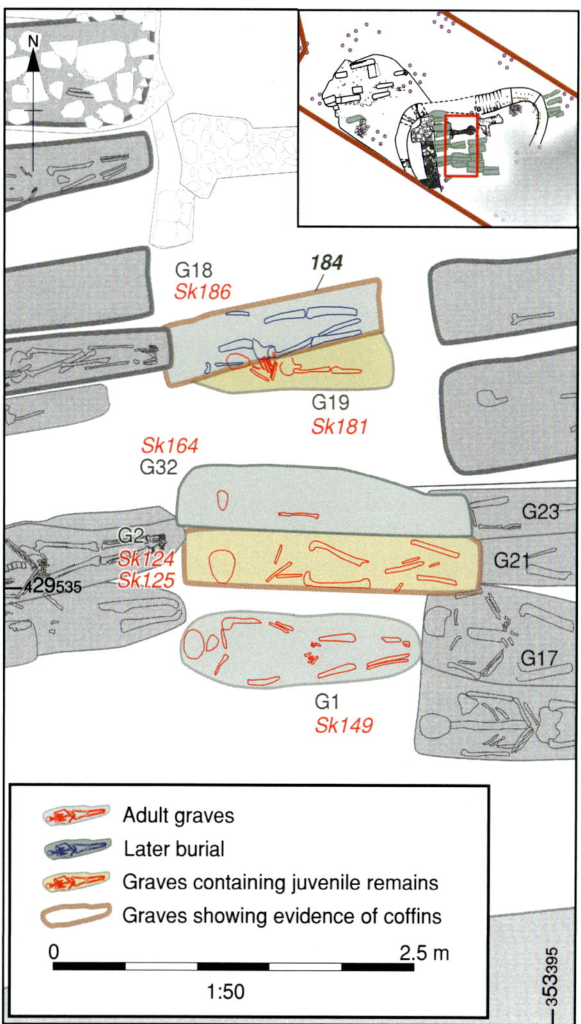

Figure 11: The graves within Row 3

general later activity, or had originally accompanied one of the women. Neighbouring grave 32 just clipped the northern edge of grave 2, and tapered at the foot end, perhaps precluding the presence of any internal wooden structure. It was also very much shallower, and contained only a few very poorly preserved skull fragments (*164*). There was a small gap between graves 2 and 1, to the south (containing adult male skeleton *149*, whose feet had been removed by the late burial in grave 17 to the east; *p 18*). It was noticeable that there was sufficient room for an additional grave in the space between graves 32 and 19, so, unless the gap had accommodated a completely robbed-out architectural element, the more intensive use and reuse of graves in this row does not seem to relate to a lack of space, *per se*.

Row 4

The most westerly row of seven graves (from south to north, graves G5, G27, G6, G20, G8, G25, and G22; Fig 12) was bounded to the north and west by walls *288* and *231*. Those that could be dated seem to be of fifteenth- or sixteenth-century date.

The southernmost grave, G5, appeared to lie at a marked angle to the other interments, and to be somewhat divorced spatially. It had been badly damaged by modern piling, and all that remained of adult skeleton *119* was its rather crumbly shin bones, whilst the coffin survived only as a fibrous soil stain. Amongst the other graves in the row, it is possible that there was a northward progression of successive burials, with graves 27 and 20 each being cut by their northern neighbours (graves 6 and 8, respectively). A gap between graves 6 and 20 was contiguous with a very similar space in Row 3, and it is possible that this area had once been occupied by an internal fixture.

As with Row 3, children were present, and there was also evidence for the disturbance/reuse of earlier graves. This was particularly notable in the case of grave 6 (Pl 4), which was somewhat more substantial than its neighbours (being some 2.07 m long, up to 0.69 m wide, and 0.3 m deep), and had clearly been cut through a much shallower earlier grave, that survived only as a scoop along its northern edge. It housed the largely complete skeleton of a mature adult (*203*), with distinctive skeletal trauma which might identify a military background (*Ch 5; pp 82-3*). The burial was accompanied by charnel deposit *202*, which comprised a single humerus placed above skeleton *203*'s left shoulder, and fragments of pelvis and three adult femurs placed upon its feet and ankles. Most of the charnel deposit presumably belonged to the earlier grave, although the third femur may have belonged to adult skeleton *213* in grave 27, to the south.

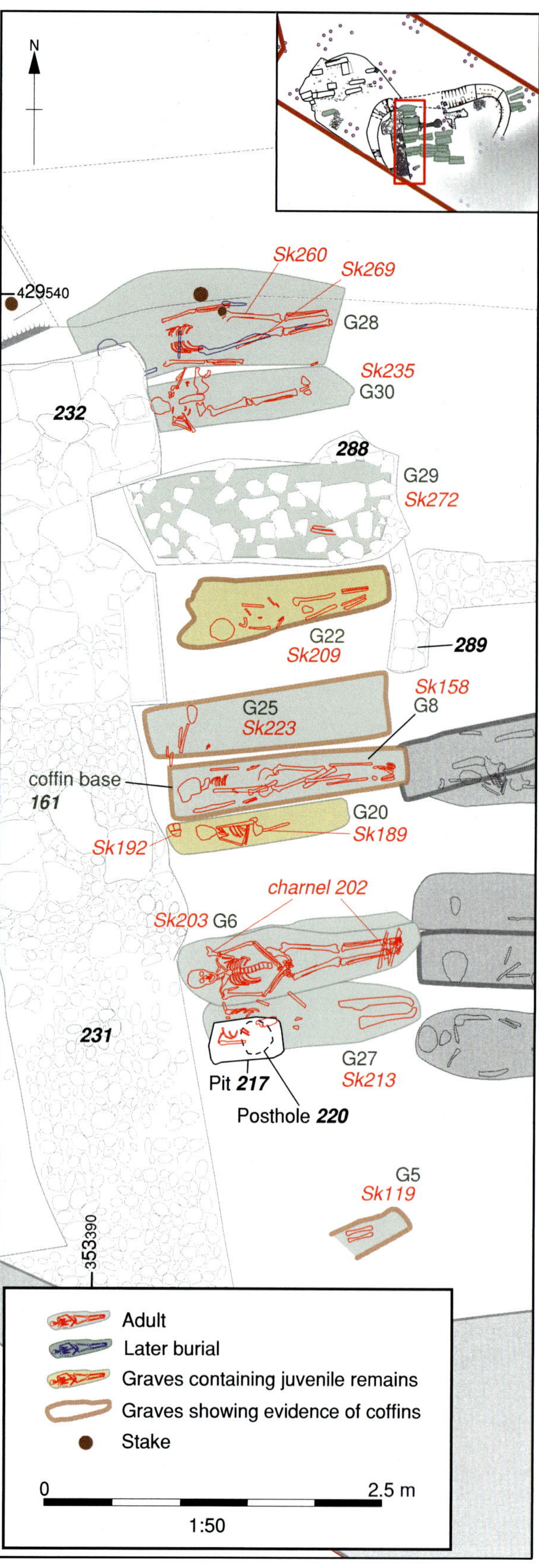

Figure 12: The graves within Row 4

Grave 8 (Pl 5) was the only one in Row 4 to retain a reasonably well-preserved coffin base (*161*), in which the adult skeleton (*158*), possibly that of a man

Plate 6: Grave 22, close to the west end of the building, perhaps defined to the west by a dressed stone

(*Ch 3, p 31*), was estimated to have died in or after *cal AD 1440–95* (Table 1). To its north was the very disturbed remains of a young man, **223**, in grave 25. Several pieces of ironwork suggest that this shallow grave had once contained a coffin.

The remains of children were identified in graves 20 and 22. Within the former, a six-to-seven-year-old (**189**) had suffered from a tumour in the left eye (*Ch 3, p 40*). The grave fill (**190**) produced a single sherd of Northern Reduced Greenware, datable to the fifteenth to sixteenth century (*Ch 4, p 44*), although whether the pottery entered the grave when it was originally backfilled, or when it was cut by neighbouring grave 8, is uncertain. If the former, when considered with the scientific dating of skeleton **158** in grave 8, it could be inferred that skeleton **189** was also interred in the fifteenth century. The circumstances of grave 22 (Pl 6), which contained 11-12-year-old child **209**, appear particularly noteworthy, in that its tomb seems to have been recessed into wall **288** (*p 20*).

Extramural burials

Several burials (graves 28-30) were identified immediately outside the north wall of the building (Fig 12). Like those inside, their alignment matched that of the structure, suggesting that it had been constructed prior to their burial. There was a good chance that the death of the stratigraphically earliest member of the group (young adult male skeleton **235** in grave 30; Pl 7; Table 1) took place in the decades on either side of 1300, which would have made it

effectively contemporary with the internal burials of Rows 1 and 2, and arguably earlier than those in Rows 3 and 4. Skeleton **235** was badly disturbed (a leg removed) by the excavation of grave 28, in

*Plate 7: Skeleton **235** in grave 30*

which lay adult male skeleton *269*, and this had been subsequently reopened for the interment of adult *260*. Evidence suggests (*Ch 3, p 32*) a familial relationship between *235* and *260*, and it is perhaps of significance that their disposition within the grave differed from that in the intramural burials, with the hands of skeleton *235* being placed on its chest, whilst those of skeleton *260* were at its sides. The fourth member of this group, adult *272*, the occupant of grave 29, was very poorly preserved, with little surviving the disturbance associated with a possible modification to the north wall of the building (*p 23*).

Undated extramural graves

Two groups of very shallow features, possibly graves, lay to the east and north-west of the building, and would appear to represent elements of a more extensive cemetery. The features shared characteristics of the graves within the building, being the same shape, with a similar range of dimensions and following the same alignment. However, there was a lack of material evidence that would allow them to be securely dated, and human remains were absent from all but one. Given the long history of development and truncation on the site, it is perhaps unsurprising that graves would have been disturbed, accelerating degradation of bone in the sandy soil, even where remains had not been conscientiously removed from former areas of development. The seven putative graves to the north-west were cut into construction horizon *229*, an irregular spread of soft, dark-red sandstone rubble (Fig 13; Pl 8). The southernmost of the group was grave 26, which was

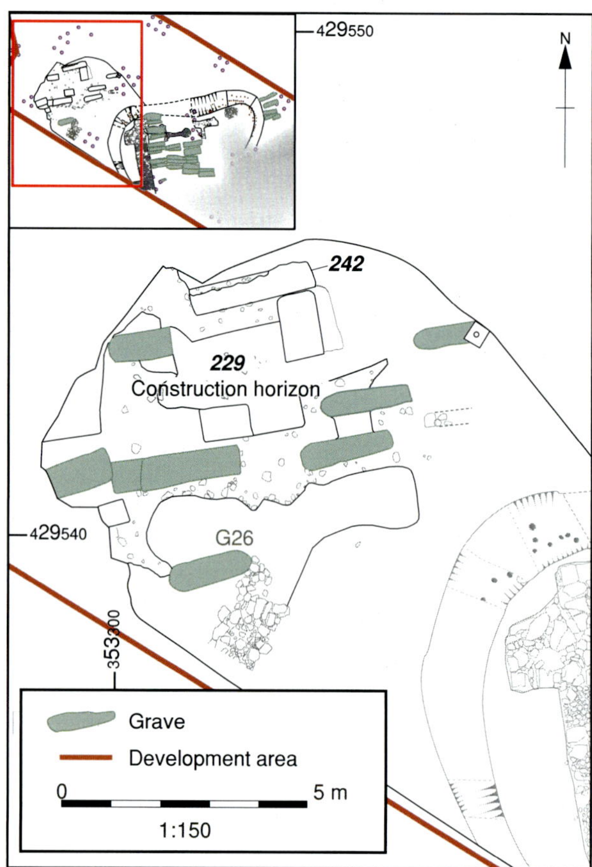

Figure 13: The empty graves forming a cemetery north-west of the building

1.68 m long, 0.5 m wide, and 0.5 m deep. It contained numerous bone fragments, including parts of the skull.

Plate 8: Graves cutting the medieval construction horizon to the north of the building, looking south-east from Marsh Lane

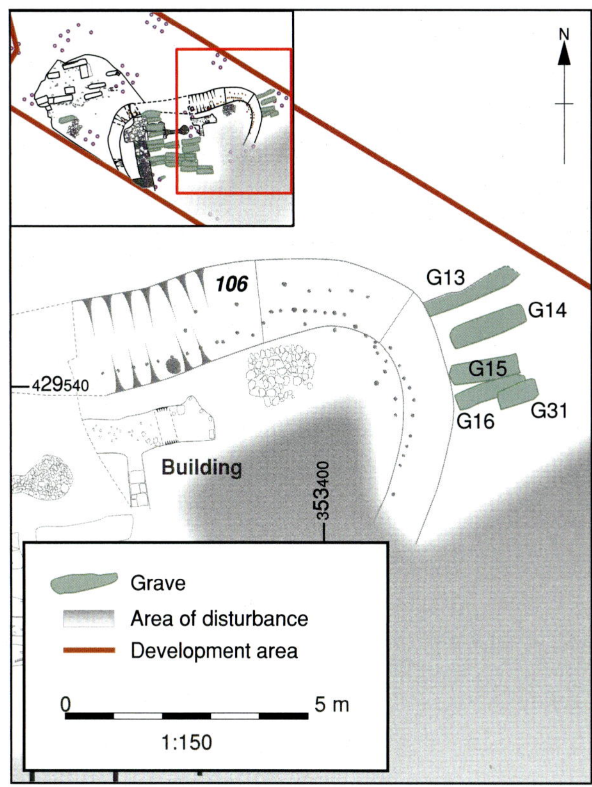

*Figure 14: The group of empty graves to the east of the building, beyond ditch **106***

To the east of the building, a further five possible graves were located immediately to the east of ditch **106** (Fig 14) and, although their situation appeared to respect that feature, it seems odd that graves should have been dug so close to an open ditch, particularly if there was a risk of collapse or disturbance. It therefore seems likely that they pre-dated the ditch, and like it, their position probably respected the building. All were less than 70 mm deep, and most were between 1.34 m and 1.93 m long. The three southern features, graves 15, 16, and 31, were successively intercutting, with the latter being only 0.88 m in length, suggesting that it may once have contained a child. The northernmost, grave 13, was only 10 mm deep, and appeared to have been cut by ditch **106**. It is, however, possible that this rather elongated feature actually represented a gully that would have fed into the ditch.

Possible structural modifications

There was some evidence that the north wall of the building had witnessed some modification following the interment of the extramural burials (*ie*, at some time during, or after, the fourteenth century). This was most evident at the western end of the wall, where a 1.8 m-long section (**288**; Fig 12) was moved northward, or perhaps reinforced, so that it disturbed and then sealed the much-reduced remains of the occupant of grave 29 (Pl 9; *p 22*). The reinforced wall footing at that point was quite unlike any of the other structures identified, and was composed of large water-worn

cobbles and boulders which had been placed in a *c* 0.3 m-deep, narrow cut that had been packed level with clay. Actual masonry, represented by several flat stones, survived only at the western end the wall. The alteration to this section of wall seems to have necessitated some adjustment of the nearby north-west buttress, which was extended northward without any cobble footings, and onto the area occupied by the head end of grave 28 (Pl 10). It was notable that this modification meant that wall segment **288** was much more closely aligned to eastern element **167** than central section **290** (Fig 9).

Plate 9: The foundations of the north wall, cutting extramural grave 29

Plate 10: The extension to the north-west buttress, without a cobble footing, covering the head end of grave 28

One result of this seems to have been the creation of what may have been a recessed tomb within the north wall (grave 22; Pl 6), bounded to the west by a piece of neatly squared stone, and to the east by narrow north/south wall *289* (Fig 12). Such a feature suggests that the child (skeleton *209*, *p 21*) inside this was from a family that enjoyed, or at least aspired to, wealth and inherited status. Six nails were located in the centre and at the ends of grave 22, indicating that it had once held a coffin, although no organic traces were observed.

Ditch and stakes

These alterations may have been associated with the excavation of a ditch, *106*, probably for drainage, that curved sinuously around the western, northern, and what was probably the eastern, sides of the building (Fig 15;

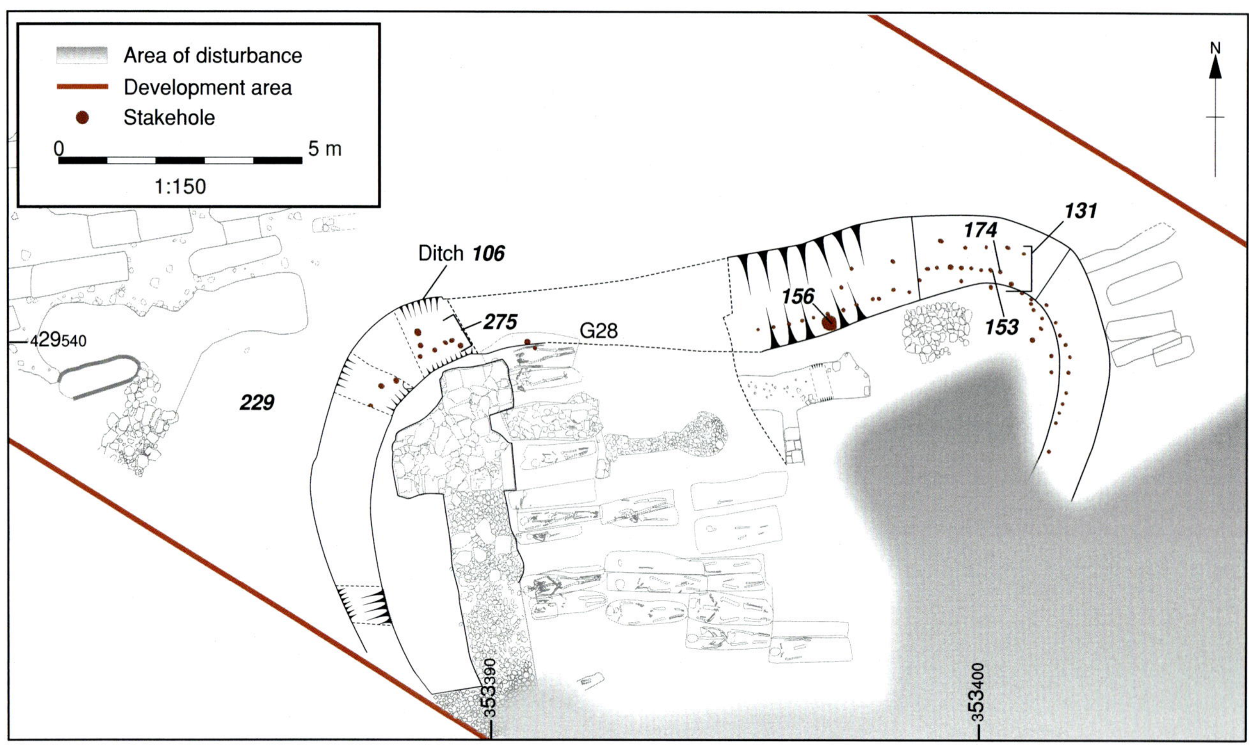

*Figure 15: Ditch **106**, with its holly stakes, which appeared to surround the building*

*Plate 11: Ditch **106**, with stakeholes in its base*

*Plate 12: Stakes extracted from ditch **106***

Material dated	Lab No	δ¹³C (‰)	Radiocarbon Age (BP)	Calibrated Date (95% confidence)	*Posterior Density Estimate (95% probability)*
Stake *153*	OxA-26233	-22.8	840±28	cal AD 1150–1270	-
Stake *132*	SUERC-39921	-27.9	565±30	cal AD 1300–1430	*cal AD 1305–1365 or 1380–1430*
Stake*154*	SUERC-39922	-24.2	635±30	cal AD 1280–1410	*cal AD 1295–1405*

Table 2: Scientific dates from the holly stakes

Pl 11). Indeed, it is the position of ditch *106*, which was some 1.98 m wide and 0.21 m deep, that provides the best evidence for the extent of the otherwise lost eastern wall of the building. It cut rubbly construction layer *229* (*p 17*), and the fill of grave 28, but otherwise respected the building. The insect assemblage from its fills suggests that it held shallow water (*Ch 4, pp 58-61*). Associated with, and in places sunk into, the ditch, were several (often paired) alignments of holly stakes (*131* and *275*), the surviving portions being up to 1.4 m long and 85 mm in diameter, with the ends sharpened to multi-faceted points that had been driven into the ground (Pl 12). That the stakes followed the inside edge of the ditch quite closely, particularly on the eastern side, suggests that the two were connected, and may have been near contemporary, although, from a practical perspective, it makes sense that the ditch should have been dug before the stakes were inserted.

Radiocarbon dating of the stakes, including an example that had penetrated extramural grave 28, suggest that they dated to the fourteenth or early fifteenth century (Table 2). They are thus unlikely to relate to the very earliest use of the building. It is difficult to be certain how long the stakes and the ditch remained as a combined fixture, as, from their rather flattened upper ends, it seems that the timbers did not rot or break off naturally, but rather that they had been deliberately cut. That this took place so close to the base of the ditch might suggest it was clean when the event happened. Further evidence that the ditch continued in use longer than the stakes is provided by the presence of fifteenth- to sixteenth-century pottery in its fills, suggesting that it was maintained right up to the Dissolution, after which it silted up naturally, seemingly within a pastoral setting (*Ch 4, p 44*).

Other, later, or undated remains

Various other features were identified during the excavation, but they generally lacked the coherence of the funerary remains, and many seem likely to reflect post-Dissolution activity (*Ch 1, pp 10-12*), especially the intensive use of the site in the last two centuries. Within the building, grave 27 (Row 4; Fig 12) was cut by posthole *220*, which was 0.3 m in diameter, 0.25 m deep, and contained small quantities of charcoal. This was cut in turn by sub-rectangular pit *217* (0.72 x 0.38 m). To the east, the skeleton within grave 9 had been cut below the waist, seemingly by the insertion of an L-shaped fixture of squared timber. Although the timber was aligned quite closely to the grave, it was dissimilar to any of the coffin wood and was not associated with any human remains, suggesting that it was more likely to relate to a later intrusion (*Ch 4, p 51*). Among the putative graves to the north-west of the building, straight-sided, elongated rectilinear cut *242* (Fig 13) had a layer of rubble in its base. It was reminiscent of a robbed foundation, but its depth, at 0.55 m, would appear greater than the foundations for the medieval building.

The 1991 Fieldwork

Only five of the trenches excavated in 1991, and the subsequent watching brief, recorded activity that could be related to the friary, or to the remains identified during the rescue excavation. Trench 8 was excavated in the former Dock Street Siding, some 45 m to the south of the 2007 site (Fig 16), whilst Trenches 9-12 were placed within an area of former railway lines between 10 m and 35 m to the south-east of Brunel Court. Sealed by well-dated post-medieval layers, Trench 8 revealed an apparently undisturbed medieval horizon at the (relatively) shallow depth of *c* 1.25 m below the ground level. No structural evidence was identified, and the horizon appeared to indicate open ground. Of particular relevance was the recovery from this horizon of two fragments of medieval tile, of a type most likely to be associated with ecclesiastical buildings (LUAU 1991a, 12). Within Trench 9, an analogous layer of grey silty loam, 0.6 m thick, contained post-medieval pottery and more medieval tile fragments. It lay above the natural geology and was interpreted as a long-lived agricultural soil. The same layer was recognised in the area of Barracks Street during the watching brief.

Although, within Trenches 10-12, this possible medieval horizon was thought to have been truncated by later activity, all three produced structural remains. At the time, these were interpreted as elements of the nineteenth-century foundry (LUAU 1991b, 9), but, with hindsight, the description of some of the structures is very similar to those identified during the 2007 investigations. Several features were revealed at the base of Trench 11, within 10 m of the 2007 site, sealed by a thin ashy layer, and a much more mixed deposit of demolition debris containing medieval pottery. A roughly north-east/south-west-aligned wall was identified in the south-facing section, where it was 0.5 m wide and survived as seven courses of roughly worked sandstone and rubble, bonded with lime mortar. A similar mode of construction was seen in an adjacent pair of five-course-high north/south-aligned walls in Trench 12, although there the depth of investigation, and unstable trench sides, precluded close investigation.

Tightly packed cobble surfaces, bedded within a layer of cinders, were identified on top of the natural silty clay in Trenches 11 and 10. The latter also revealed an active drain, lined with stones and capped with slabs.

Several walls and culverts, some built of brick, others of stone, were identified during the watching brief on the Ringway route. The quality of many of the brick-built structures, which were described as 'retaining much of their strength' (LUAU 1991b, 7), would suggest that they were relatively modern. The majority of the culverts were again brick-built, but had been capped with sandstone slabs. An extensive and extremely robust composite brick and dressed sandstone structure (blocks of 1.1 x 1.2 x 0.5 m), which had been sealed by a black sooty layer, may have related to the Cable Street Mill, or perhaps to the Canal Foundry (*Ch 1, p 13*).

Later deposits across the friary site

The medieval remains were sealed by a series of made-ground deposits that included reworked natural sandy clay, and horizons containing burnt material and other industrial waste. In the area of Brunel Court, these were cumulatively around 2.2 m thick, but clearly increased in depth to the south and south-east. Similar deposits in evaluation Trench 12 (50 m to the south-east of the 2007 excavation), were 2.9 m thick, whilst in Trenches 1-8, on the Dock Street siding (between 50 m and 150 m to the south of the 2007 excavation), comparable deposits were as much as 3.75 m thick. This overburden can be attributed to the construction of the canal in 1798 (*Ch 1, p 13*), and to subsequent redevelopment over the following two centuries (LUAU 1991a, 12; 1991b, 9).

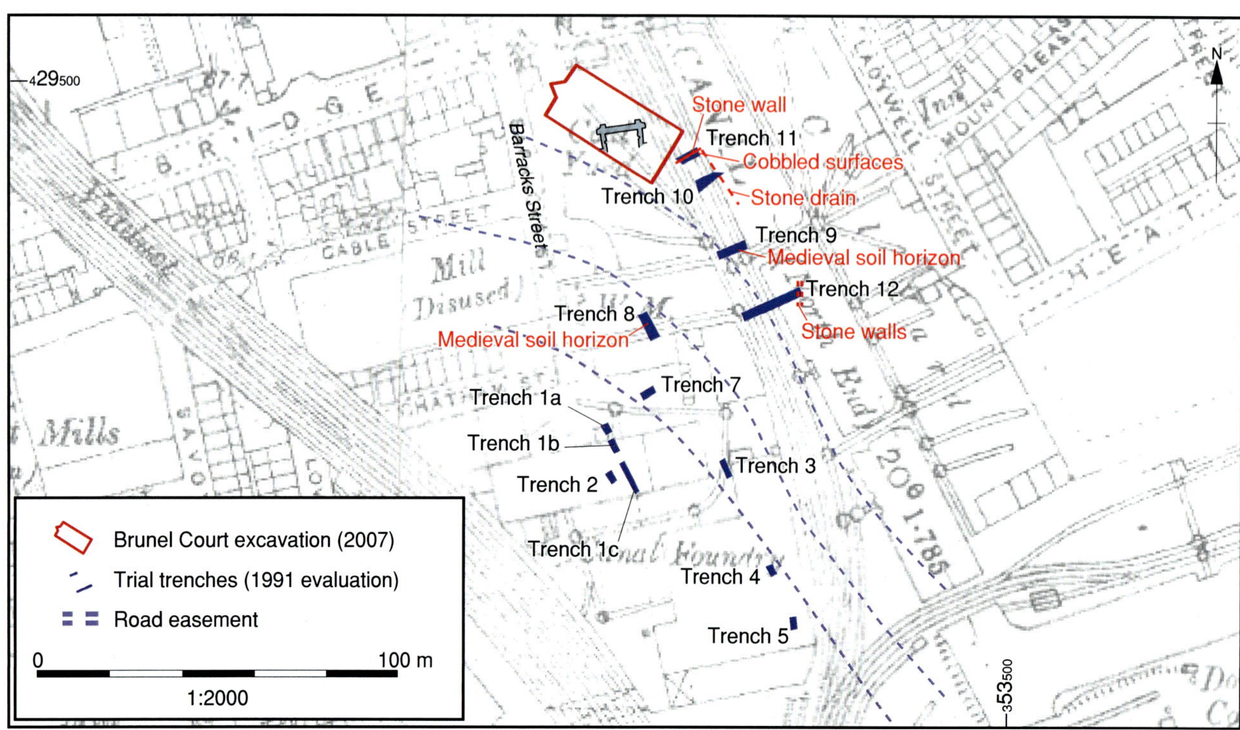

Figure 16: The 1991 evaluation trenching, superimposed on the 1893 Ordnance Survey map

3

THE HUMAN REMAINS

Mark Gibson, Roişin McCarthy, and Louise Loe

Methodology

Osteological analysis was undertaken on all 24 articulated skeletons, and a charnel deposit that represented the discrete remains of a single individual. The analysis followed published guidelines (Brickley and McKinley 2004) and involved the macroscopic examination of each cleaned skeleton. This recorded the preservation status, an inventory of the bones and teeth present, and, where preservation allowed, an estimation of age and sex, scoring of the presence and absence of non-metric traits, recovery of metrical data, and a full record of pathological lesions observed.

Preservation was considered in terms of the percentage of a skeleton's bones that were a) present (*ie* completeness), b) fragmented, or c) affected by taphonomic erosion (McKinley 2004, 16). Adult age estimates observed late-fusing skeletal elements, and degenerative changes of the auricular surface and pubic symphysis of the pelvis, supported by observations of the overall degree of cranial closure (Scheuer and Black 2000; Brooks and Suchey 1990; Lovejoy *et al* 1985; Buckberry and Chamberlain 2002; Meindl and Lovejoy 1985), with skeletons assigned to one of six broad age categories. Juvenile skeletons were aged using dental development, epiphyseal fusion, and long-bone length, predominantly of the femur (Moorees *et al* 1963; Scheuer and Black 2000).

Biological sex was determined from dimorphic traits of the skull and pelvis (Phenice 1969; Bass 1987; Buikstra and Ubelaker 1994), with adults assigned to one of seven possible determinations, comprising indeterminate and three probability levels for each of 'male' and 'female'. The terms 'female' and 'male' refer to all sexed individuals, including possible and probable cases. No attempt was made to estimate the sex of juvenile skeletons (individuals less than 18 years), because there are still no nationally accepted standards for this (Brickley 2004, 23).

The presence of non-metric traits was recorded (minor anomalies of skeletal anatomy that may be genetically or environmentally induced; Mays 1998), with the standard 23 cranial (Berry and Berry 1967) and 29 post-cranial traits (Finnegan 1978) scored for each skeleton. When preservation allowed, metrical analysis was also carried out. Only limited numbers of post-cranial measurements were possible, and none could be taken from the skulls. Adult stature was calculated by employing complete long-bone lengths of sexed individuals, and applying them to the appropriate regression formula for Caucasian populations (Trotter 1970, based on Second World War data; Waldron 1998, 75).

A full dental record, including major pathologies, was undertaken with the aid of published guidelines (Brothwell 1981, 155; Ogden 2008, 293; Lukacs 1989; Buikstra and Ubelaker 1994). Any pathological lesions or bony abnormalities were described, photographed as appropriate, and differential diagnoses explored with reference to standard texts (*eg* Aufderheide and Rodríguez-Martín 1998; Ortner 2003; Resnick 1995a). Systematic examination and description for cribra orbitalia, endocranial lesions, and maxillary sinusitis followed the schemes of Stuart-Macadam (1991, 101-13), Lewis (2004, 90), and Boocock *et al* (1995) respectively.

Basic statistical comparisons were made using calculations of crude and true prevalence rates. The 'crude prevalence rate' (CPR) refers to the number of cases of a condition out of the total number of individual people in the sample population. The 'true prevalence rate' (TPR) refers to the number of cases of a condition relative to the total number of skeletal elements present on which the condition could possibly occur.

Comparative assemblages

In order to explore patterns of demography and pathology in a wider context, the results were compared with broadly contemporary monastic skeletal assemblages from England, Scotland, and Ireland (Table 3). Due to the variation in reporting methods and data presentation, however, some datasets could not be used for all comparisons of demography/pathology. A further source for

Site	Site type	No skeletons	Reference
Warrington Friary, Cheshire	Monastic	110 (30 pre-1539)	Boylston and Weston 2001
Carmarthen Greyfriars, Wales	Monastic	193 (church burials)	James 1997
Dominican Friary, Beverley	Monastic	12	Armstrong and Tomlinson 1987
Greyfriars, Gloucester	Monastic	23	Oyler 2001
Hospital of St Mary Magdalen, Partney, Lincolnshire	Rural hospital connected to monastic estate	32	Anderson 2010
Dominican Friary, Perth, Scotland	Monastic	23	Bowler *et al* 1995
Austin Friar's, Leicester	Monastic	25	Stirland 1981
Blackfriars Friary, Ipswich	Monastic	250	Mays 1991a
Carmelite Friary, Aberdeen	Monastic	68	Kerr *et al* 1988
Dominican Friary, Guildford	Monastic	113	Henderson 1984
Dominican Priory, Chelmsford	Monastic	138	Bayley 1975
Eynsham Abbey, Oxfordshire	Monastic	9	Boyle 1998
Hulton Abbey, Staffordshire	Monastic	24	Wise 1985
Mottisfort Abbey, Romsey	Monastic	12	McKinley 1995
St Gregory's Priory, Canterbury	Monastic	91	Anderson and Andrews 2001
Tintern Abbey, Co Wexford	Monastic	88	O'Donnabhain 1991
Whitefriars, Buttermarket, Ipswich	Monastic	15	Mays 1991b

Table 3: Monastic cemetery sites used for comparison with the Brunel Court assemblage

comparison was the data presented by Roberts and Cox (2003), which provide the average rates for a variety of pathological conditions, for British monastic and lay assemblages, from *c* 1050 to *c* 1550 (*op cit*, 221-86). These were calculated by combining the prevalence rates gleaned from a multitude of osteological reports and, whilst the rates presented are often (but not always) crude, the data serve as a rough measure for the period.

Preservation and Completeness

There are several factors known to affect the preservation status of human bone, including soil acidity, depth of burial, and *in-situ* compression, as well as post-depositional disturbance (Brothwell 1981, 7-9). The age, sex, and bone health of the individual can also affect preservation levels, as might the use of absorbent materials placed in the bases of graves and/or coffins, such as sawdust and bran (Cox 1996, 112). Most skeletons were incomplete (Fig 17) and highly fragmentary (Fig 18), although over a quarter (seven skeletons) were greater than 50% complete, and the same number had low or moderate levels of fragmentation. Despite the overall incomplete and fragmentary condition of much of the assemblage,

most skeletons had bone surfaces that were reasonably well preserved, albeit with varying grades (1-4) of moderate erosion (McKinley 2004, 16; Fig 19).

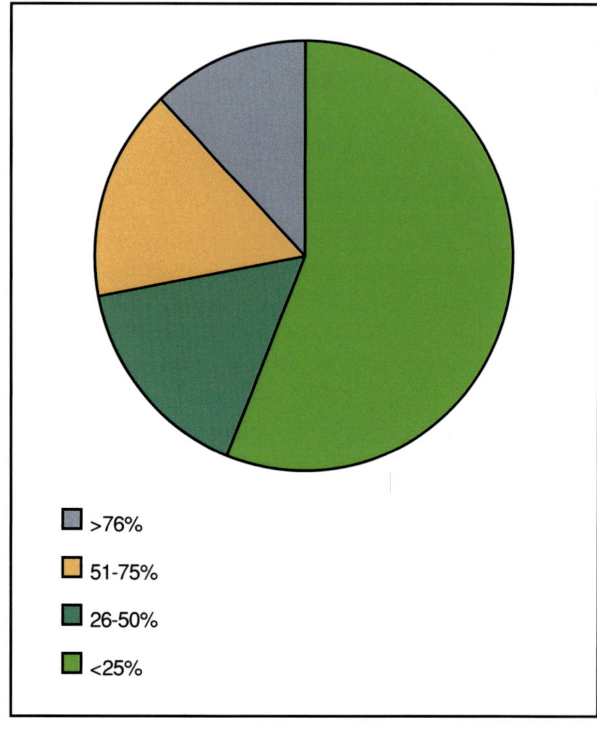

Figure 17: Completeness of the skeletons

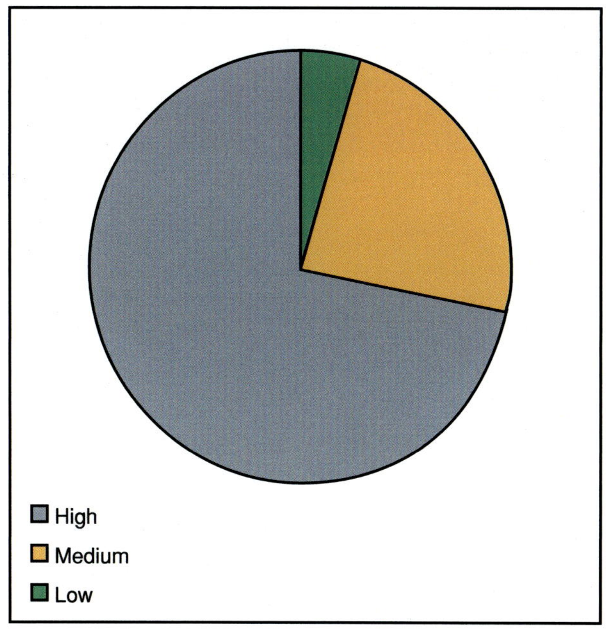

Figure 18: Fragmentation levels

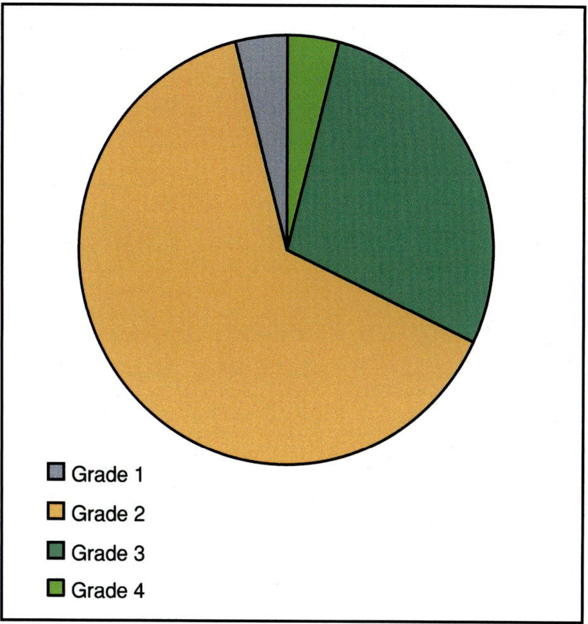

Figure 19: Taphonomic erosion, according to McKinley's (2004) grading system

Demography

Of the 25 individuals in the assemblage, 21 (84%) were adult and four (16%) were juvenile. Among the adult skeletons that could be sexed, there was a higher proportion of men than women, seven and four individuals, respectively, giving a male to female ratio of 1.75:1. However, sex could not be estimated for the remaining ten adults, owing to missing elements and/or ambiguous morphological features. The same factors also meant that, where sex could be estimated, it could not always be confidently assigned, particularly in the case of several men (Fig 20). Although the number of sexed individuals is small, at face value, the ratio of men to women at Preston is lower than in other monastic assemblages, both from the north and south of Britain, with the exception of the Dominican Friary at Perth (Bowler *et al* 1995; Table 4).

Ages ranged from approximately one to four years (two young children), to greater than 45 years (three skeletons; Table 4; Fig 21). Ten adult skeletons (47.6%) could not be assigned a more specific age, but, of the remainder, most died in mature adulthood (35-45 years; five individuals), closely followed by the 'prime' and 'older adult' age categories (25-35 years and 45+, respectively). A similar

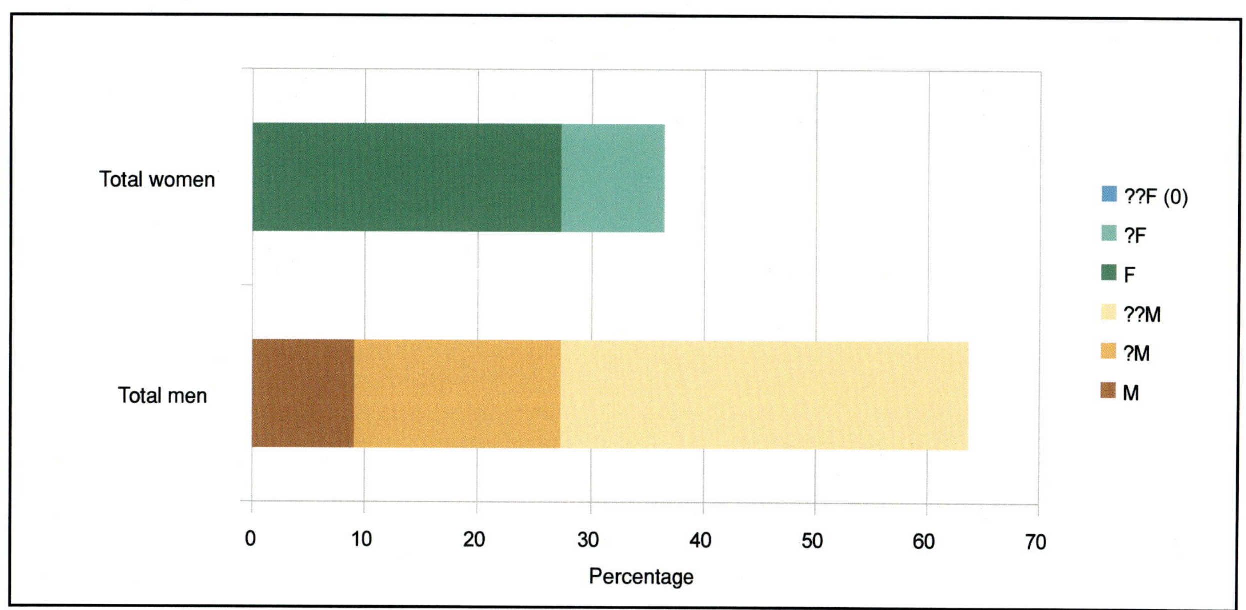

Figure 20: Proportions of women and men within the sexed adult assemblage (n=11)

Age category	Age range	Man	Woman	Indeterminate /NR (%)	Totals (%)
Pre-term		-	-	0 (0%)	**0 (0%)**
Neonate		-	-	0 (0%)	**0 (0%)**
Infant		-	-	0 (0%)	**0 (0%)**
Young child	1-5 years	-	-	2 (8%)	**2 (8%)**
Older child	6-12 years	-	-	2 (8%)	**2 (8%)**
Adolescent	13-17 years	-	-	0 (0%)	**0 (0%)**
Juvenile (unspecified)	<18 years	-	-	0 (0%)	**0 (0%)**
Young adult	18-25 years	1 (4%)	0 (0%)	1 (4%)	**2 (8%)**
Prime adult	26-35 years	1 (4%)	2 (8%)	0 (0%)	**3 (12%)**
Mature adult	36-45 years	3 (12%)	1 (4%)	1 (4%)	**5 (20%)**
Older adult	>45 years	1 (4%)	1 (4%)	1 (4%)	**3 (12%)**
Adult (unspecified)	>18 years	1 (4%)	0 (0%)	7 (28%)	**8 (32%)**
Totals		***7 (28%)***	***4 (16%)***	***14 (56%)***	***25 (100%)***

Table 4: Age and sex distribution of the assemblage (N=25)

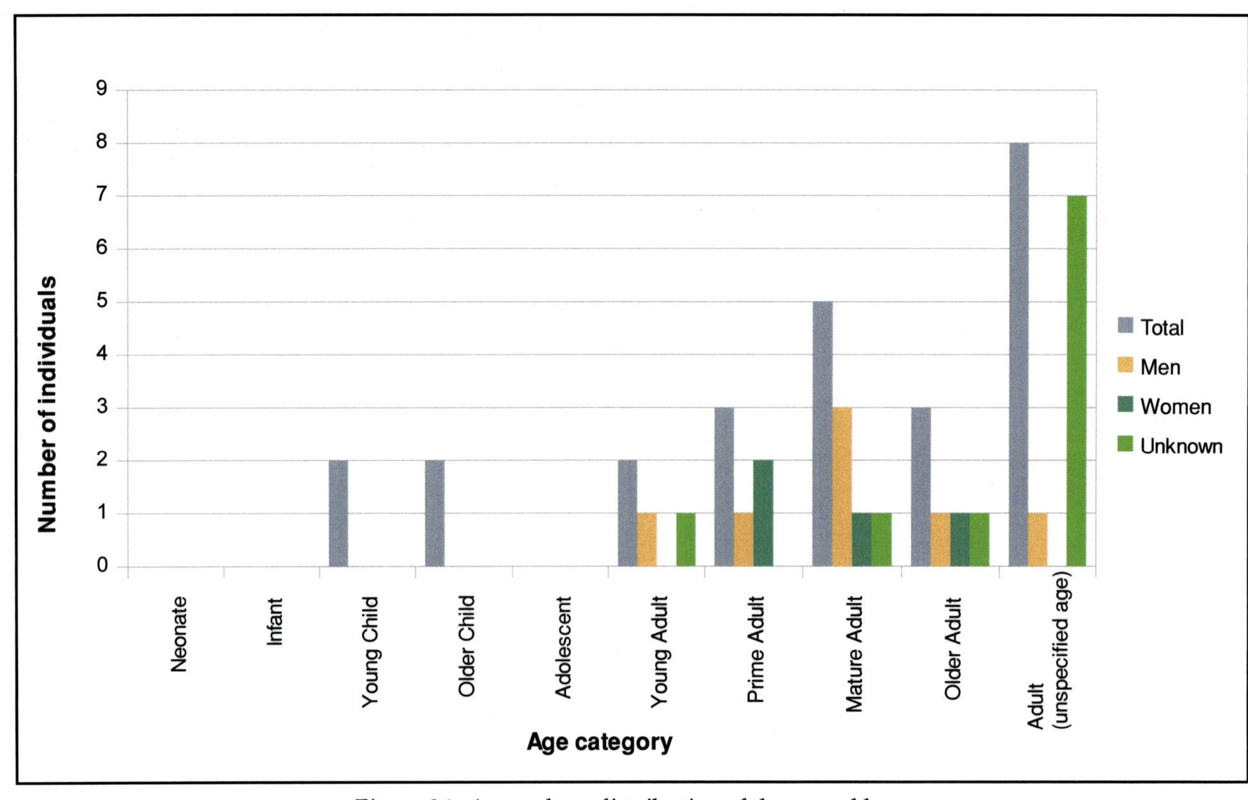

Figure 21: Age and sex distribution of the assemblage

trend of proportionally fewer young and elderly adults was observed among those interred in the chapel and burial ground belonging to St Mary Magdalen, Partney, Lincolnshire (Anderson 2010). Elderly adults were also low in number from the cemetery of the Dominican friars at Kinnoull Street, Perth (Bowler *et al* 1995), and from the chapter house, cloisters, and church of the Austin Friars, Leicester (Stirland 1981), as well as from the cloister alleys and chapter house of the Greyfriars, Carmarthen (James 1997). However, these patterns were not seen among either the extramural burials, or those from the church, at Warrington Friary, where fairly even numbers of young, middle-aged, and elderly adults were identified overall, and there was good representation of elderly adults within the pre-1539 assemblage (Boylston and Weston 2001; 2002). In addition, adults over the age of 45 were common among the burials excavated from the church and cloister walk at the Dominican Friary, Beverley (Armstrong and Tomlinson 1987) and the church of the Gloucester Greyfriars (Ferris 2001).

Metrical Data

As a result of the overall fragmentary and incomplete nature of the assemblage, the amount of metrical data which could be gathered was very limited. Only prime adult male skeleton *158* (grave 8; *Ch 2, p 20*) could be measured for stature, estimated to have been 1.74 m tall (5 ft 8 ins). This is 30 mm taller than the mean for the medieval period (Roberts and Cox 2003, 248), and a little taller than the average male height from comparative assemblages (1.73 m at the Dominican Friary, Guildford (Henderson 1984, 13), and Blackfriars, Ipswich (Mays 1991a, 16), and 1.72 m at Whitefriars, Ipswich (Mays1991b, 3)).

Non-metric Traits

Non-metric traits are minor anomalies in the morphology of the skeleton, and are generally of no pathological significance. They may be present as localised deficiencies of bone (for example, as extra blood vessel openings, or foramina), or as extra bones (for example, as small wormian bones in the cranial sutures). Traits which involve variations in joint surfaces tend to be more environmentally influenced, a reflection of mechanical factors operating on the bones (Mays 1998, 110). Those involving the skull, such as retention of the metopic suture into adulthood, and the presence of lambdoid ossicles, tend to have a more genetic basis (Torgersen 1951a; 1951b; Sjøvold 1984) and have thus been used to explore familial ties within cemetery populations.

A range of four cranial and seven post-cranial traits was observed (Table 5). One skeleton (26-35-year-old female *145*, grave 9; *Ch 2, p 18*) had retained the metopic suture, which divides the two halves of the frontal bone of the forehead in the mid-line and usually fuses in early childhood. This anomaly is often encountered in archaeological remains, where its incidence varies greatly, indicating a genetic basis to its manifestation (Scheuer and Black 2000). Male skeleton *235* (grave 30; *Ch 2, p 21*) and neighbouring unsexed adult *260* (grave 28; *Ch 2, pp 21-2*) both had supra-orbital foramen, an opening above the eye socket created by bony bridging of the supra-orbital notch. Accessory infra-orbital foramina (an additional opening near the eye socket) were also seen on skeletons *235*, and *124a* (grave 2; *Ch 2, pp 19-20*), the remains of a woman more than 45 years old at death.

Among the post-cranial traits were Poirer's facets, or articular capital extension, a developmental trait of the hip joint (affecting skeletons *124a* and *186b*, in graves 2 and 18 (*Ch 2, pp 18-19*), respectively; S Anderson *pers comm*). The trait manifests on the femur (thigh bone), with an extension of the femoral head onto the superior surface of the femoral neck. It has been suggested that this trait arises as a result of extreme flexion of the hip joint, when the ilio-femoral ligament or ilio-psoas tendon repeatedly comes into contact with the acetabular labrum (the margin of the hip socket; Angel 1964). Three other traits were observed on the femur, including Allen's fossa (a region of exposed inner, woven, bone tissue, occurring on the anterior surface, just below the border of the rounded head of the joint; Finnegan 1978; skeleton *124a*); third trochanters (a bony tubercle on the upper end of the muscle attachment for the buttock; *ibid*;

	Brunel Court (n/N)		Blackfriars Friary, Ipswich (Mays 1991a) (n/N)	
Cranial trait	*Left*	*Right*	*Left*	*Right*
Metopism	25.0% (1/4)		9.9% (17/172)	
Accessory infra-orbital foramen	25.0% (1/4)	50.0% (1/2)	12.1% (8/66)	11.4% (8/70)
Supra-orbital foramen	0.0% (0/3)	66.6% (2/3)	27.3% (41/150)	23.3% (35/150)
Double condylar facet	50.0% (1/2)	0.0% (0/2)	3.8% (3/78)	2.6% (2/77)
Post-cranial trait				
Atlas – facet double form	25.0% (1/4)	0.0% (0/5)	13.2% (12/91)	17.6% (18/102)
Humerus – supra-condyloid process	25.0% (2/8)	0.0% (0/8)	0.0% (0/164)	0.0% (0/159)
Femur – Allen's fossa	25.0% (1/4)	0.0% (0/4)	12.4% (16/129)	17.9%) (25/140)
Femur – Poirer's facet	50.0% (2/4)	25.0% (1/4)	No data	No data
Femur – third trochanter	33.3% (2/6)	0.0% (0/4)	No data	No data
Femur – Hypotrochanteric fossa	0.0% (0/10)	10.0% (1/10)	No data	No data
Calcaneus – double anterior facet	20.0% (1/5)	25.0% (1/4)	44.3% (78/176)	39.8% (72/181)

Table 5: Comparison of true prevalence rates for non-metric traits within the adult sample at Brunel Court and that from Ipswich

skeletons *124a* and *203*, graves 2 and 6; *Ch 2, pp 19-20*); and a hypotrochanteric fossa (a vertical groove on the posterior surface of the shaft, just to the outside of the muscle attachment for the buttock; skeleton *235*; grave 30; *Ch 2, pp 21-2*).

Other non-metric traits affected the first vertebra, known as the atlas, the elbow joint, and the calcaneus (heel). In the case of the first vertebrae of skeleton *203*, the traits were double atlas facets, which appear as two (rather than one) distinct facets, separated by a groove or ridge, on the surface of the joint that articulates with the base of the skull (*ibid*). The elbows of skeletons *124a* and *235* (graves 2 and 30) had supra-condyloid processes, which are small bony processes on the humerus (upper arm bone), just above the elbow joint (*ibid*). Skeletons *158* and *178* (graves 8 and 7; *Ch 2, p 18, p 21*) both had double anterior calcaneal facets, where two, rather than a single, discrete facets are observed on the upper surface of the calcaneus (*ibid*).

Comparative data for non-metric traits are limited, although the frequencies of post-cranial traits observed at Brunel Court are similar to comparative groups from Ipswich (Mays 1991a; Table 5). The frequency of the cranial traits is notionally higher than the assemblages from Ipswich Blackfriars (*ibid*), although consideration needs to be given to the skewing effect of the small number of skeletons from Preston. Given the strong genetic component in the aetiology of cranial traits, it may be significant that skeletons *235* and *260* were buried next to one another (*Ch 2, p 22*). Of further interest is the fact that skeletons *235* and *124a*, although buried in different parts of the building, also had supra-condyloid processes on their humeri.

Dental Disease

In the adult assemblage, 52.4% of individuals (11/21) had observable dentitions (teeth and/or jaws), including six men, two women, and three individuals of unknown sex. Of a possible 672 teeth (based on 21 adults, each with an expected full complement of 32 teeth), 25% (168 teeth, including 120 belonging to men and 26 to women) were present (Table 6). There were 79 observable tooth sockets (including 54 male and

Site	AMTL (n/N)	Caries (n/N)	Periapical cavities (n/N)	TPR/CPR Calculus (n/N)	TPR/CPR Periodontitis (n/N)	TPR/CPR DEH (n/N)
Brunel Court, Preston	20.3% (16/79)	12.5 % (21/168)	1.3 % (1/79)	58.9% (99/168)/ 72.2% (8/11)	2.5% (2/79)/ 22.2% (2/9)	8.4% (14/167)/ 18.2% (2/11)
Blackfriars Friary, Ipswich	17.4% (731/4205)	10.4% (302/2917)	5.2% (231/4436)	74.3% (127/171)	20.0% (50/250)	35.6% (53/149)
Carmelite Friary, Aberdeen	No Data	5.1% (55/1088)	No Data	No Data	No Data	No Data
Dominican Friary, Guildford	No Data	No Data	No Data	73.2% (30/41)	100% (40/40)	No Data
Eynsham Abbey, Oxfordshire	9.1% (12/132)	4.2% (5/119)	No Data	66.7% (4/6)	No Data	No Data
Hulton Abbey, Staffordshire	No Data	No Data	No Data	4.2% (1/24)	50.0% (8/16)	20.8% (5/24)
Tintern Abbey, Co Wexford	17.7% (150/849)	14.3% (86/602)	No Data	93.3% (28/30)	74.2% (23/31)	No Data
St Gregory's Priory, Canterbury	21.7% (279/1286)	11.9% (118/993)	4.4% (56/1274)	No Data	100.0% (42/42)	47.6% (20/42)
Whitefriars, Buttermarket, Ipswich	No Data	15.1% (41/271)	No Data	75.0% (9/12)	75.0% (9/12)	6.7% (1/15)
Partney, Lincolnshire	5.7% (23/404)	1.6% (6/371)	1.2%	No Data	No Data	No Data

Note: AMTL (ante-mortem tooth loss; *p 33*); TPR/CPR (true prevalence rate/crude prevalence rate); for definitions of caries, periapical cavities, calculus, periodontitis, and DEH (dental enamel hypoplasia) see *pp 33-4*. Corrected CPR is only given for calculus, peridontitis, and DEH in comparative assemblages.

Table 6: Comparison of true prevalence rates for dental pathology at Brunel Court, with contemporary assemblages

16 female sockets), from which 16 teeth had clearly been lost ante-mortem. There was no evidence of non-eruption or agenesis of third molars (*ie* teeth that had formed in the jaw but had not grown into the gums, or had failed to form altogether).

Calculus

Dental plaque, a dense accumulation of micro-organisms on the tooth surface, is responsible for the most common dental diseases to affect teeth once they have erupted (Hillson 1996, 254). Calculus is mineralised plaque, attached to the surface of the tooth, and is most common close to the ducts of the salivary glands (*op cit*, 255-6). As well as providing information on oral hygiene practices, it has been linked to diets high in protein and/or carbohydrates.

In total, 72.2% of adult dentitions (8/11) and 58.9% (99/168) of all teeth had calculus deposits. The CPR is comparable to those of most of the contemporary sites studied, which range from 73.2% to 93.3% of dentitions being affected (Table 5). Compared with the rates calculated for the period by Roberts and Cox (2003, 262), the CPR is higher (72.2% compared with 59.2%), as might be expected for a small sample, but the TPR is similar (58.9% compared with 54%; *ibid*).

Caries

Dental caries is a destruction of enamel, dentine, and cement, resulting from acid produced by bacteria in dental plaque, leading to cavity formation in the tooth crown or root surface (Hillson 1996, 269). Diets high in sugar have a well-established association with acidogenic bacteria, and are, therefore, a major factor in the formation of caries (Lukacs 1989, 261). Severe caries can cause large cavities, which can lead to dental abscesses and, ultimately, tooth loss. Carious lesions were observed in 36.4% (4/11) of adult dentitions. In total, 21 teeth were affected, a TPR of 12.5% (21/168). In general, the rate of caries is closer to those given for urban assemblages (Table 6) and is more than double that observed at the rural Carmelite Friary near Aberdeen (5.1%; Kerr *et al* 1988), or at Eynsham Abbey, Oxfordshire (4.2%; Boyle 1998), and the 5.6% TPR calculated for the period as a whole (Roberts and Cox 2003, 259).

Periodontitis

Periodontal disease is brought on by chronic inflammation of the tissues of the mouth, specifically the gums, periodontal ligament, and alveolar bone of the jaws, and may be linked to genetics, environment, diet, and/or oral hygiene (Hillson 1996, 262, 269). Early stages of the disease involve the gums only, and are classified as gingivitis. The last stage involves all the periodontal tissues, including the alveolar bone, and is classed as periodontitis. Detachment of the periodontal ligament and progressive resorption of alveolar bone

can ultimately lead to tooth loss, after which the tooth socket will remodel (*op cit*, 266).

Of the nine individuals with observable sockets, two had mild periodontitis, equating to grade two on Ogden's scale (2008, 293; CPR: 22.2%; TPR: 2.5%, 2/79). This is similar to the 20% CPR observed at Blackfriars, Ipswich (Mays 1991a), but the average for the period is rather greater, at 37.5% (Roberts and Cox 2003, 261). Indeed, it would appear that, typically, a high proportion of burials associated with monastic sites display periodontal disease (Table 6), with every individual at the Dominican Friary, Guildford (Henderson 1984), and St Gregory's Priory, Canterbury (Anderson and Andrews 2001), being affected.

Periapical cavities

Assisted by periodontal disease and calculus, caries, excessive attrition, or trauma to the tooth crown can lead to infection of the pulp cavity (colloquially an abscess) and a resultant build-up of pus (Hillson 1986, 316). As pus accumulates, pressure increases, and a periapical cavity (a small sinus, or fistula) will form in the wall of the jaw at the apex of the tooth socket, allowing extrusion of the pus (*op cit*, 317; Roberts and Manchester 1995, 50). Periapical cavities can also be caused by the bone remodelling away from periapical granulomata and apiceal periodontal cysts. These arise from the development and subsequent inflammation of tumour-like masses of granular tissue in response to infection.

Periapical cavities were identified only on skeleton *158* (grave 8; *Ch 2, pp 20-1*; CPR: 11.1%, 1/9; TPR: 1.3%, 1/79), although poor preservation precluded determination of the type and cause of the cavity. At Blackfriars, Ipswich (Mays 1991a), and St Gregory's Priory, Canterbury (Anderson and Andrews 2001), periapical cavities were more frequent, but these are larger assemblages than that from Brunel Court (Table 6). Roberts and Cox (2003, 260) report an average CPR of 3.1% for the period.

Ante-mortem tooth loss

Ante-mortem tooth loss can result from caries, abscesses, and periodontal disease, but also from dentistry and trauma (Roberts and Cox 2003, 324). Five of nine adult jaws were affected, involving 16 teeth (CPR: 55.6%; TPR: 20.3%, 16/79). The TPR is very close to the 19.4% calculated for the period (Roberts and Cox 2003, 263), whilst the fairly high CPR is similar to the range observed at other monastic sites (Table 6). Most cases at Brunel Court were among the older age categories (35+ years), which is consistent with the degenerative nature of the disease process (Hillson 1996, 198). All of the skeletons affected also had caries, which may have been an important causative factor, but in the case of skeleton *158* (grave 8), the tooth loss may have related to the abnormal attrition observed on the remaining teeth (*below*).

Dental enamel hypoplasia

Dental enamel hypoplasia is a defect on the buccal (cheek) or labial (lip) surface of the affected tooth crown, and may appear as lines, pits, or grooves (Hillson 1986, 129). These defects are caused by thinning of the enamel, and reflect an interruption of its development, up to around 12 years of age (Brickley *et al* 2006, 144). Prolonged episodes of illness and/or malnutrition, lasting at least three weeks, are thought to result in such defects; thus it may be used as an indicator of non-specific physiological stress during this period of childhood (Hillson 1996, 166). Whether its presence denotes individuals who were compromised physiologically or, because the presence of such defects indicates recovery, individuals who had a good immune response, is an ongoing debate (Duray 1996; Lewis and Roberts 1997).

Some 167 teeth from 11 adults were observable (excluding teeth where crowns were obscured by calculus, or were largely lost to caries or severe attrition). In total, 14 teeth (8.4%) displayed dental enamel hypoplasia, which in all cases took the form of a faint horizontal line or groove. Only corrected CPRs were available for comparison. The CPR for Brunel Court (18.2%; 2/11) is in keeping with the majority of those observed at contemporary sites (20.8-47.6%; Table 6), although the 6.7% CPR from Whitefriars, Buttermarket, Ipswich, was notably low (Mays 1991b).

Dental anomalies

A few dental anomalies were recorded. The right second lower premolar in 25-35-year-old male skeleton *158* (grave 8; *Ch 2, pp 20-1*) was rotated 135º clockwise, whilst the molars of adult male skeleton *269* (grave 28; *Ch 2, pp 21-2*) had an unusual pattern of attrition on the occlusal (biting) surfaces. This was heavy on the upper and lower third molars, moderate on the second molars, and light on the first molars. This is the reverse of the normal pattern, where dental attrition is heaviest on the first molars and relatively light on the third molars, consistent with the amount of time during which these teeth have been erupted and in occlusion. All of skeleton *269*'s surviving premolars were free from caries, and the surviving right mandible was free from periapical cavities, although the right lower first molar had been lost ante-mortem. Extra-masticatory wear, such as the use of the teeth as a tool or a third hand, is unlikely, because the more easily accessible anterior dentition is usually favoured (Gibson 2002), and, in the present case, they showed no unusual attrition.

Juvenile dental health

Two of the four juvenile individuals had observable dentitions, comprising five deciduous and 32 permanent teeth that were either fully erupted, erupting, or loose. Unerupted teeth in sockets (n=5), even if partially visible, were not counted for analysis, nor were those that consisted of a root only, due to post-mortem damage. In total, 15 sockets/tooth positions were observable, of which two were recorded as having lost teeth post-mortem. Caries were observed in both juvenile dentitions, affecting single deciduous and permanent teeth, whilst 11-12-year-old *209* (grave 22; *Ch 2, p 21*) had two permanent teeth with calculus deposits (Table 7). Six-to-seven-year-old *189* (grave 20; *Ch 2, p 21*) had two permanent teeth with dental enamel hypoplasia.

Skeletal Pathology

A wide variety of skeletal manifestations of disease was encountered in the Brunel Court assemblage. These have been classified into one of the following categories, according to their primary aetiology (cause; Table 8; Fig 22):

Skeleton	No crowns observable		No sockets observable	No crowns/sockets with							
				Caries		Calculus		DEH		PC	AMTL
	Perm	Decid		Perm	Decid	Perm	Decid	Perm	Decid		
189	11	5	13	0	1	0	0	2	0	0	0
209	21	0	2	1	0	2	0	0	0	0	0
Total	*32*	*5*	*15*	*1*	*1*	*2*	*0*	*2*	*0*	*0*	*0*
TPR %				3.1 (1/32)	20.0 (1/5)	6.3 (2/32)	0 (0/5)	6.3 (2/32)	0 (0/5)	0 (0/15)	0 (0/15)
CPR %				50.0 (1/2)	100 (1/1)	50.0 (1/2)	0 (0/1)	50.0 (1/2)	0 (0/1)	0 (0/2)	0 (0/2)

Notes: Perm=permanent teeth; Decid=deciduous teeth; DEH=Dental enamel hypoplasia; PC=Periapical cavity; AMTL=ante-mortem tooth loss.

Table 7: True and crude prevalence rates for juvenile dental pathology

- Circulatory disorders
- Non-specific inflammation
- Metabolic disorders
- Spinal joint disease
- Extra-spinal joint disease
- Trauma
- Neoplastic disease
- Miscellaneous disease (*ie* diseases of unknown aetiology)
- Undiagnosed conditions.

No specific infections or congenital/developmental anomalies were observed.

Pathological lesions were identified on the skeletons of two out of four juveniles and 12 of 21 adults (56.0% of the assemblage as a whole; 14/25), over half of whom (8/14) were affected by more than one category of disease. All of the 11 individuals with no pathological changes were less than 25% complete, and 81.8% of them were highly fragmented (9/11), suggesting that the observation of pathological conditions might have been higher had preservation been better.

Spinal joint disease was the most frequently observed type of pathology, followed by non-specific inflammation. This differs from other sites, and the

	Adults	Juveniles	Total
Circulatory disorders	9.5% (2/21)	0.0% (0/4)	8.0% (2/25)
Non-specific inflammation	23.8% (5/21)	25.0% (1/4)	24.0% (6/25)
Metabolic disorders	19.0% (4/21)	25.0% (1/4)	20.0% (5/25)
Extra-spinal joint disease	14.3% (3/21)	0.0% (0/4)	12.0% (3/25)
Spinal joint disease	42.9% (9/21)	0.0% (0/4)	36% (9/25)
Trauma	9.5% (2/21)	0.0% (0/4)	8.0% (2/25)
Neoplastic disease	0.0% (0/21)	25.0% (1/4)	4.0% (1/25)
Miscellaneous	4.8% (1/21)	0.0% (0/4)	4.0% (1/25)
Undiagnosed conditions	4.8% (1/21)	0.0% (0/4)	4.0% (1/25)

Table 8: Crude prevalence rates of pathological conditions by disease category

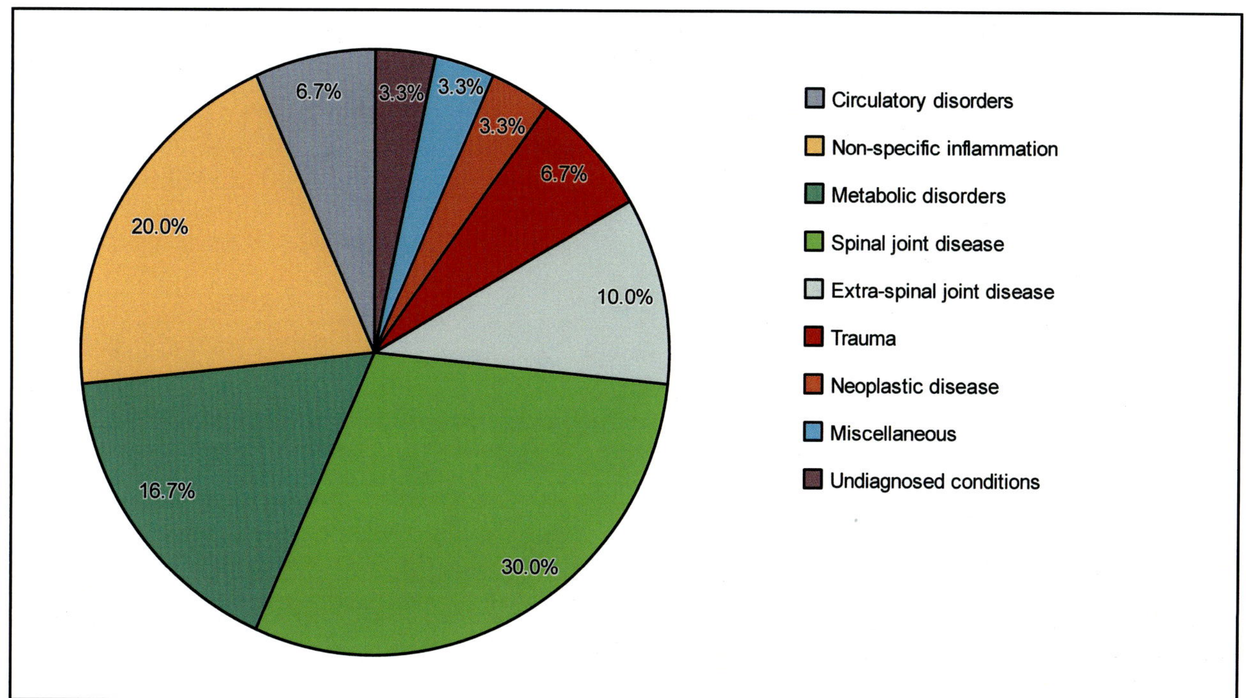

Figure 22: Percentage of cases of skeletal pathology, according to primary aetiology

unusually low occurrence of extra-spinal joint disease (*ie* away from the backbone; Rogers 2000, 163) at Brunel Court is probably due to the low representation of well-preserved joint surfaces. In common with most archaeological populations, neoplastic and miscellaneous conditions were not well represented.

Circulatory disorders

Obstruction to normal blood flow can be caused by numerous factors, including infections, trauma to the arteries and veins, and auto-immune conditions. Whilst in most instances the arterial lesion is too small to be easily observed, it can result in cellular death (necrosis) of the tissue it normally perfuses. If the individual survives the condition, the skeletal tissue is usually absorbed, resulting in a cortical defect (Aufderheide and Rodríguez-Martín 1998, 77). Several such conditions were observed within the Brunel Court assemblage.

One probable and one possible case of Legg-Calve-Perthes' (abbreviated to Perthes') disease was observed, a condition that is not uncommon in archaeological material (Roberts and Cox 2003), including two cases from Blackfriars Friary, Ipswich (CPR: 0.8% 2/250; Mays 1991a). Perthes' disease results from an obstruction of the blood supply to the head of the femur during childhood, and is probably initiated by trauma (Ortner 2003, 346). This can cause necrosis, deformation, and a widened and flattened femoral head and neck, as well as flattening and elongation of the corresponding hip socket (the acetabulum; Aufderheide and Rodríguez-Martín 1998, 84). The condition was observed on the right hip of mature adult female *198* (grave 23; *Ch 2, p 18*; CPR: 4.0%, 1/25), the femur having a mushroom-shaped head and a shortened, flattened, neck, and the acetabulum was flattened. Considerable porosity, eburnation (polishing), osteophytosis (additional bone growth), and bony contour change were also present on and around the joint, and are consistent with secondary osteoarthritis. Similar deformities may also occur in slipped femoral capital epiphysis, although that is an unlikely diagnosis for skeleton *198* because there

is no inferior displacement of the femoral head, the joint surface is not smooth and intact, the depression for the *ligamentum teres* is not well defined, and the radiographic appearance of the bone shows a poorly organised trabecular structure (Ortner 2003, 346-9).

Prime adult (26-35 years) male skeleton *158* (grave 8; *Ch 2, pp 20-1*) also exhibited (minor) pathological changes on his femoral heads, which may have been caused by disruption to the circulatory system. The diagnosis is unconfirmed, however (*p 41*).

Mature adult male skeleton *203* (36-45 years old; grave 6; *Ch 2, p 20*) had a large, crescent-shaped, erosive lesion on the anterior margin of the twelfth thoracic vertebra, consistent with Scheurmann's disease (CPR 4.0% 1/25). This had caused anterior wedging of the vertebral body, the height of which was reduced by 6 mm. This characteristic wedging can lead to scoliosis or kyphosis (curvature of the spine), where numerous vertebrae are involved (Aufderheide and Rodríguez-Martín 1998, 87; Helms 1989), although skeleton *203* was unlikely to have been so afflicted; two cases (CPR 0.8% 2/250) were found at Blackfriars, Ipswich (Mays 1991a). The onset of the disease is usually between the ages of 12 and 18, though it has been reported as starting as late as 23 (Aufderheide and Rodríguez-Martín 1998, 87).

Non-specific inflammation

Non-specific bone inflammation was the second most common type of pathology observed at Brunel Court, accounting for 20.7% of all cases of disease, and being observed on almost a quarter of skeletons (24.0%, 6/25; Table 9). Bone inflammation has three main causative factors: extension of a soft-tissue infection to the bone; part of a more generalised disease process; or involvement from infection of the underlying bone (osteitis or osteomyelitis; Aufderheide and Rodríguez-Martín 1998, 172).

Five adults from Brunel Court had periostitis, which occurs as thin layers of new bone that are deposited as a result of inflammation of the periosteum, the

Site	Periostitis Total CPR (n/N)	Osteitis Total CPR% (n/N)
Brunel Court, Preston	20.0% (5/25)	4.0% (1/25)
Dominican Friary, Guildford	7.1% (8/113)	2.7% (16/589)
Dominican Priory, Chelmsford	2.9% (4/138)	-
Tintern Abbey, Co Wexford	4.6% (4/88)	-
St Gregory's Priory, Canterbury	-	13.2% (12/91)

Table 9: Inter-site comparison of non-specific bone inflammation (periostitis) and osteitis CPRs (crude prevalence rates)

thin sheath that covers the outer surfaces of bones. As well as infection, trauma, neoplastic disease, and haemorrhage may all produce periosteal new bone (*op cit*, 172). As healing occurs, the new bone is remodelled and may eventually be completely resorbed. For this reason, the number of cases of periostitis recorded in archaeological bone in a population probably under-estimates the true prevalence, as many fully healed cases would be unobservable (Brickley *et al* 2006, 113). The overall CPR at Brunel Court (20.0%, 5/25 individuals, or 23.8% for 5/21 adults) is much higher than at other monastic sites, and is closer to the 14.1% CPR calculated for the medieval period in general (Roberts and Cox 2003, 235).

Analysis of non-specific bone inflammation (periostitis) by skeletal element showed several typical trends (Fig 23). Not surprisingly, given its proximity to the skin and its susceptibility to recurrent minor trauma (Roberts and Manchester 1995, 130), the tibia (shin bone) was the most commonly affected element (TPR: 25.0%, 6/24). The tibia was also the most commonly affected element among the skeletons from Warrington Friary, where 60% and 58% of right and left male tibias, respectively, were affected (Boylston and Weston 2001, 176; 2002).

Multiple elements were affected by periostitis in three cases. Mature adult (36-45 years) female *198* (grave 23; *Ch 2, p 18*) had periostitis involving her right tibia and right femoral neck, the latter of which also had changes associated with Perthes' disease (*Ch 2, p 36*; although it is not possible to say whether the two conditions were necessarily related). In adult males skeletons *158* and *235* (graves 8 and 30; *Ch 2, p 20, p 21*), small patches of dense new bone growth, indicating healed periostitis, were observed on multiple elements, including both femoral shafts and the left tibial shaft of skeleton *158* and the right femoral, tibial, and fibular shafts, and the proximal second metatarsal, of skeleton *235*. Multiple periosteal lesions may refer to systemic

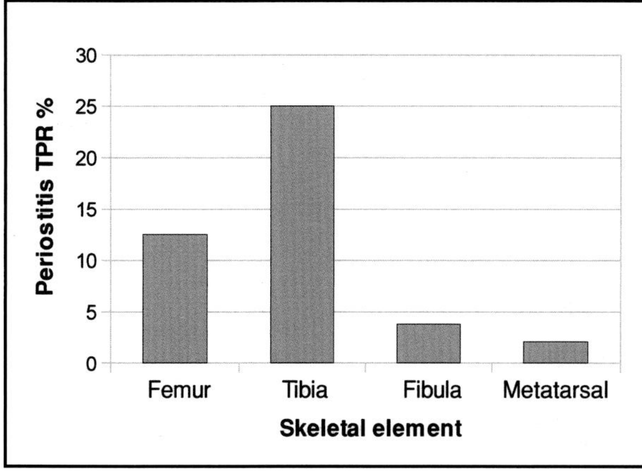

Figure 23: True prevalence rate (TPR) of periostitis, by skeletal element

conditions, but the patterns and distributions of lesions seen in these skeletons are not specific to a particular disease process.

Only one individual, older child *189* (grave 20; *Ch 2, p 21*), had osteitis (total CPR: 4.0%; juvenile CPR: 25.0%), an inflammation of the bone cortex. Osteitis can accompany non-infectious conditions, can occur with or without infection of the underlying medullary cavity (osteomyelitis), and can be hard to differentiate from the latter condition (Aufderheide and Rodríguez-Martín 1998, 172; Resnick and Niwayama 1995). In the case of child *189*, the left ulna and radius were affected (TPR: 4.0%, 1/25; and 3.4%, 1/29, respectively) and the condition may have been related to possible neoplastic disease, involving the orbit (*below*). Osteitis has been recorded in several of the comparative assemblages (Table 9), where a similar prevalence rate is reported for the Dominican Friary, Guildford (Henderson 1984), but a much higher rate was seen at St Gregory's Priory, Canterbury (Anderson and Andrews 2001). The overall CPR calculated for the medieval period is 2.7% (Roberts and Cox 2003, 240).

Metabolic disorders

Metabolic disorders may manifest as a disruption of bone formation, bone remodelling, and/or bone mineralisation, with the most common forms related to some form of vitamin or mineral deficiency (Brickley 2000, 337; Roberts and Cox 2003, 304-10). The principal metabolic condition at Brunel Court appeared to be iron-deficiency anaemia, which manifested as cribra orbitalia. In this condition, the roof of the eye socket becomes thin and porous, probably due to pressure from the expansion of the marrow-rich underlying trabecular bone, as the body seeks to produce more red blood cells (Stuart-Macadam 1982; 1991; Roberts and Manchester 1995, 167). Aside from a diet deficient in iron, excessive blood loss through injury, chronic disease such as cancer, and parasitic infection of the gut may all have played a significant part in iron deficiency during this period (Roberts and Manchester 1995, 166). Cribra orbitalia is commonly most fully developed in infancy, but the degree of healing may be indicative of ongoing physiological stress into adulthood, and it is likely that the most minimal examples in older individuals represent a healing stage of a previously more severe lesion (Aufderheide and Rodríguez-Martín 1998, 349).

In total, 20.0% (5/25) of the Brunel Court assemblage displayed this condition. However, only nine skeletons actually had at least one observable orbit, giving a rather higher corrected CPR of 55.6% (5/9 individuals) and a TPR of 42.9% (6/14 eye sockets). The overall CPRs are similar to those calculated for Blackfriars and Whitefriars, Ipswich (Mays 1991a; 1991b; Table 10),

Site	CPR (n/N)
Brunel Court, Preston	20.0% (5/25)
Blackfriars Friary, Ipswich	19.2% (10/52)
Hulton Abbey, Staffordshire	4.2% (1/24)
St Gregory's Priory, Canterbury	3.3% (3/91)
Tintern Abbey, Co Wexford	13.6% (12/88)
Whitefriars, Buttermarket, Ipswich	20.0% (3/15)

Table 10: Inter-site comparison of cribra orbitalia rates

but are extremely high compared with other sites, including Hulton Abbey, Staffordshire (Wise 1985), St Gregory's Priory, Canterbury (Anderson and Andrews 2001), and the medieval average CPR of 10.8% (Roberts and Cox 2003, 235).

A single possible instance of rickets was observed (CPR: 4.0%, 1/25). Although some cases may have a hereditary basis, this childhood disease is caused principally by a prolonged deficiency in dietary, or naturally synthesised, vitamin D, preventing the efficient absorption of calcium and resulting in soft, poorly mineralised limb bones that can become bent or distorted by the weight of the individual (Pfitzner *et al* 1998; Waldron 2009, 127-9; Roberts and Manchester 1995, 174). So-called healed or 'residual' rickets may be cautiously identified in adult skeletons by the presence of bilaterally bowed leg bones (Waldron 2009, 129), and this may have been the case of skeleton *193* (grave 17; *Ch 2, p 18*). Both femora of this older adult (45+ years) man were slightly bowed anteriorly, and the tibial shafts were slightly flattened in the medio-lateral plane. Given that these changes were only slight, it has not been possible to attribute them to rickets with confidence. For example, the changes may relate to post-mortem plastic deformation as a result of taphonomic processes.

Spinal joint disease

Lesions of joint disease in the spine are considered separately from those of the extra-spinal skeleton, given the greater complexity of joint disease aetiology and the variety of joint types in this region. The term covers various age-related and degenerative conditions, including:

- osteoarthritis (OA): the progressive degradation of the synovial joints, leading to pitting, development of bony osteophytes, and, eventually, the bone-on-bone polishing known as 'eburnation'. Symptoms may include pain, swelling, and, in more severe cases, limited movement of the affected joint (Aufderhide and Rodríquez-Martín 1998, 93; Ortner 2003, 93; Rogers and Waldron 1995, 43-5; Roberts and Manchester 1995, 106);

- spondylosis deformans (SD): degeneration of the intervertebral discs, often associated with prolonged labour-intensive physical activities, causing the growth of horizontal bony osteophytes on the upper and lower margins of the vertebral bodies, which can themselves also become pitted and bear reactive bone growth (Jurmain 1977, 353-6; Lovell 1994; Kahl and Smith 2000, 433; Rogers and Waldron 1995, 27; Ortner 2003, 555);

- Schmorl's nodes (SN): distinct depressions on the upper and lower surfaces of the vertebral bodies, created as bone resorbs away from the pressure of a herniated (ruptured and protruding) intervertebral disc, often caused by a sudden impact, and producing the conditions lumbago and, eventually, sciatica (Rogers and Waldron 1995, 27; Lovell 1997, 159; Martini *et al* 2003);

- ankylosing spondylitis: the inflammation of spinal joints, which frequently ankylose (fuse with new bone growth), and which can occur in young men in their second decade (Rogers and Waldron 1995, 65).

Spinal joint disease was only seen within the adult assemblage, where it affected eight out of 13 individuals (61.5%) with one or more observable vertebrae (*ie* with at least 50% of a body surface and/ or at least two apophyseal joint surfaces observable; Table 11). The overall CPR of 38.1% (8/21) is rather

Spinal region	Osteoarthritis (OA) TPR% (n/N)	Schmorl's nodes TPR% (n/N)	Marginal osteophytosis TPR% (n/N)
Cervical	10.7 (3/28)	0.00 (0/26)	15.4 (4/26)
Thoracic	5.3 (2/38)	60.0 (42/70)	44.3 (31/70)
Lumbar	0.0 (0/30)	38.5 (10/26)	15.4 (4/26)
Total	*9.3* *(22/236)*	*46.7* *(52/214)*	*38.8* *(83/214)*

Note: For OA, N=total number of observable vertebral arches with observable apophyseal joint facets; for all other conditions, N=total number of observable vertebral bodies.

Table 11: True prevalence rates (TPR) of spinal joint disease, showing distribution by spinal region

higher than those for Eynsham Abbey, Oxfordshire (11.1%; Boyle 1998), and the medieval average of 20.9% (Roberts and Cox 2003, 281).

Three adults had spinal osteoarthritis involving the apophyseal joints and/or the articular facets for the ribs (Table 12). The cervical spine was the most frequently affected region, with no cases observed in the lumbar and sacral spine. The CPR, although similar to that for extra-spinal osteoarthritis from the assemblage, is lower than that for both of the comparative sites (especially so in the case of Blackfriars, Ipswich; Mays 1991a) and for the medieval period overall (Roberts and Cox 2003, 282). That the three cases at Brunel Court were observed on a mature adult and two older adults (35-45 and 45+ years) reflects the degenerative nature of the disease.

Marginal osteophytosis was observed in seven adults, occurring on over a third of observable vertebrae (CPR: 33.3%, 7/21; 87.5% (7/8) individuals with vertebral bodies). The thoracic region was most frequently affected, followed by both the lumbar and cervical regions (Table 11). Although the CPR exceeds the medieval average of 12.8% (Roberts and Cox 2003, 282), it is considerably lower than at Mottisfort Abbey, Romsey (66.7%, 8/12; McKinley 1995).

A third of adults had Schmorl's nodes (CPR: 33.3%, 7/21, or 87.5% of eight adults with observable vertebral bodies). Of the 52 vertebrae so affected, the vast majority was seen on the thoracic, followed by the lumbar, spine, in keeping with published trends (TPR: 46.7%, 52/214; Rogers and Waldron 1995, 27). None was observed in the cervical spine. The rate of Schmorl's nodes is comparable to that of Blackfriars, Ipswich (Mays 1991a), but is more than double that of Whitefriars, Buttermarket, Ipswich (Mays 1991b; Table 12).

Extra-spinal joint disease

The only extra-spinal joint disease observed was osteoarthritis (cases of osteophytosis (the development of bony growths without the full suite of indicators) are not included in this discussion, but are recorded in the project archive). Extra-spinal osteoarthritis was observed in three adults (CPR: 14.3%, 3/21) and affected 3.2% (5/155) of adult joints. Only Tintern Abbey, Co Wexford (O'Donnabhain 1991), has a notably higher rate, whilst Hulton Abbey, Staffordshire (Wise 1985), and St Gregory's Priory, Canterbury (Anderson and Andrews 2001), had broadly similar overall rates to Brunel Court (Table 12), and are closer to the medieval average of 16.8% (Roberts and Cox 2003, 283). The positive correlation of osteoarthritis with increasing age is reflected at Brunel Court by its incidence only in mature female skeleton *198* (36-45 years old; *Ch 2, p 18*), and two out of the three older adults (45+ years; male *193* and female *124a*; *Ch 2, p 18, p 19*; Rogers and Waldron 1995, 32; Roberts and Manchester 1995, 106; Table 13).

Only one of the cases appeared to be secondary to another disease, and concerned the right hip of skeleton *198* (grave 23; *Ch 2, p 18*). There, considerable osteophytes, porosity, change to the joint contours, and eburnation were observed, and were secondary to Legg-Calve-Perthes' disease (*p 36*). Unusually, eburnation was observed on the pelvis of skeleton *124a* (grave 2), occurring on the superior demi-facet of both of the iliac auricular surfaces. Whilst the sacro-iliac joint is not usually considered as a true synovial joint, the superior demi-facet is synovial, and therefore has been included in the statistics for this site.

Trauma

Trauma, broadly defined as an injury to living tissue inflicted by a force external to the body itself (Lovell 1997, 139), was identified on three individuals,

Site	Spinal osteoarthritis CPR (n/N)	Adult Schmorl's nodes CPR (n/N)	Extra-spinal osteoarthritis CPR (n/N)
Brunel Court, Preston	14.3% (3/21)	33.3% (7/21)	14.3% (3/21)
Blackfriars Friary, Ipswich	60.0% (150/250)	30.5% (69/226)	-
Whitefriars, Buttermarket, Ipswich	-	16.7% (2/12)	-
Mottisfort Abbey, Romsey	41.7% (5/12)	-	16.7% (4/24)
Hulton Abbey, Staffordshire	-	-	17.6% (16/91)
St Gregory's Priory, Canterbury	-	-	
Tintern Abbey, Co Wexford	19.3% (17/88)	-	40.1% (36/88)

Table 12: Inter-site comparison of rates of spinal osteoarthritis, adult Schmorl's nodes, and extra-spinal osteoarthritis

Skeleton	Age category	Sex	Joint		TPR		
			Left	Right	Left	Right	Total
124a	Older adult	F	Sacro-iliac	Sacro-iliac	14.3% (1/7)	12.5% (1/8)	13.3% (1/19)
193	Older adult	M	Wrist	Wrist	20.0% (1/5)	25.0 (1/4)	22.2% (2/9)
198	Mature adult	F	-	Hip	0.0% (0/8)	9.1% (1/11)	5.3% (1/19)

Table 13: Distribution of osteoarthritis by joint, sex, age, and side

Site	CPR (n/N)
Brunel Court, Preston	9.5% (2/21)
Blackfriars Friary, Ipswich	18.1% (41/226)
Whitefriars, Buttermarket, Ipswich	33.3% (4/12)

Table 14: Inter-site comparison of crude prevalence rates (CPR) of adult fractures

including two fractures (CPR 8.0%; 2/25), and one case of cortical defects (skeleton *203*; grave 6; *Ch 2, p 20*). Prime adult (26-35 years old) male skeleton *158* (grave 18; *Ch 2, pp 20-1*) had a healed fracture on the distal shaft of the right fibula, probably caused by indirect trauma, such as forcible rotation of the foot, although a direct blow cannot be ruled out (TPR: 3.8%; 1/26; Galloway 1999, 203). Unsexed 18-25-year-old *223* (grave 25) had a fractured right radius (mid-shaft), also healed (TPR: 4.5%; 1/22). The radius fracture was oblique, its pattern and location suggestive of a high energy-direct trauma, such as an assault (*op cit*, 137).

Overall, the CPR for fractures among the Brunel Court skeletons is low compared with those observed among the two Ipswich assemblages (Mays 1991a; 1991b; Table 14) and Warrington Friary (Boylston and Weston 2001; 2002), where nine individuals (six men and three women) had sustained fractures, including several blade injuries. However, in common with these and other assemblages, no fractures were observed amongst the juveniles. It is likely that juveniles of the past sustained fractures as frequently as they do today, but their tendency to suffer incomplete (greenstick) fractures, and to heal rapidly, means that evidence of this is hard to detect archaeologically (Brickley *et al* 2006, 120-1).

Mature adult male skeleton *203* (grave 6; *Ch 2, p 20*) had cortical defects on both of his clavicles (collar bones), at the site of the costo-clavicular ligament. Among archaeological remains, this is a common location for cortical defects, which occur where strong muscles attach to bone, and are believed to be the result of repeated micro-avulsions (tearing away) of the bony cortex due to intense mechanical stress (Bufkin 1971, 492; Hawkey and Merbs 1995). The identification of the condition relies on well-preserved bone surfaces, and, accordingly, the presence and frequency of cortical defects in the Brunel Court assemblage was not routinely scored.

Neoplastic disease

Neoplasms are the uncontrolled growth of tissue cells, and include various benign and malignant tumours (Roberts and Manchester 1995, 186). A single case was observed on the upper quadrant of the left eye socket of six-to-seven-year-old child *189* (grave 20; *Ch 2, p 21*), in the form of a large kidney-shaped lytic (destructive) lesion that measured approximately 17 mm (medial to lateral) by 8 mm (superior to inferior; Pl 13). There was no macroscopic evidence for expansion of the cortical bone or reactive bone growth. The base of the lesion comprised sclerotic (additional) bone, the superior margin being irregular and porous, and the inferior margin was smooth. The area outside the lesion was unaffected, except for some slight porosity.

The sclerotic base to the lesion is indicative of a slow, but expansive, neoplastic disease, such as an aneurysmal bone cyst, which occurs in individuals between five and 12 years of age. In this disease, which is the most common tumour to affect the orbits in children (M Lewis *pers comm*), the cortex does not expand in the initial stages. Although this is similar to the case of child *189*, radiographic investigation is

*Plate 13: Neoplastic lytic lesion on the left orbit of six-seven-year-old child **189***

required to determine whether the margin of the lesion is sclerotic, and to confirm the diagnosis. Differential diagnoses include a haemingioma, which invades the cortical bone, and rhabdomyosarcomas, which can invade bone and sinuses. However, the latter is primarily a soft-tissue disease and the former usually affects the spine and results in lesions that are punched outward, and not inward, as is the case with skeleton *189*. Other candidates are the metastatic tumours, neuroblastoma (the most common metastatic tumour to affect the eye), and Ewing tumour, but are thought to be unlikely because they result in multiple lytic lesions (Resnick 1995a; 1995b), which were not seen in the present case.

Langerhans' cell histiocytosis is a good possibility for the cause of this lesion, because the disease is often found in children, where it may well result in solitary lesions, and commonly involves the skull, ribs, and long bones (Resnick 1995c, 2214-15). In the palaeopathological literature, Langerhans' cell histiocytosis is variously classified as a hematological disorder, or a disorder of the immune system, and has only fairly recently been linked with neoplastic disease (Aufderheide and Rodriguez-Martin 1998; Ortner 2003). Of significance here is the fact that the radiographic characteristics of this disease include bone lesions that can resemble osteomyelitis (Resnick 1995c, 2214-15), and the left ulna and radius of skeleton *189* had inflammatory changes (osteitis; *Ch 2, p 21*), in addition to the lesion in the orbit. In conclusion, Langerhans' cell histiocytosis, or an aneurysmal bone cyst, are the preferred diagnoses for the changes seen on skeleton *189*.

Miscellaneous conditions

Young adult skeleton *223* (grave 25; *Ch 2, p 21*; CPR: 4.0%, 1/25) displayed pseudo-osteochondritis dessicans on the proximal joint surface of the first phalanx of the foot. The condition manifests as small pits or porous lesions located on the concave surfaces of joints (Rogers and Waldron 1995, 29-30). The aetiology of the lesion is unclear, but, unlike 'real' osteochondritis dessicans (*op cit*, 28-30) on the convex surface of a joint, the condition is not thought to result from trauma. Rather, it may possibly be caused by small developmental defects during ossification.

Undiagnosed conditions

Both femoral heads of 26-35-year-old male skeleton *158* (grave 8; *Ch 2, pp 20-1*) had a single, shallow, kidney-shaped depression, just adjacent to the fossa for the *ligamentum teres* (Pl 14). It is unlikely that this lesion relates to Perthes' disease (*p 36*), because the femoral heads were not flattened and the morphologies of the femoral necks were unaltered. Whilst the changes may refer to a circulatory condition, or trauma, which had resulted in necrosis of bone tissue, it is possible that the abnormalities are normal morphological variation in the joints, because they are unaccompanied by other changes.

*Plate 14: Undiagnosed defect on the femoral head of prime adult skeleton **158***

Stable Isotope Measurements

Peter Marshall, Chris Bronk Ramsey, Gordon Cook, and Fiona Brock

Stable isotope analysis indicated that, in common with many medieval sites in England, the people buried at Preston Friary incorporated marine and freshwater foods into a predominantly terrestrial diet (Müldner and Richards 2007). The isotopic data are similar to those from other medieval religious establishments, such as Whithorn, Scotland (Müldner *et al* 2009), Fishergate, York (Müldner and Richards 2007), and Furness Abbey, Cumbria (Marshall and Beavan 2012), and suggest that these individuals consumed more marine and freshwater protein than the rest of the population (Fig 24).

Conclusion

The osteological and biochemical analysis of this small, but significant, assemblage has provided important insights into the lives of some of the medieval inhabitants of Preston. It has identified that they represent a mixed population, with adults of both sexes, as well as children, some of whom have traits suggestive of genetic relationships. They display a range of more and less common lesions of pathology, some of which may relate to aspects of lifestyle, whilst stable isotope measurements have provided a rare opportunity to examine the diet of medieval people in the North West. Such information is enhanced by its integration with the other forms of data recovered (*Ch 5, p 83*).

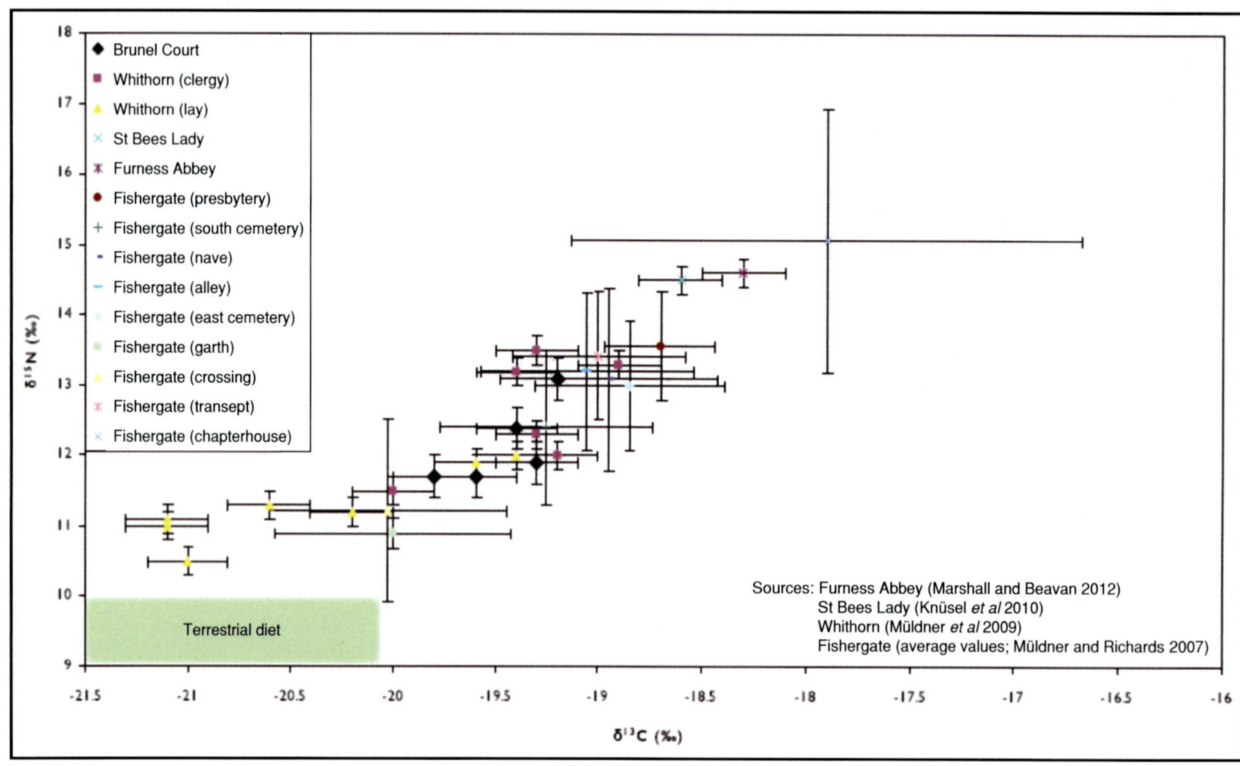

Figure 24: Distribution of isotope results in comparison with other sites

4

ARTEFACTS, ECOFACTS, SCIENTIFIC DATING, AND PALAEOENVIRONMENTAL REMAINS

Methodologies

The size of the finds assemblages recovered reflects the truncated and disturbed nature of the remains, being rather sparse, often badly damaged, and sometimes surviving in poor condition. Perhaps the most important evidence with regard to the medieval building comes from the small, but well-preserved, group of floor tiles. Their analysis followed standard recording procedures (Stopford 1990) and involved comparison with a range of other assemblages from the region, as well as further afield. Other groups of finds add some information to illustrate the appearance of the buildings on the site, and to an understanding of the objects used in daily life. These finds were recorded and analysed in accordance with standard practice (CIfA 2014), with the analysis of the medieval pottery following the Medieval Pottery Research Group guidelines (Slowikowski *et al* 2001). The broad grouping of fabrics was undertaken with reference to the collections of medieval pottery from earlier excavations in Preston and the surrounding area (*eg* Wood *et al* 2008).

The wooden coffins are of particular importance, adding to an understanding of a poorly known facet of medieval practices of the disposal of the dead. Individual fragments of coffin timbers were recorded as scaled digital images, with an outline written record, and the larger fragments were also drawn at 1:1, with any notable features, including toolmarks, illustrated. Timber species were identified microscopically with the use of reference specimens and standard reference texts (Schweingruber 1990; Hather 2000).

A key aim of the project was to undertake a programme of scientific dating that would permit the best understanding of the chronology of the site and its individual components, aiding an interpretation of the sequence of burial, and of the site as a whole. The nature of the remains permitted the utilisation of two complementary scientific dating techniques: tree-ring dating (dendrochronology) of the better-preserved oak coffin timbers; and radiocarbon dating of the

human bone, and of the holly stakes from ditch **106** (*Ch 2, p 25*). When integrated with the stratigraphic sequence, these scientific dates provided a useful chronological framework that not only placed activity within the known occupation dates of Preston Friary (*ie*, the later thirteenth to mid-sixteenth century), but also provided some clues to the sequence of burial within the building excavated.

Palaeoenvironmental samples were taken from a range of features during the fieldwork, but assessment indicated that only the waterlogged material from fill **127** of grave 4 (*Ch 2, p 18*) and fill **107** of ditch **106** (*Ch 2, pp 24-5*) had any potential, through analysis, to be informative about the local environment. The extracted waterlogged plant and insect remains were therefore examined and quantified using binocular microscopes, identification being aided by comparison with modern reference collections, and with the use of standard texts (Katz *et al* 1965; Cappers *et al* 2006; Stace 2010 for plants; and Duff 2012a; 2012b; Bantock and Botting 2012, for insects). Beetle (Coleoptera) and bug (Hemiptera) taxa were divided into broad ecological groups for interpretation (Kenward *et al* 1986; Kenward 1997), with waterside and marginal taxa included among terrestrial forms. The state of preservation of the insect remains was recorded using the system of Kenward and Large (1998), where fragmentation and erosion are scored on a scale from 0.5 (superb) to 5.5 (extremely decayed or fragmented).

Day-to-day Life

Most of the evidence for day-to-day life is drawn from the pottery, although this was a very small assemblage. It seems to reflect domestic activity, with at least the earliest coming from very local sources.

Medieval and later pottery
Jeremy Bradley
In total, 21 sherds of medieval pottery were recovered from eight stratified contexts, and also unstratified, with individual contexts producing three or fewer sherds. All fragments were 80 mm or less in

maximum dimension, but diagnostic sherds were well represented, in the form of rims, a base, and a handle. Three pottery fabrics were identified: Gritty ware (eight fragments); Northern Reduced Greenware (seven sherds); and Midlands Purple-type ware (six fragments). These spanned, very broadly, the twelfth to seventeenth centuries.

Amongst the Gritty wares, there were two possible sub-fabrics; a single sherd was in the Northern Gritty-ware tradition, which can be dated to the twelfth or thirteenth century (McCarthy and Brooks 1988), from fill *199* of grave 23 (*Ch 2, p 18*). The remainder was in a yellowish-red gritty fabric with a reduced core and an olive-green glaze. The sherds from fill *107* of ditch *106* (*Ch 2, p 25*), and from rubbly deposits *241* and *243* (respectively the fill of possible robber trench *242* and of an empty grave in the north-western graveyard; *Ch 2, p 25, p 22*), may well have been products of the Samlesbury kiln site to the east of Preston. If so, they would have a slightly later, thirteenth- to fourteenth-century, date (Wood *et al* 2008).

Three vessels in the Northern Reduced Green-ware tradition were identified: a jug handle and a jar, both from ditch *106* (*Ch 2, p 25*; Fig 25.1); and a possible fragment from a spouted dripping dish, from fill *190* of grave 20 (*Ch 2, p 21*; Fig 25.2). This vessel is distinguished by having an inturned rim and resembles a similar fragment of fifteenth-century Toynton ware from Lincolnshire. The Lincolnshire example has a zoomorphic spout (Young *et al* 2005, 175), and although this is missing from the Preston sherd, there is a clear scar where the spout was once attached. These specialised vessels and, indeed, the majority of the sherds, were in a dark grey, fine, sandy fabric, with occasional oxidised surfaces; the dark olive-green glaze was thickly applied and smooth. This fabric, however, does not resemble those commonly found in North Lancashire (Miller and White forthcoming) or Cumbria (McCarthy and Brooks 1992, 29); nor was this tradition represented at the Samlesbury kiln site (Wood *et al* 2008), but it remains possible that they were local products or regional imports. Two sherds from ditch *106*, in a softer light grey fabric, belong to the Silverdale-ware tradition of the fifteenth century and later (White 2000).

The Midlands Purple-ware tradition began in the late fifteenth century (Boyle and Rowlandson 2009), and is characterised by a hard-fired, almost stoneware-like fabric, usually grey in colour, with a purplish-brown, sometimes rather dull, glaze. Two vessels were identified: an unstratified jar with an applied thumb strip (Fig 25.3); and a hollow-ware vessel with handles, from fill *258* of ditch *106* (*Ch 2, p 25*; Fig 25.4). The latter vessel resembles a cistern from Ticknall, South Derbyshire (*op cit*, fig 8).

Some 71 sherds of post-medieval pottery were recovered, but, apart from the Midland Purple-type sherds, none could have been of sixteenth-century date. Although such a dearth is not unusual in the North West (Lewis 2002), other seventeenth-century material was largely absent from the site, at best being represented by the base of a possible early Blackware cup, from evaluation Trench 11 (*Ch 2, p 26*). Mottled

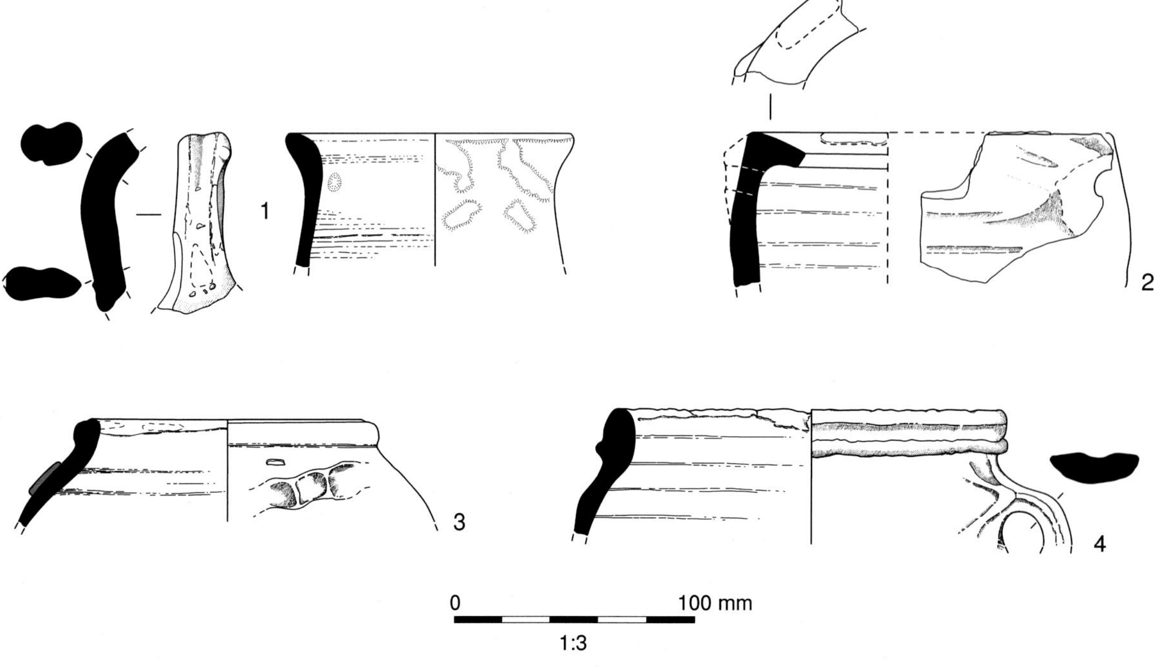

0   100 mm

1:3

Figure 25: Medieval pottery

ware, usually ascribed to the later seventeenth and first part of the eighteenth century (Barker 2008), was present in demolition deposit **230**, and on top of medieval cobble foundation **231** (*Ch 2, p 16*), suggesting that these had been exposed or, more likely, the overlying building robbed of stone, at that time. The only unequivocally eighteenth-century material came from a layer within evaluation Trench 9, which produced two refitting sherds of a white salt-glazed stoneware foot-ring, and a fragment of slip-coated ware. Rather, the majority of the pottery spanned the late eighteenth to the middle of the nineteenth century, and comprised kitchen- and fine table-wares.

Other finds
Christine Howard-Davis and Andrew Bates
Other medieval or later finds reflecting day-to-day life are extremely sparse. A single medieval fiddle-key horseshoe nail came from fill **224** of grave 25 (*Ch 2, p 21*), presumably entering the fill by accident, rather than being a deliberate addition. Seven unmodified animal bones, together weighing 300 g, were also recovered from the site. Six came from fill **107** of ditch **106** and, where identifiable to species, were of cattle and pig. Although mostly well preserved, and thus likely to have been incorporated within the ditch fill towards, or at, the end of its use, one very abraded

piece may relate to the reworking of earlier fills, as suggested by the associated pottery (*p 44*). A single calcined fragment came from rubble deposit **241** in possible robber trench **242** (*Ch 2, p 25*).

There were also 11 small fragments of industrial residue, the largest *c* 60 mm in maximum dimensions, and together these weighed less than 100 g. Stratified fragments came from ditch fill **107**, and fill **127** of grave 4 (*Ch 2, p 18*); the remainder was unstratified. It is assumed that the assemblage reflects occasional small-scale blacksmithing on the site, possibly in the course of construction. Apart from the handful of fragments of post-medieval pottery (*p 44*), there were two small and undiagnostic fragments of post-medieval clay tobacco-pipe stem.

One timber fragment associated with grave 9 stood out in being significantly thicker (32 mm) than any of the coffin boards therein, and, uniquely, had been sawn rather than axe-cut. Its consistent width (60 mm) suggested that it had survived close to its original dimensions and was, therefore, a dressed timber rather than any part of a coffin (Pl 15). It was most likely to have been associated with the later disturbance that removed the lower half of skeleton **145** in the grave (*Ch 2, p 25*).

Plate 15: The remains of the timber board in grave 9, with a later fragment above it

The Building and its Appearance

Seemingly so little was excavated of the building, and its state of preservation was so poor, that it is almost impossible to consider its form or construction; the ground plan is incomplete, and the walls were reduced to their footings. There are, however, slight indications of the internal decorative schemes, albeit not found in situ; these were provided by structural components, such as floor tiles, stonework, and window glass.

The floor tiles
Jennie Stopford

Although small (parts of just 30 tiles were recovered, scattered among a large number of contexts), this assemblage is an important group, making a contribution to knowledge of tile production in north-west England, and being the first from Preston. The majority fall within a single tile group (Stopford 2005), and, from their manufacturing characteristics and fabric, are thought to be the products of a single workshop. Typologically, they are of fourteenth- to fifteenth-century date. Although none of the tiles was found *in situ*, it seems likely that they had originally been laid as a floor, not far from where they were found. The coherence of the group, and the varied wear, with some still in very good condition, would argue against their being the remains of reused paving.

Line-impressed mosaic tiles

One of the tiles is apparently of the same design as an example shown in an antiquarian drawing from Holm Cultram Abbey, Cumbria (Gilbanks and Oldfield 1900), a group of line-impressed mosaic tiles that has been assigned to tile group 14 (reproduced in Stopford 2005, 192, fig 17.5). All but one of the examples from Brunel Court fall into that group, but the six different designs are newly identified, and numbered accordingly as 14.1-6 (Fig 26). Only eight of the 30 tiles recovered were complete: three were completely worn, with no decoration visible; but most of the remainder were unworn, or only slightly worn. One example was obscured by mortar on the upper surface as a result of redeposition. There were no wasters.

Various shapes and sizes were observed, although the majority were either *c* 125 mm-wide squares, or smaller triangles. In at least eight cases, these had been split from the square tiles by scoring across the upper surface before firing, and snapping off afterwards. A broken circular tile (100 mm in diameter; from fill *258* of ditch *106*; *Ch 2, pp 24-5*) must have been used in a mosaic, whilst a single example (from fill *199* of grave 23; *Ch 2, p 18*) may have originally been rectangular. The thickness of the unworn examples was unusually variable, ranging between 25 mm and 40 mm, and none had nail holes or keys cut into their bases. Many of the lower surfaces were uneven, and only some were sanded. The circular tile had roughly trimmed sides, visible as a series of facets sloping inwards from top to bottom, but the remainder had slightly, or steeply, bevelled sides.

Design 14.2 was the best represented, with 12 examples, of which six were either largely, or partly, complete. The three broken tiles of design 14.3 included the example obscured by mortar. The circular tile was line-impressed with design 14.1, whilst designs 14.4-6 were each represented by single examples only. Four other fragments were probably also stamped with a design, but were unidentifiable, whilst three small scored and split triangles, and the broken rectangle, had not been incised.

All were slipped and/or glazed, with most glazed either yellow/brown over a yellow slip, or dark green, dark

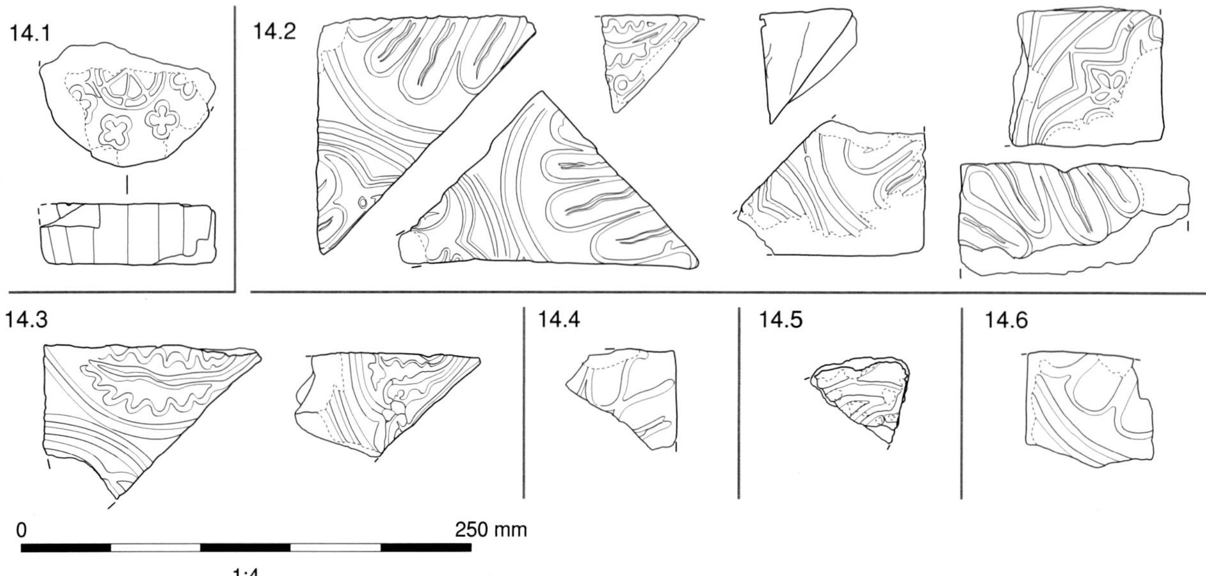

Figure 26: The designs of the line-impressed glazed tiles

brown, or black, directly over the body fabric. In some cases, however, the glaze applied over the yellow slip had fired dark green or dark brown (for example, on the broken rectangle, on the fragment of design 14.6, and on some pieces of design 14.2). It appears that two different glazes were used and, in some cases, the dark glaze had been either mistakenly, or carelessly, applied over slipped tiles. As a result, the dark glaze on these tiles had fired to an opaque metallic sheen, rather than the usual translucence. The slip coating was *c* 0.5 mm deep and successfully covered the upper surface of the yellow tiles. However, on the unworn yellow examples of design 14.2, the glaze appeared pitted.

Despite the diversity of the designs, the fabric appeared consistent, being roughly formed and laminated, with voids and many inclusions, ranging from large pebbles to quartz and grog (of both red and white clay). The body fabric of most tiles was fully oxidised, but some examples had a slightly reduced core, whilst some of the dark-glazed tiles appeared highly fired.

Unassigned tile

A single poor-quality half tile in two pieces, from the subsoil, could neither be assigned to a tile group, nor find comparators in other assemblages. It was 126 mm across, 30 mm deep, and had a laminated fabric, with pebbles and quartz inclusions, which had been oxidised on the surfaces but reduced at the core. The indistinct design comprised a stamped and slipped *fleur-de-lis*, but differentiation between the design and its background was not achieved during manufacture. Little glaze remained, but appeared yellow-brown throughout. There were no nail holes, or keys in its sandy base.

Other ceramic building material
Jeremy Bradley
The investigations in 1991 and 2007 together produced 15 fragments of ceramic building material, which comprised pieces of medieval roof tile, possible moulded brick, and post-medieval bricks. Amongst the roof tile (from evaluation Trench 9; *Ch 2*, Fig 16) there were two glazed fragments, one from a ridge tile, and the other part of a flat roof tile. A further three small glazed tile fragments could have been either flat roof tile or floor tile. One example, from evaluation Trench 11 (*Ch 2, p 26*), was clearly reused, having been shaped into a rough disc (54 mm in diameter). Such discs are fairly common on sites with tiled buildings, and can be found on sites as far apart as Southampton and Hull (Brown and Hardy 2011, 153, fig 5.21; Watkin 1987, 190, fig 108). Their use has variously been interpreted as pot lids (probably too small for such a purpose in this case), or gaming pieces.

A single example of a possible moulded chamfered brick was unstratified. It is, perhaps, an unusual find in the context of this particular establishment, as the archaeological remains and historical accounts (Whittle 1837, 126) suggest that stone was the main building material. However, such moulded bricks occur commonly on medieval sites elsewhere in the country (Potts 1996, 107). The remainder of the assemblage comprised handmade brick fragments of eighteenth- and nineteenth-century date.

Worked stone
Christine Howard-Davis
Of the three fragments of dressed stone, all unstratified, none appears to reflect sculptural or architectural detail. It would, however, seem reasonable that they derive from the fabric of buildings on the site, and most probably from that of the building investigated.

Worked stone found in the nineteenth century
Jeremy Bradley and Christine Howard-Davis
A group of seven worked stones from the area was published in Fishwick's *History of the Parish of Preston* (1900, 201-3), although their present location is not known, except for a male figure with crossed arms, which is currently on display in the Harris Museum, Preston. The workmanship appears quite crude, compared to contemporary stonework from Furness Abbey or Norton Priory, for instance (see Harrison *et al* 1998; Harrison 2008), and might contradict Whittle's rather florid description of the friary church as 'a building splendid and glorious' (1837, 126).

The images reproduced by Fishwick (Pl 16; clockwise from bottom left) are thought to represent a fragment of tracery; a possible corbel (male figure with crossed

Plate 16: Decorative stonework from south of Marsh Lane, found in the nineteenth century (reproduced from Fishwick 1900; not to scale)

arms, clearly intended to be seen from below), rather than a depiction of Christ, as described by the Harris Museum; and a voussoir with the head of Christ. The voussoir is reminiscent of depictions of St Veronica's Veil (or handkerchief), a motif much in vogue in the fourteenth century (MacGregor and Langmuir 2000), with the grooves on the facing reflecting the folds of cloth seen in many depictions. The final two stones are grotesques, probably corbels. Fishwick (1900, 202-3) also presents line drawings of a Holy Water stoup, which is shown as being bell-shaped with fluted decoration, and a sundial, apparently from the 'south wall of the Grey Friars' (*op cit*, 203).

Glass and metalwork
Christine Howard-Davis
Evidence for the presence of glazed windows in the medieval buildings is provided by a very small group (13 fragments) of window glass, all but one fragment coming from the subsoil. Their size (the largest being 30 mm across) and poor condition upon excavation (completely demineralised and crumbling) precluded any analysis. They are all flat window glass, probably greenish 'forest glass', and one piece has evidence of enamelled decoration. There is also, however, a small amount of medieval lead window kame, strongly suggesting that the glass derived from leaded lights. Elaborate lights of coloured glass were discouraged by the Franciscan General Constitution of 1260 (Little 1917, 66), and, with this in mind, the use of relatively inexpensive English-made forest glass, rather than expensive imported glass, might point to plain windows, or at the most elaborate, grisaille decoration. More elaborate pictorial windows, however, were allowed in the principal window of the friary church, behind the high altar (*op cit*, 67).

A fragment of short H-profile kame, probably of medieval date, was twisted tightly into a loop, and another small fragment (from fill *262* of grave 28; *Ch 2, p 21*) was part-melted. Both of these point to reclamation of the lead at some point, most obviously the extensive stripping and reclamation of metal that presumably accompanied the Dissolution, when lead was frequently stripped from windows and melted down on the spot (Brown and Howard-Davis 2008, 402). It must be noted, however, that unless the fragment from the fill of grave 28 is intrusive, then it probably precedes this event.

Other unstratified lead objects are also likely to have come from structures on the site, although they cannot be unequivocally assigned to the medieval buildings. For instance, there is a large run-in gallet, and a fragment of lead sheathing. The latter was probably run-in to a square-sectioned hole to support an item with the same shaped section. There were also two small pieces of much later kame, both with

a deep H-shaped profile and clearly milled, which are probably of late eighteenth- or nineteenth-century date, coming from late structures on the site. Although some of the iron nails were probably used in the buildings, mainly, from their size, in fixtures and fittings rather than securing substantial timbers, most seem to be associated with the wooden coffins (*below*).

Wooden stakes
Christine Howard-Davis
Several rows of roundwood stakes were noted in close association with ditch *106* (*Ch 2, pp 24-5*), of which a representative sample of four, including stake *116*, which had been driven into the backfill of grave 28 (*Ch 2, p 21*), was retained for examination. All were of relatively small diameter, cut from holly (*Ilex*) roundwood, and sharpened to a multi-facet point by more than ten blows. The wood had not survived well, none of the stakes being its full original length, and, beyond the shaped points, the surfaces were too poorly preserved to allow any detailed surface treatment or tool signatures to be recognised. Scientific dating (*p 54*) indicated that they were of early fourteenth- to early fifteenth-century date.

The longest stakes survived to *c* 1.4 m in length, but this merely represented the part that had been sunk into the ground; all were undoubtedly originally longer. They varied in diameter, with stake *116* being the smallest at *c* 62 mm, and the other three (*132, 153*, and *154*) all between 80 mm and 85 mm. This relative consistency of size might suggest an element of selection. Unless it simply reflects the pragmatic utilisation of whatever was available, the use of holly in a (presumably) wet ditch might suggest that the structure was not intended to be long-lived, as holly is regarded as a perishable hardwood, vulnerable to insect attack, and today it is rarely used for anything but decorative veneers and inlays, turned vessels, and trinkets (Meier 2019).

The Coffins

Christine Howard-Davis

Probably the most important medieval finds from the site were the timber coffins or grave linings, which, preserved in largely anaerobic conditions, were recovered from graves 2, 4, 8, 9, and 18 within the building (*Ch 2, p 17*). In all, some 165 fragments of riven boards were examined; the vast majority were of oak (*Quercus*), although one of the boards from coffin *161* in grave 8 (*Ch 2, p 20*) was identified as ash (*Fraxinus*). The assemblage was in fair to good condition, although often fragmented, and all surfaces were degraded to some degree. Dendrochronological dating was possible on three examples (*p 51*), and indicated that the timbers ranged in date from the mid- to late thirteenth century (*155* in grave 9; Pl 15) to the mid- to late fourteenth century (coffins *123* and *184* in graves 2 and 18, respectively; *Ch 2, pp 19-20*).

In most cases, only the fragmented base timbers had survived (Pl 17), although, in the instance of the coffins from graves 2 and 18, elements of the sides, ends, and, in the case of the latter, the lid, had also survived in part. The overall impression was that the coffins had been manufactured from long, radially riven boards that had probably been dressed with axes or adzes to reduce the originally triangular cross-section to one that was more-or-less rectangular. The boards were generally *c* 17-27 mm thick, and between 150 mm and 200 mm in width, although some were up to 300 mm wide. Two such timbers were placed side by side for the bases, whilst, in the very rare cases where sides had survived, these appeared to be single, wider, boards. The structures were thus typically rectangular, and ranged from 0.35 m to 0.39 m (*155*) across, and were 1.602-1.877 m long, by perhaps 0.3 m deep. However, coffin *184* (grave 18; *Ch 2, p 19*) was somewhat

Plate 17: Base timbers from grave 18

trapezoidal, being some 0.54 m wide at the head, but only 0.37 m wide at the foot. The preserved remains included a fragmentary lid, which was *c* 17 mm thick.

The degree of surface erosion meant that there were few surviving toolmarks, although, where preserved, these suggested the use of axes, with blade widths of 30 mm+, 43 mm+, and 60 mm+. It was possible that one board fragment from coffin *155* (grave 9; *Ch 2, p 18*) had been deliberately bevelled, presumably to reduce its width.

There was no indication of sophisticated joints, with the sides presumably nailed over the cut edges of the base boards at the head and foot. Single nail holes, placed centrally at one end, *c* 12 mm in from the edge, were identified on the base boards of coffin *123* (grave 2; *Ch 2, p 19*). Further nails were identified with the associated skeleton (*126*), whilst, from the backfill, a fragment of relatively narrow iron strip, with at least two nail holes, could have been reinforcing from the coffin. Possible evidence for the carrying of the laden coffin was observed in the form of single small (13 mm in diameter) holes in coffins *130* and *155* (graves 4 and 9, respectively; *Ch 2, p 18, p 25*). These may have served to accommodate a carrying handle, perhaps made of rope, although there was no firm evidence for this.

Dendrochronology
Ian Tyers

Sixteen of the 24 samples of oak boards, from graves 2, 9, and 18 (*Ch 2; pp 18-19*), were suitable for dendrochronological analysis. In the simplest terms, the process involves counting and measuring the sequence of tree rings present on a cross-section of each timber. Such rings represent annual growth, and the width of individual rings is a reflection of the conditions in which the trees grew, which can vary from year to year, producing a distinct pattern (English Heritage 1998). Comparing the pattern for each timber with an overall reference sequence, built up from many trees of prehistoric and historical date from throughout Britain and northern Europe, allows the dendrochronologist to ascertain the date of a specific set of tree rings on a sample. Where parts of the same sequence of tree rings are identified on several timbers, this is referred to as a cross-match.

At Brunel Court, 12 timbers had cross-matches (Table 15), indicating that either the timber derived from the same tree, or that part of the parent tree's growth period was contemporary with that of another represented at the site. As the cross-matches often occurred at different places on each timber, it was possible to arrange the samples according to their synchronised positions, and to build up a composite sequence of 351 years in length (Fig 27).

Sample	Size (mm)	Type	Rings	Sap and Bark	Date of measured sequence	Interpreted result
123.36	80 x 15	Oak	*c* 50 *	–	unmeasured	–
123.43	145 x 20	Oak	100	–	undated	–
123.50	130 x 20	Oak	75	–	undated	–
123.51/61a	265 x 15	Oak	176	–	AD 1160–1335	after AD 1345
123 51/61b	170 x 15	Oak	127	–	AD 1209–335	after AD 1345
123.54	225 x 20	Oak	157	–	AD 1161–1317	after AD 1327
123.55/56	140 x 20	Oak	126	–	AD 1199–1324	after AD 1334
123.57/58a	160 x 20	Oak	118	–	AD 1211–1328	after AD 1338
123.57/58b	135 x 20	Oak	126	–	AD 1209–1334	after AD 1344
123.59	55 x 15	Oak	*c* 50 *	–	unmeasured	–
123a	55 x 10	Oak	52	–	undated	–
123b	295 x 25	Oak	247	–	AD 1008–1254	after AD 1264
123c	85 x 15	Oak	*c* 60 *	–	unmeasured	–
123d	85 x 15	Oak	*c* 60 *	–	unmeasured	–
123e	85 x 15	Oak	*c* 60 *	–	unmeasured	–
123f	65 x 10	Oak	*c* 50 *	–	unmeasured	–
130a	155 x 15	Oak	86	–	undated	–
130b	100 x 15	Oak	*c* 31	–	unmeasured	–
130c	40 x 5	Oak	*c* 15	–	unmeasured	–
155a	155 x 15	Oak	88	–	AD 985–1072	after AD 1082
155b	200 x 15	Oak	160	–	AD 1073–1232	after AD 1242
184a	105 x 15	Oak	86	–	AD 1217–1302	after AD 1312
184b	90 x 10	Oak	79	–	AD 1218–1296	after AD 1306
184c	110 x 10	Oak	83	–	AD 1217–1299	after AD 1309

Notes: Rings: *c* indicates estimated numbers of rings in unmeasured samples, * indicates sample with unresolved band of narrow rings.

Table 15: The dendrochronological samples from the coffins

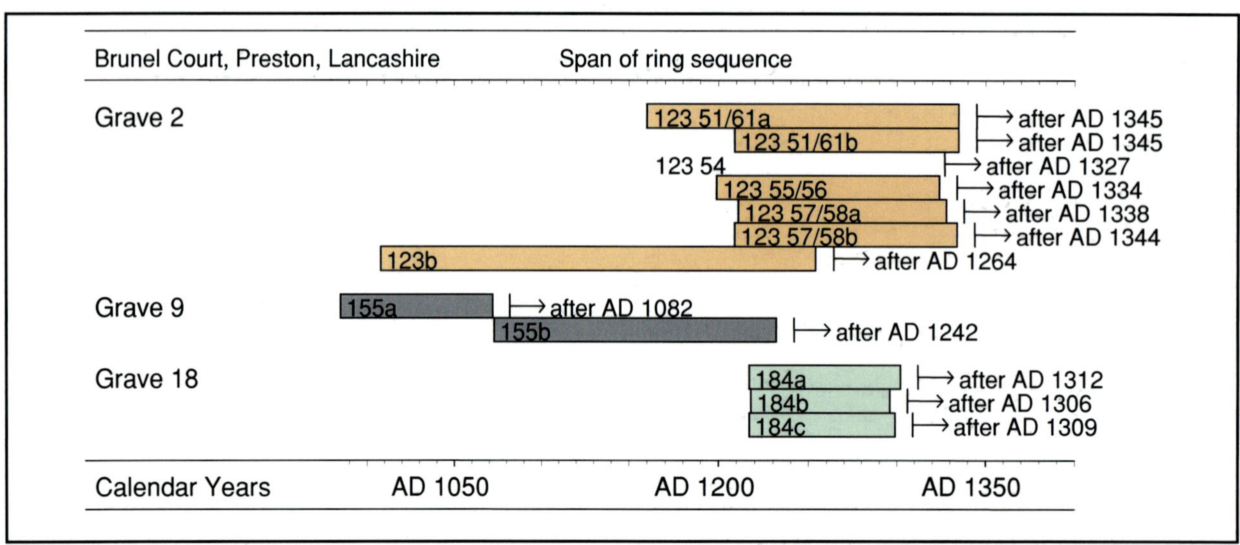

Figure 27: The calendar positions of the measured and dated tree-ring sequences

Several statistically significant matches were obtained, primarily with contemporaneous chronologies from northern and western England. These indicate the composite sequence is AD 985–1335 inclusive, and that long-living oak trees from the region were utilised. This dating position also independently confirmed the internal cross-matching, particularly when there were only short overlaps between individual timbers from the site. The boards retained no sapwood (*ie* the outermost, and therefore, youngest, part of a log), so no precise felling dates could be gained for the timbers, and hence for the construction of the coffins.

Grave 2

Seven samples were taken from the numerous plank fragments that represented the sides, base, and ends of coffin *123* from grave 2 (*Ch 2, p 19*). Two pairs of samples, from the base (fr 51/61) and one of the sides (fr 57/58), were sufficiently alike to indicate each pair was derived from the same parent log, or original board. The seven samples consisted entirely of heartwood, and, for these, *terminus post quem* dates were calculated using a ten-year minimum for missing sapwood (Table 15; Fig 27). However, the clustering of the end-dates of six of the seven boards, which derived from several different trees, suggests that the degradation of this material may only have resulted in the loss of the sapwood. The result indicates the coffin can be no earlier than *c* 1345. It thus seems reasonable to assume that this coffin is mid- to later fourteenth-century in date.

Grave 9

Two samples were measured from coffin *155* from grave 9 (Table 15; *p 49; Ch 2, p 18*). The precise juxtaposition of the measured series, one ending in 1072, the other starting at 1073, strongly suggests that they were derived from a single board, originally *c* 355 mm wide. This would have been from a tree more than 250 years old when felled. The end-date of the most recent part of the board indicates the timber can be no earlier than *c* 1242. Given that the friary was founded in *c* 1260 (*Ch 1, p 9*), it thus seems possible that this coffin is from relatively early in the life of the house.

Grave 18

Three samples from coffin *184* from grave 18 (*p 49; Ch 2, p 19*) were sufficiently alike to indicate that they probably derived from the same original board (Fig 27). The result indicates the coffin can be no earlier than *c* 1312. Although it may be reasonable to assume that this is likely to date from the mid- to later fourteenth century, it should be noted that the analysed section of this board is only *c* 110 mm wide, so that if the preservation has been uneven across the lid/base, this could represent only the inner part of a much wider, and hence later, board.

Chronology

Peter Marshall

Principles of radiocarbon dating

There are three principal isotopes of carbon which occur naturally: ^{13}C and ^{12}C (both stable), and ^{14}C (unstable or radioactive). The naturally occurring radioactive isotope of carbon (^{14}C) is formed in the upper atmosphere when cosmic radiation interacts with nitrogen atoms and is unstable, with a half-life of 5730±40 years (Bayliss and Marshall forthcoming).

Once produced, radiocarbon mixes rapidly through the atmosphere and enters the terrestrial food chain through photosynthesis. This means that the ^{14}C content of plants which live on land, and the animals who eat them, are in equilibrium with the contemporary atmosphere. When an organism dies it ceases to take up radiocarbon, and so over time the proportion of ^{14}C in the dead organism decreases. By measuring the proportion that remains, the elapsed time since death can be estimated. The ratio of ^{14}C in the material of unknown age to that in a modern standard is multiplied by the half-life to determine the age (*ibid*).

Human bone pre-screening programme

Human bone is 30% organic and 70% inorganic. The organic component is mostly collagen (90–95%), a fibrous protein, which provides strength and flexibility to bones. The protein component of bone samples is preferred in radiocarbon dating because it is relatively acid insoluble. The burial environment can, though, cause bone to degrade. As collagen decays, its strands untwist and become vulnerable to contamination by humic acids (*ibid*).

Given the waterlogged conditions under which several of the inhumations at Brunel Court were preserved, and the likelihood of post-depositional loss of bone collagen, a pre-screening programme was undertaken on 20 skeletons at the Oxford Radiocarbon Accelerator Unit to determine whether human bone samples suitable for radiocarbon dating survived. The results indicated that preservation was variable across the site but that some samples would yield sufficient collagen for dating.

The samples

Samples of human bone and waterlogged wood were submitted to the Oxford Radiocarbon Accelerator Unit (OxA-) and the Scottish Universities Environmental Research Centre (SUERC) for Accelerator Mass Spectrometry (AMS) dating. AMS is increasingly used for measuring the amount of radiocarbon in samples (Bayliss and Marshall forthcoming). Typically, a sample is combusted to carbon dioxide and then converted to a graphite target for loading into the Accelerator Mass Spectrometer (AMS). In this AMS, the carbon atoms in the target are given a series of electric charges and accelerated to very high speeds, which allows the ^{14}C to be isolated on the basis of weight using a series of powerful magnets.

Results

The radiocarbon results (Table 16) are reported as conventional radiocarbon ages measured on the radiocarbon timescale in units 'BP'. Such ages have been calculated using standards that have been internationally agreed (Stuiver and Polach 1977). Full details of the radiocarbon dating programme are given in the archive report (Marshall *et al* 2015).

Lab number	Sample reference	Material and context	δ^{13}C (‰)	δ^{15}N (‰)	C/N ratio	Radio-carbon Age (BP)	Weighted mean	Calibrated Date (95% confidence)	*Posterior Density Estimate (95% probability)*
OxA-26219	Skel *196*	Left femur, from articulated human leg, grave 21, Row 2	-19.4	12.4	3.2	536±24		cal AD 1325–1435	*cal AD 1320–1350*
OxA-26233	Skel *198* A	Left femur from articulated human skeleton, grave 23, Row 2	-19.2	13.1	3.3	662±26	678±20 (T'=0.9; v=1; T'(5%)=3.8)	cal AD 1275–1385	*cal AD 1280–1315*
SUERC-39417	Skel *198* B	As OxA-26233	-19.4	13.0	3.3	700±30			
OxA-26220	Skel *193*	Right femur from articulated human skeleton, grave 17, Row 2	-19.8	11.7	3.2	459±25		cal AD 1410–1460	*cal AD 1415–1460*
OxA-26221	Skel *235* A	Right femur, from articulated human skeleton in grave 30, which lay in the north-east angle of the buttress and the north wall	-19.2	12.0	3.2	679±25	653±18 (T'=2.4;v=1; T'(5%)=3.8)	cal AD 1280–1390	*cal AD 1280–1320 (81%) or 1355–1385 (14%)*
OxA-26222	As OxA-26221	As OxA-26221	-19.3	11.7	3.2	625±25			
GU26805	Skel *235* B	As OxA-26221				Failed – insufficient carbon			
OxA-26224	Skel *158*	Right femur, from human skeleton in grave 8, Row 4	-19.6	11.7	3.2	385±25		cal AD 1440–1630	*cal AD 1440–1495*
OxA-26233	Stake *153*	Waterlogged wood, *Ilex*, outer rings; driven into ditch *106*, which clipped the edge of grave 30	-22.8			840±28		cal AD 1150–1270	-
SUERC-39921	Stake *132*	Waterlogged wood, *Ilex*, outer rings; driven into ditch *106*, which clipped the edge of grave 30	-27.9			565±30		cal AD 1300–1430	*cal AD 1305–1365 (44%) or 1380–1430 (51%)*
SUERC-39922	Stake *154*	Waterlogged wood, *Ilex*, driven into ditch *106*, which clipped the edge of grave 30	-24.2			635±30		cal AD 1280–1410	*cal AD 1295–1405*
P31311	Skel *203*	Right femur from articulated human skeleton, grave 6, Row 4				Failed due to low yield		-	
P31308	Skel *124b* A	Right femur from human skeleton, grave 2, Row 3				Failed due to no yield			
GU26806	Skel *124b* B	As P31308				Failed – insufficient carbon			

Notes: δ^{13}C (‰): ratio of stable carbon isotopes ^{12}C and ^{13}C, in parts per thousand; δ^{15}N (‰): ratio of stable nitrogen isotopes ^{14}N and ^{15}N, in parts per thousand; C/N ratio: ratio of carbon and nitrogen; Radiocarbon age: the age of the sample as calculated from the breakdown of radio-active carbon isotopes, and expressed in years prior to 1950.

Table 16: Radiocarbon and stable isotope results

Stable isotope measurements

Reservoir effects occur when the carbon that is incorporated into a sample during life is not in equilibrium with the contemporary atmosphere. This gives the sample an apparent radiocarbon age which is older than that of a contemporary terrestrial sample (Bayliss and Marshall forthcoming). Most samples requiring reservoir correction derive from the marine environment. On average, the apparent age of marine samples is about 400 radiocarbon years older than the contemporary atmosphere. This offset is caused by the time it takes atmospheric radiocarbon to exchange into ocean bicarbonate, and by the dilution effect caused by the mixing of surface waters with very old upwelling deep water (*ibid*).

Carbon and nitrogen stable isotope analysis was undertaken on the human bone samples submitted to both laboratories, as there is potential for diet-induced radiocarbon offsets if an individual has taken up carbon from a reservoir not in equilibrium with the terrestrial biosphere (Lanting and van der Plicht 1998), and this might have implications for determining the actual date of their death. Carbon stable isotope analysis (^{13}C:^{12}C, measured as δ^{13}C) is used to distinguish between the consumption of marine versus terrestrial organisms in an individual's diet. The expected isotope values for a 100% terrestrial diet (green box) can be compared with the more enhanced δ^{13}C values, getting less negative, which indicate a greater marine proportion to the diet (*Ch 3*, Fig 24).

Nitrogen stable isotope (^{15}N:^{14}N, measured as δ^{15}N) analysis identifies the trophic (nutrition) level of an individual and the amount of aquatic resources in the diet. Again, the expected isotope values for a 100% terrestrial diet (green box) can be compared with those from Brunel Court. The highest δ^{15}N ratios are usually expected from populations using aquatic sources as a main staple in the diet, because the foodchains in aquatic ecosystems are more extended than those of terrestrial ones (*ibid*).

Terrestrial foods, as would be expected for England, made up the largest proportion of the diet of the people buried at Brunel Court. However, the data do, like those of many medieval sites in England, indicate the incorporation of marine and freshwater foods into a predominantly terrestrial diet (Müldner and Richards 2007). The Brunel Court human isotopic data, along with that from other religious establishments (Whithorn, Scotland (Müldner *et al* 2009), Fishergate, England (Müldner and Richards 2007), and Furness Abbey, Cumbria (Marshall and Beavan 2012)), suggest that these individuals consumed more marine and freshwater protein than the rest of the population.

Although the scale of the marine offset in the coastal waters around England is relatively well understood (Harkness 1983), there is no information on freshwater radiocarbon offsets for fish in north-west England. Some freshwater aquatic sources do appear to be in equilibrium with the atmosphere, but others have appreciable hard-water offsets (Keaveney and Reimer 2012) of 100–1000s of years. Given this, the radiocarbon result has simply been calibrated on human bone with the terrestrial calibration curve (*below*), acknowledging that the calibrated age quoted provides a maximum age for the death of the individual and that the true age could be younger.

Calibration

Calibration is an essential step in using radiocarbon measurements to estimate the calendar date of samples. As the production rate of radiocarbon in the atmosphere is not constant, but varies through time, the radiocarbon measurement ('BP' age) of a sample needs to be converted to the calendar scale using a calibration curve made up of radiocarbon ages on samples of known calendar date. Fortunately, there is now a set of internationally agreed consensus calibration curves for the whole range of the radiocarbon method. The terrestrial calibration curve for the mid-latitude northern hemisphere (IntCal09; Reimer *et al* 2009) has been used for the samples dated from Brunel Court (Table 16; Fig 28).

Chronological modelling

Bayesian statistics provide a probabilistic method for combining different sorts of evidence to estimate the dates of events that happened in the past and for quantifying the uncertainties of these estimates. The basic idea is encapsulated in Bayes' theorem (McGrayne 2011), which simply states that the new data collected about a problem ('the standardised likelihoods') should be analysed in the context of existing experience and knowledge about that problem (our 'prior beliefs'). This enables a new understanding to be arrived at which incorporates both existing knowledge and new data (our 'posterior belief').

In the Bayesian chronological model for Brunel Court (Fig 29), the radiocarbon and dendrochronological dates form the 'standardised likelihoods'. They are the data which are reinterpreted in the light of archaeological 'prior beliefs'. These are no more than a formal expression of our understanding of the archaeological context of the problem which is being modelled. For example, when one dated grave clearly cuts another, there is strong archaeological evidence of the relative chronology of the samples that have been dated. The 'posterior beliefs' that are output by a Bayesian model are known as posterior density estimates (distributions in black) and are expressed in italics to distinguish them clearly from date estimates that have not been produced by modelling.

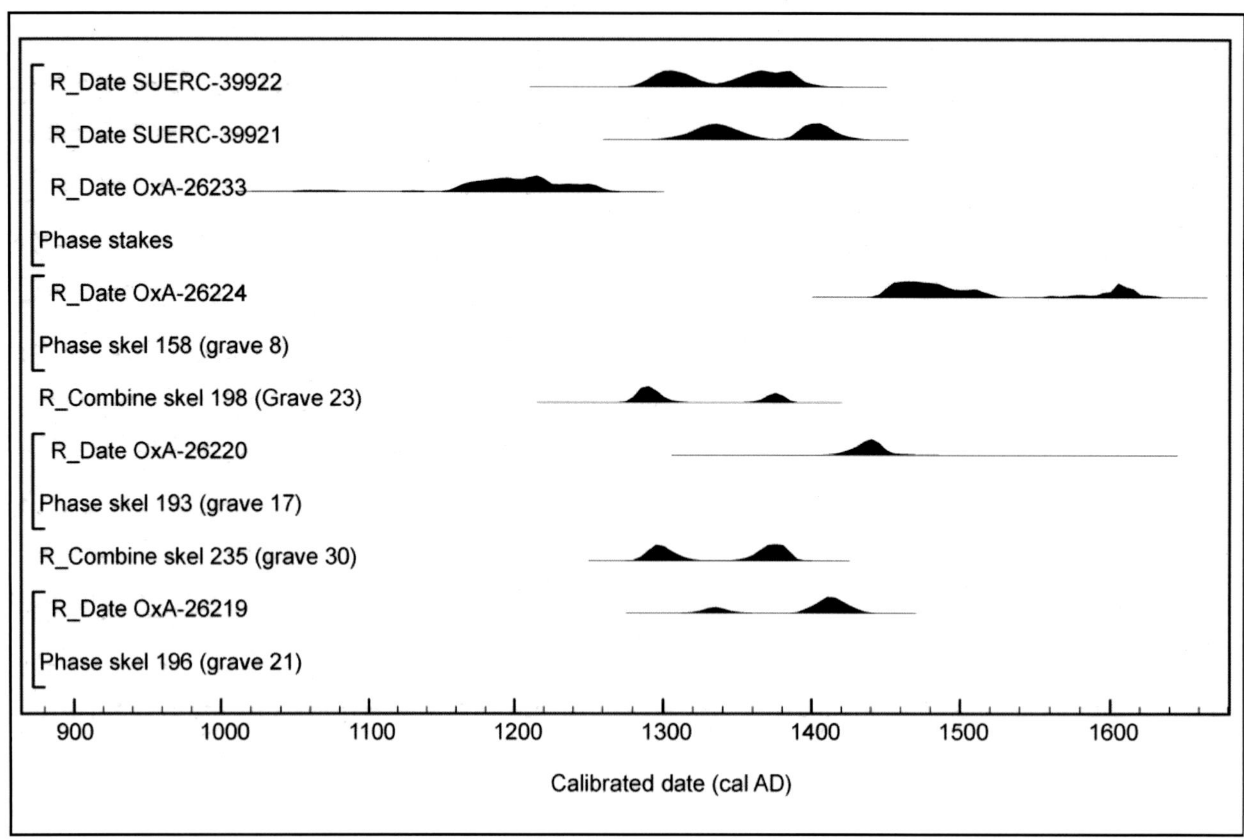

Figure 28: Probability distributions of the dates, the distributions being the result of simple radiocarbon calibration (Stuiver and Reimer 1993)

The model shows good agreement between the radiocarbon and tree-ring dates, and the stratigraphy, and estimates, albeit from a very limited number of samples, that burial activity started in *cal AD 1265–1305 (95% probability; start_brunel_court)*. Skeleton 235, buried in the outlying grave 30, dates to the early part of the use of the site as a cemetery (*cal AD 1280–1320 (81% probability; grave_30)*). The holly stakes inserted into ditch **106** clearly pre-date the Dissolution, the best estimate for their insertion being *cal AD 1320–1425 (95% probability)*. The latest dated burial, Skeleton **158** in grave 8, was probably buried in *cal AD 1440–1495 (95% probability; OxA-26224)*.

Palaeoenvironmental Remains

Elizabeth Huckerby and Enid Allison

Two assemblages were targeted for analysis, one from a grave in Row 2 (*Ch 2, p 18*), and the other from the ditch (**106**) surrounding the building (*Ch 2, pp 24-5*).

Grave 4

The plant assemblage from fill **127** of grave 4 (*Ch 2, p 18*) included species from a range of environments, although generally damp conditions were indicated by numerous seeds of soft rush/compact rush-type (*Juncus effusus/Juncus conglomeratus*-type) and common water-

starwort (*Callitriche* cf *stagnalis*; Table 17). These taxa inhabit marshes, ditches, bogs, wet meadows, damp woods, and muddy places by rivers and lakes (Stace 2010), suggesting that the grave was located on wet or muddy ground. Common nettle (*Urtica dioica*) seeds, indicative of nitrogen-rich waste or cultivated ground, were frequent, but other plants from cultivated ground were present in small numbers. These included seeds of fat hen (*Chenopodium album*), fragments of wild radish fruits (*Raphanus raphinistrum*), and a single undifferentiated charred cereal grain. A few seeds from woodland plants, such as red campion (*Silene dioica*), and wood sorrel (*Oxalis acetosella*), and grassland (for example common sorrel (*Rumex acetosa*) and sheep's sorrel (*Rumex acetosella*)) were also identified.

It is possible that some of these plants, together with marsh marigold (*Caltha palustris*), marsh cinquefoil (*Comarum palustre*), and creeping buttercups (*Ranunculus repens*), may represent flowers that had accompanied the burial in one form or another. However, it is perhaps more likely that the assemblage as a whole represents the diverse habitat within which the friary precinct was initially set out, which was sealed by the construction of the building.

Ditch *106*

Samples from fill **107** of ditch **106** produced evidence of plants from wet-ground and aquatic environments,

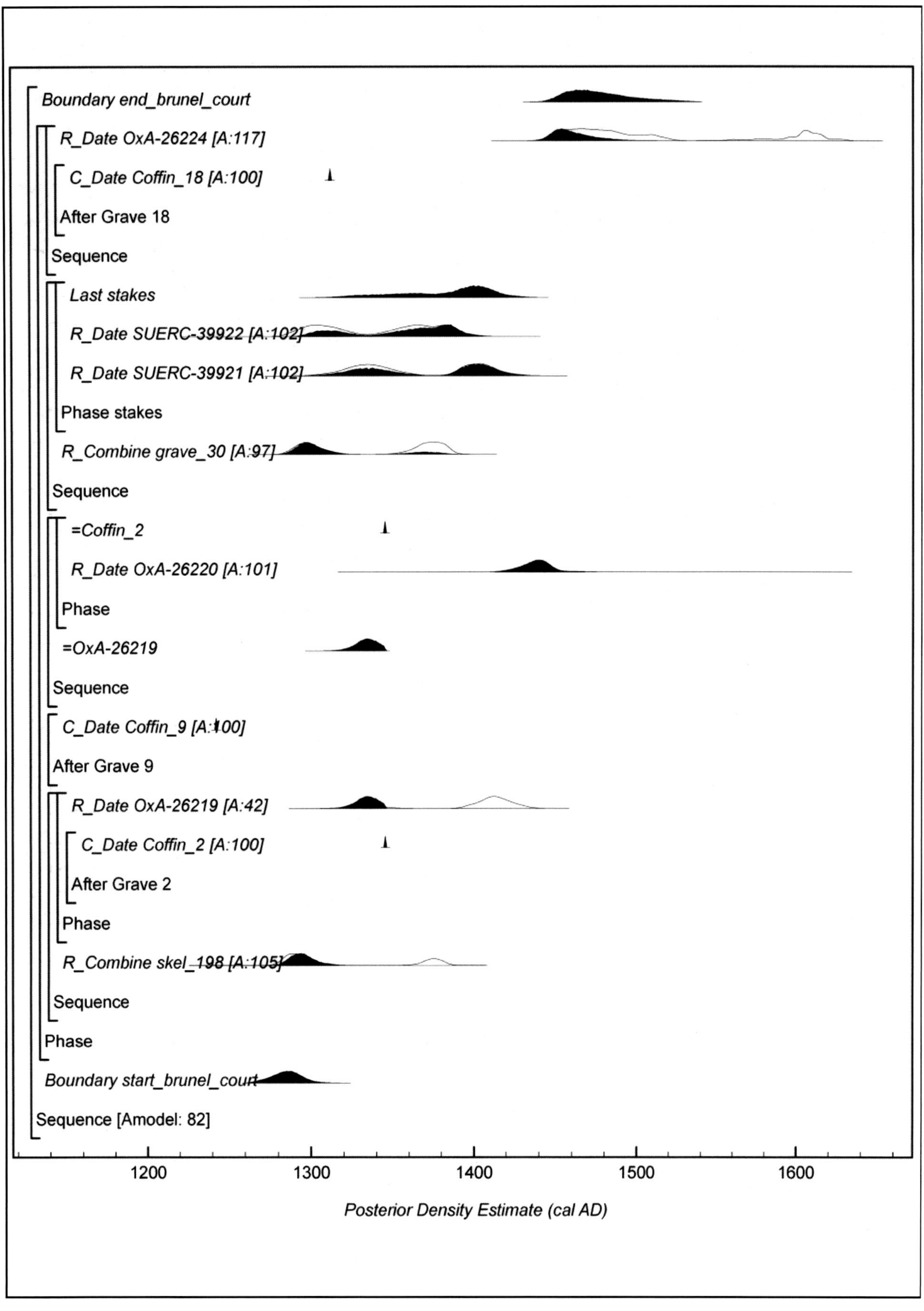

Outline= simple radiocarbon calibration; solid= chronological model.

Figure 29: Probability distribution model

Sample No		1	2	101
Context No		*107*	*107*	*127*
Feature Type		Ditch *106*	Ditch *106*	Grave 4
Sample volume litres		20	50	10
Flot volume millilitres		600	25	
Annual weeds of waste and cultivated ground				
Anthemis cotula	Stinking chamomile		1	
Chenopodium album	Fat-hen	>100	9	10
Euphorbia sp	Spurge		1	
Fumaria sp	Fumitory	8		
Glebionis segetum	Corn marigold	8	1	
Papaver	Poppy	10		
Persicaria lapathifolia	Pale persicaria	1		
Raphanus raphinistrum pod fragments	Wild radish			4
Spergula arvensis	Corn spurrey		1	
Stellaria media	Common chickweed	>100	15	3
Urtica urens	Small nettle	8		
Ruderal communities (found growing on waste or fallow ground)				
Matricaria discoidea	Pineapple-weed			2
Matricaria sp	Mayweeds	>100		
Prunella vulgaris	Selfheal	72		
Rumex obtusifolius	Broad-leaved dock	97		
Sonchus asper	Prickly sow-thistle	16		
Taraxacum	Dandelions	16		
Urtica dioica	Common nettle	>100	>100	>100
Grassland plants				
Bellis perennis	Daisy	8		
Poaceae with seeds >4 mm	Grasses with large seeds			1 *
Rumex acetosa	Common sorrel	>100		7
Rumex acetosella	Sheep's sorrel			7
Stellaria graminea	Lesser stitchwort	>100		
Woodland/scrub plants, including those from woodland clearings and hedgerows				
Betula sp	Birch	8		
Prunus/Crataegus thorns	Blackthorn/hawthorn thorns	+		
Oxalis acetosella	Wood sorrel			1
Silene dioica	Red campion	>100		6
Rubus/Rosa thorn	Bramble/rose thorns	++	+	
Wet ground and aquatic plants				
Callitriche cf *stagnalis*	Common water-starwort	>100	20	>100
Caltha palustris	Marsh-marigold	1		1
Carex trigonus	Sedges	16		14
Carex lenticular	Sedges	16		1
Comarum palustre	Marsh cinquefoil	8		4
Eleocharis palustris	Common spike-rush	8		7
Eriphorum	Cottongrass spindle			1
Isolepis	Bristle club-rush	>100	>100	2
Juncus effusus-type	Common rush	>100	>100	>100
Juncus seed capsule				1
Scrophularia/Verbascum	Figwort/mullein	10	48??	

Table 17: The plant remains

Sample No		1	2	101
Context No		*107*	*107*	*127*
Feature Type		Ditch *106*	Ditch *106*	Grave 4
Sample volume litres		20	50	10
Flot volume millilitres		600	25	
Food and economic taxa				
Rubus sect 2 *Glandulosus*	Bramble	>100	64 +fragments	
Sambucus nigra	Elder	17	12 +fragments	3
Cerealia undifferentiated, charred	Charred cereal grain			1
Plants belonging to broad groupings				
Atriplex/Chenopodium	Goosefoots/oraches		2	
Asteraceae undifferentiated	Daisy family			1
Epilobium sp	Willowherb	>100	12	
Galeopsis tetrahit	Common hemp-nettle	1	1	
Polygonum undifferentiated	Knotweeds		1	1 charred
Potentilla sp	Cinquefoils			1
Ranunculus repens-type	Creeping buttercup-type	>100		8
Ranunculus sardous	Hairy buttercup			
Scrophularia/Verbascum	Figwort/mullein	10	48	
Viola	Violet/pansy		1	
Matrix Scale of abundance				
Amorphous plant remains			+	
Wood fragments		++	++	++
Roundwood and twiggy pieces		++		
Bark		+		
Buds		++		
Leaf fragments		+	+	
Charcoal fragments		+	++ oak and diffuse porous	+
Bryophyte fragments	Moss fragments	+	+	
Mammal bone		+		+
Small mammal bone		+		
Fly puparia		+		
Insect fragments		++	++	+
Fungal sclerotia			+	
Earthworm egg cases		+	+	+
Daphnia ephippia			+	
Coal		+	++	+
Heat-affected vesicular material			+	
Coarse sand and gravel		++	++	
Silty/clay		+		

Notes: Plant nomenclature follows Stace (2010). The ecological groupings are similar to those defined by Huntley and Hillam (2000, 356-7). The components of the matrix were noted and scored on a relative scale of 1-5, + = present and ++ = abundant.

Table 17: The plant remains (cont'd)

with those taxa identified in grave 4 joined by common figwort (cf *Scrophularia nodosa*; W Carruthers *pers comm*). The seeds of common nettles, brambles (*Rubus* sect 2 *Glandulosus*), elder (*Sambucus nigra*), and fruits of broad-leaved dock (*Rumex obtusifolius*) were very abundant, and are likely to have been growing on the sides of the ditch. These were accompanied by large numbers of wood fragments, including roundwood, and buds from woody plants, together with some bark, leaf fragments, charcoal, moss remains, and animal bone.

The plant remains suggested that the environment away from the ditch was likely to have been a mosaic of cultivated and/or waste ground, with fat-hen, corn marigold (*Glebionis segetum*), common chickweed (*Stellaria media*), selfheal (*Prunella vulgaris*), and mayweeds (*Matricaria*) all growing nearby. The presence of some grassland is suggested by the frequent presence of plants such as common- and sheep's sorrel, and lesser stitchwort (*Stellaria graminea*). Red campion might also indicate the presence of some nearby woodland. Although some of these plants have medicinal qualities, including common chickweed, broad-leaved dock, and common figwort (Grieve 1971), they are most likely to be local weeds.

An assemblage of 254 beetles (Coleoptera) and bugs (Hemiptera) of 147 taxa was recovered by paraffin flotation from a single sample from ditch fill **107** (Table 18). Preservation was generally good, but larger species were, in the main, highly fragmented, notably

ANNELIDA:	
Oligochaeta sp (earthworm egg capsules)	+
CRUSTACEA:	
Ostracoda sp (carapaces)	++
INSECTA:	
Dermaptera sp (earwigs)	+
Hemiptera: (bugs)	
Stygnocoris sabulosus (Schilling) [oa -p]	3
Dufouriellus ater (Dufour) [u]	1
Saldidae sp [oa-d]	2
Heteroptera spp	2
Delphacidae spp [oa-p]	10
Auchenorhyncha spp [oa-p]	8
Psyllidae sp indeterminate [oa-p]	1
Aphidoidea sp	+
Trichoptera sp (caddis fly larval fragments)	+
Diptera: (flies)	
Diptera spp (puparia)	++
Hymenoptera: (bees, wasps, and ants)	
Formicidae spp	++
Apis mellifera Linnaeus	+
Hymenoptera Parasitica spp	++
Coleoptera: (beetles)	
Agabus bipustulatus (Linnaeus) [oa-w]	1
Hydroporinae spp [oa-w]	1
Carabus sp [oa]	1
Cychrus caraboides (Linnaeus) [oa]	1
Leistus sp [oa]	1
Nebria cf *brevicollis* (Fabricius) [oa]	1
Notiophilus sp [oa]	1
Elaphrus cupreus Duftschmid [oa-d]	1
Loricera pilicornis (Fabricius) [oa]	1
Poecilus sp [oa]	1
Pterostichus niger (Schaller) [oa]	1
Pterostichus (*Pseudomaseus*) sp [oa-d]	1
Pterostichus vernalis (Panzer) [oa-d]	1

INSECTA:	
Paranchus albipes (Fabricius) [oa-d]	1
Carabidae spp [ob]	4
Helophorus grandis Illiger [oa-w]	2
Helophorus spp [oa-w]	8
Anacaena globulus (Paykull) [oa-w]	4
Hydrobius fuscipes (Linnaeus) [oa-w]	1
Laccobius bipunctatus (Fabricius) [oa-w]	1
Hydrophilinae spp [oa-w]	1
Cercyon haemorrhoidalis (Fabricius) [rf-sf]	4
Histerinae sp [rt]	1
Limnebius truncatellus (Thunberg) [oa-w]	4
Ochthebius bicolon Germar [oa-w]	8
Ochthebius dilatatus Stephens [oa-w]	3
Ochthebius minimus (Fabricius) [oa-w]	2
Ptenidium sp [rt]	1
Acrotrichis sp [rt]	2
Choleva or *Catops* sp [u]	1
Silphidae sp [u]	1
Lesteva longoelytrata (Goeze) [oa-d]	2
Olophrum sp [oa]	2
Omaliinae spp [u]	1
Megarthrus sp [rt]	2
Micropeplus porcatus (Paykull) [rt]	1
Tachinus sp [u]	1
Tachyporus spp [u]	2
Cratataea suturalis (Mannerheim) [rt-st]	1
Aleochariinae spp [u]	20
Anotylus nitidulus (Gravenhorst) [rt-d]	1
Anotylus rugosus (Fabricius) [rt]	4
Anotylus sculpturatus group [rt]	3
Anotylus tetracarinatus group [rt]	2
Oxytelus laqueatus (Marsham) [rf]	1
Oxytelus sp indeterminate [rt]	1
Carpelimus sp [u]	1
Scydmaeninae spp [u]	2

*Table 18: Insects and other invertebrates recorded from fill **107** of ditch **106***

INSECTA:			Corticariinae spp [rt]	1
Stenus spp [u]	6		Mycetophagidae sp [u]	1
Lathrobium sp [u]	1		Ciidae sp [l]	1
Othius punctulatus (Goeze) [rt-sf]	2		*Donacia* or *Plateumaris* sp [oa-p-d]	1
Xantholinus linearis or *longiventris* [rt-sf]	3		*Chrysolina* sp [oa-p]	1
Staphylininae spp [u]	6		Alticini sp [oa-p]	1
Geotrupinae sp [oa-rf]	1		Apionidae spp [oa-p]	2
Aphodius rufipes (Linnaeus) [oa-rf]	1		*Notaris acridulus* (Linnaeus) [oa-p-d]	1
Aphodius ater (De Geer) [oa-rf]	1		*Nedyus quadrimaculatus* (Linnaeus) [oa-p]	1
Aphodius fimetarius (Linnaeus) [ob-rf]	2		*Rhinoncus perpendicularis* (Reich) [oa-p]	1
Aphodius prodromus or *sphacelatus* [ob-rf]	17		*Rhinoncus* sp [oa-p]	1
Aphodius contaminatus (Herbst) [oa-rf]	5		Ceutorhynchinae sp [oa-p]	1
Aphodius spp [ob-rf]	2		Cossoninae sp [l]	1
Onthophagus ?similis (Scriba) [oa-rf]	1		*Philopedon plagiatum* (Schaller) [oa-p]	3
Phyllopertha horticola (Linnaeus) [oa-p]	2		*Barynotus* sp [oa-p]	2
Byrrhidae sp [u]	3		*Otiorhynchus ?singularis* (Linnaeus) [oa-p]	1
Dryops sp [oa-d]	1		*Phyllobius pomaceus* Gyllenhal [oa-p]	1
Agriotes sp [oa-p]	5		*Phyllobius* or *Polydrusus* spp [oa-p]	2
Elateridae spp [ob]	5		*Sitona* sp [oa-p]	2
Elateridae sp (larval apex) [ob]	+		Entiminae sp [oa-p]	1
Tipnus unicolor (Piller and Mitterpacher) [rd-ss]	5		*Leiosoma* cf *deflexum* [oa-p]	2
Ptinus fur (Linnaeus) [rd-sf]	2		*Hylesinus varius* (Fabricius) [l]	1
Grynobius planus (Fabricius) [l]	1		Curculionidae sp [oa-p]	7
Anobium punctatum (De Geer) [l-sf]	3		Coleoptera spp and sp indeterminate [u]	3
Brachypterus sp [oa-p]	2		Insecta spp indeterminate, larval fragments	+
Mycetaea subterranea (Fabricius) [rd-ss]	1		ARACHNIDA:	
Latridius minutus group [rd-st]	1		Acarina spp (mites)	+++
			Total beetles and bugs	**254**

Notes: A minimum number of individuals (MNI) has been given for beetles (Coleoptera) and bugs (Hemiptera), and abundance of other invertebrates estimated on a three-point scale as + present, ++ common, or +++ abundant.

Ecological codes (Kenward *et al* 1986; Kenward 1997) are shown in square brackets: **d** – damp ground or waterside taxa; **l** – wood-associated taxa; **oa** – certain outdoor taxa (unable to live and breed within buildings or in accumulations of organic material); **ob** – probable outdoor taxa; **rd** – dry decomposers; **rf** – foul decomposers; **rt** – generalised decomposers; **p** – strongly plant-associated taxa; **sf** – facultative synanthropes (favoured by human activities but found in man-made and natural habitats); **st** – typical synanthropes (typically present in man-made habitats but capable of living in natural situations); **ss** – strong synanthropes (very rare in natural habitats); **u** – uncoded taxa; **w** – aquatics.

Table 18: Insects and other invertebrates recorded from fill **107** *of ditch* **106** *(cont'd)*

ground beetles (Carabidae), click beetles (Elateridae), and some weevils (Curculionidae), and this limited their identification.

Ostracod carapaces, remains of caddis fly (Trichoptera) larvae, and an assemblage of aquatic beetles indicated that the ditch held shallow water for at least some of the time. The generally uneroded condition of most of the insect material suggested that conditions within the ditch remained constantly wet. Water beetles (including *Ochthebius bicolon*, *Ochthebius dilatatus, Limnebius truncatellus, Anacaena globulus, Laccobius bipunctatus,* and *Dryops*) made up 14% of the beetle and bug assemblage, and chiefly indicated running water and wet mud. Beetles and bugs from waterside habitats and damp, or wet, ground accounted for 6% of the terrestrial fauna, and included *Notaris acridulus*, a weevil found on tall semi-aquatic grasses, particularly reed sweet-grass (*Glyceria maxima*; Morris 2002, 3), and *Elaphrus cupreus*, a ground beetle found on sparsely vegetated damp soils near water (Duff 2012b).

Several other ground beetles, such as *Loricera pilicornis*, *Pterostichus vernalis*, *Pterostichus niger*, and *Cychrus caraboides* (a specialised snail predator), were typical of damp or shaded ground, with shade provided either by long vegetation, trees, or shrubs, or perhaps a hedgerow. At least some trees probably grew close to the ditch, and there were dead and rotten wood habitats: the bark beetle, *Hylesinus varius*, burrows under the bark of ash (*Fraxinus*; Duff 2012b, 498); *Dufouriellus ater* is a tiny bug found beneath tree bark (Southwood and Leston 1959, 187); Ciidae species are found on bracket fungi (fungi with multiple, roughly circular plate- or shelf-like fruiting bodies, often found on tree trunks and branches; Harde 1984, 206); cossonine weevils are usually in rotten wood (Morris 2002, 38); and *Grynobius planus* is found in the dry, dead wood of deciduous trees (Harde 1984, 210).

Plant-feeding insects were common (29% of the terrestrial assemblage), suggesting richly vegetated damp and drier areas, with some species providing clues to specific plants. *Brachypterus*, *Nedyus quadrimaculatus*, and *Phyllobius pomaceus* are all found on nettles (*Urtica* sp; Davis 1983). Two species of *Rhinoncus*, found on docks (*Rumex*) and persicarias, were recorded, one being *Rhinoncus perpendicularis*, usually associated with the terrestrial form of amphibious bistort (*Persicaria amphibia*, f *terrestris*; Morris 2008, 93). *Leiosoma* cf *deflexum* is found in damp places on wood anemone (*Anemone nemorosa*) and members of the buttercup family (Ranunculaceae), especially creeping buttercup (*Ranunculus repens*) and marsh marigold (*Caltha palustris*; Morris 2002, 55). *Sitona* species are typical of grassy habitats, where they feed on various members of the legume family (Fabaceae), many of them on clovers, trefoils, and vetches (Morris 1997, 50-9).

Soils away from the ditch were probably relatively dry. This was suggested by several *Stygnocoris sabulosus* (a small ground bug (Lygaeidae)), and a number of beetles with root-feeding larvae that would not survive in waterlogged ground. The latter included the fragmentary remains of at least ten click beetles (Elateridae), including a minimum of five *Agriotes*. The 'wireworm' larvae of these beetles feed on roots, especially in grassland, and *Agriotes* can be serious pests of root crops (Brickell 1992, 566). *Phyllopertha horticola*, a small chafer known colloquially as the 'June bug', has larvae that feed on turf roots, and is characteristic of open, poor-quality pasture land on light soils, where there is a diversity of flowering plants and a high proportion of weeds (Raw 1951; Jessop 1986, 29).

Decomposers associated with foul organic matter, principally scarabaeid beetles, accounted for 16% of the terrestrial fauna, and half of the total decomposer component. *Aphodius* were particularly common, and included *A prodromus* or *sphacelatus* (the most numerous of the group), *A contaminatus*, *A rufipes*, *A fimetarius*, and *A ater*. *Onthophagus* ?*similis* and a dor beetle (Geotrupidae) were also recorded. *Aphodius* primarily exploit herbivore dung, but some of those recorded less commonly exploit decaying plant material (Jessop 1986, 20-5). *Cercyon haemorrhoidalis* and *Oxytelus laqueatus* (a rove beetle) were the only non-scarabaeid foul decomposers recorded, and both are also mainly associated with dung (Hansen 1987, 147; Skidmore 1991, 148-9; Lott 2009, 37).

A modern study has indicated that the proportion of scarabaeid dung beetles in insect assemblages from small bodies of water can reflect the intensity of local grazing (Smith *et al* 2010), suggesting that dung beetles may make up more than 10% of the terrestrial fauna when large or dense populations of grazing animals are present nearby, but less than 5% when there are natural populations of grazing animals or 'naturalistic' grazing by domestic animals. The situation on occupation sites is often complicated by the presence of foul habitation waste, but at Brunel Court, the predominance of taxa specifically associated with dung relative to other types of decomposer almost certainly indicates a significant population of grazing animals in the area. The *Aphodius* species in the assemblage exploit most types of domestic herbivore dung, but *Onthophagus* ?*similis* is usually found in sheep or horse dung in dry, open, insolated (sunny) locations (Jessop 1986, 27; Skidmore 1991, 149).

A further group of beetles associated with relatively dry decomposing organic material (5% of the terrestrial fauna) suggested that some material from within buildings had entered the ditch fill, either by direct deposition, or in run-off. Notable among this group were the spider beetles, *Tipnus unicolor* and *Ptinus fur*. The former, represented by at least five individuals, is a particularly strongly synanthropic species, and is not very common in natural habitats, although it has sometimes been recorded from birds' nests (*eg* Hinton 1941; Linsley 1944; Palm 1959). In reviewing its archaeological occurrence, Harry Kenward (2009, 308-10) concluded that it is generally a good indicator of long-lived, relatively high-status buildings, with numbers appearing to increase in proportion with general cleanliness. It is often particularly well represented in post-medieval domestic assemblages.

Several other beetle taxas, that are often associated with *T unicolor* and *P fur* in archaeological 'house' faunas, were the *Latridius minutus* group, woodworm beetle (*Anobium punctatum*), and *Mycetaea subterranea* (Hall and Kenward 1990; Kenward and Hall 1995; Carrott and Kenward 2001). Woodworm beetles are strongly associated with structural timber, although they could have infested outdoor wooden structures nearby, or naturally occurring dead wood. *M subterranea* is another strong synanthrope. Modern records are mainly from decaying straw and wood in dry cellars, barns, and stables, and in association with the dry-rot fungus, *Merulius lacrymans* (Hinton 1945; Palm 1959).

Other remains of note included leg segments of a honey bee (*Apis mellifera*). The tiny bug, *Dufouriellus ater*, is generally found beneath bark, but also occurs in beehives, where it feeds on small commensal insects (psocids; Southwood and Leston 1959, 187), although the connection could not be demonstrated here. Hives were often kept at ecclesiastical establishments (Buchmann and Repplier 2005, 51), and feral populations may have persisted after the Dissolution. However, the single record could equally indicate hives or feral colonies further afield.

Conclusions

It is likely that the plant remains identified within the fill of grave 4 (*Ch 2, p 18*) derive largely from the environment that immediately preceded the construction of the building, whilst the sediments within ditch *106* (*Ch 2, pp 24-5*) were probably the last to accumulate following the cessation of maintenance activities around the time of the building's abandonment. As such, the similarities between the two plant assemblages would indicate that the area was prone to dampness, and that the shallow, running, probably rather muddy, water within the ditch would have been present throughout its use, reflecting its efficacy as a drainage feature. As the ditch silted up, it seems to have trapped material from the surrounding environments, as these are indicative of the area becoming overgrown. Damp ground close to the ditch was probably shaded, at least in places, either by long herbaceous vegetation or by shrubs or deciduous trees.

The wider surroundings were likely to have been a richly vegetated mosaic of different environments, including relatively open, flowery, grassy areas close by, some on drier ground, and some poorer areas with a high proportion of weeds (Raw 1951). A significant group of dung beetles indicated that open, drier ground in the vicinity was almost certainly used as pasture for domestic animals. Essentially, the site would appear to have been reverting to its former agrarian state.

Direct evidence for human occupation, including the incorporation into the ditch of foul matter, is generally lacking, although the ditch does seem to have received limited amounts of material from within buildings, possibly of relatively high status, either directly or as run-off. This may relate to the final clearing out, or decay, of such structures in the vicinity.

Plate 18: The construction of the north and west walls of the building, with both intra- and extramural graves

5

DISCUSSION

Stephen Rowland, Jeremy Bradley, and Christine Howard-Davis,
with Mark Gibson, Louise Loe, Jennie Stopford, and Ian Tyers

The Nature and Identity of the Site

The evidence from Brunel Court makes it clear that the excavations revealed significant medieval remains which are, within an urban context, rare in the North West (Newman 2006, 13), and unprecedented within Preston. Although heavily truncated, frequently disturbed, often poorly preserved, and, at times, disparate, they still form a coherent and inter-related entity, thus representing a highly significant contribution to the archaeology of the region. There are few stratified, datable, artefacts, but in combination with scientific dating of the skeletons, their wooden coffins, and some other artefacts, they indicate that the principal activity dates from the later thirteenth to the fifteenth centuries, with a marked dearth of finds from any later period.

The most significant structural element found was the poorly preserved remnant of what seems to have been a stone building, constructed on well-laid cobble footings, and reinforced with buttresses (*Ch 2, pp 15-16; Pl 18*), which contained a group of well-dated burials (*Ch 3*, Table 1). Any substantial stone structure would be notable in a northern medieval town, where the majority of the buildings, even those of the wealthy, would most likely have been of timber construction (Higham 2004, 153). Thus it is likely to imply elevated status, and resources that were enjoyed by only the wealthiest individuals, municipal bodies, parish churches, or other religious houses.

The presence of formal graves, both within its walls and surrounding it, are key to the interpretation of the building as an ecclesiastical structure. All of the graves were aligned broadly west/east, as would be expected in a Christian context, with those inside, and those outside closest to the building, echoing its orientation with most precision.

If these remains were indeed those of a church and its accompanying cemetery, then, with hindsight, evidence (albeit fragmentary) for the presence of other structures can now be identified in several of the evaluation trenches excavated in 1991, emphasising the likelihood that they represent fragments of a considerably more extensive precinct, which is probably monastic in origin. As the locations of the few other medieval institutions in and around Preston are well-known (St Wilfrid's church, the hospital of St Mary Magdalen, and, arguably, the Savigniac abbey at Tulketh), it can be concluded with relative confidence that these excavations examined part of a church or chapel, and small elements of other buildings within a larger establishment, which is most likely to be the Franciscan friary founded in *c* 1260 (*Ch 1*). Finds made during nineteenth-century construction works nearby seem to reinforce this conclusion (*p 67*), being recorded from a coalyard belonging to Pearson and Coles (Hewitson 1883, 280; *Ch 1, p 13*). Indeed, the only coalyard shown in this area on both the 1849 and the 1893 OS Town Plans was in the area now occupied by Brunel Court. Both Hewitson (1883) and later historians (Fishwick 1900; Clemesha 1912) associated these early finds with the Franciscan friary.

The Friary Church

Design and layout

In architectural and spatial terms, the heart of every mendicant order was the church. It was the epicentre of devotion, both in life and, particularly in the case of the lay community, in death. Death and resurrection are central to Christian belief, as, during the later Middle Ages, was the benefit afforded to the dead by the prayers of the living (Jupp and Gittings 1999, 110). Moreover, the desirability of burial within ecclesiastical buildings, particularly the church itself, especially for people of status, had been recognised as early as the Council of Mainz in 813 (O'Sullivan 2013a).

A small church, always oriented east-west, was generally the first building to be erected on any friary site (Bruzelius 2012, 369). The nave, freely accessible to the laity, and vital to the Franciscans' proselytising aims, was thus often a later addition (*ibid*; Dickinson 1961, 46). Early Franciscan churches tended to be very

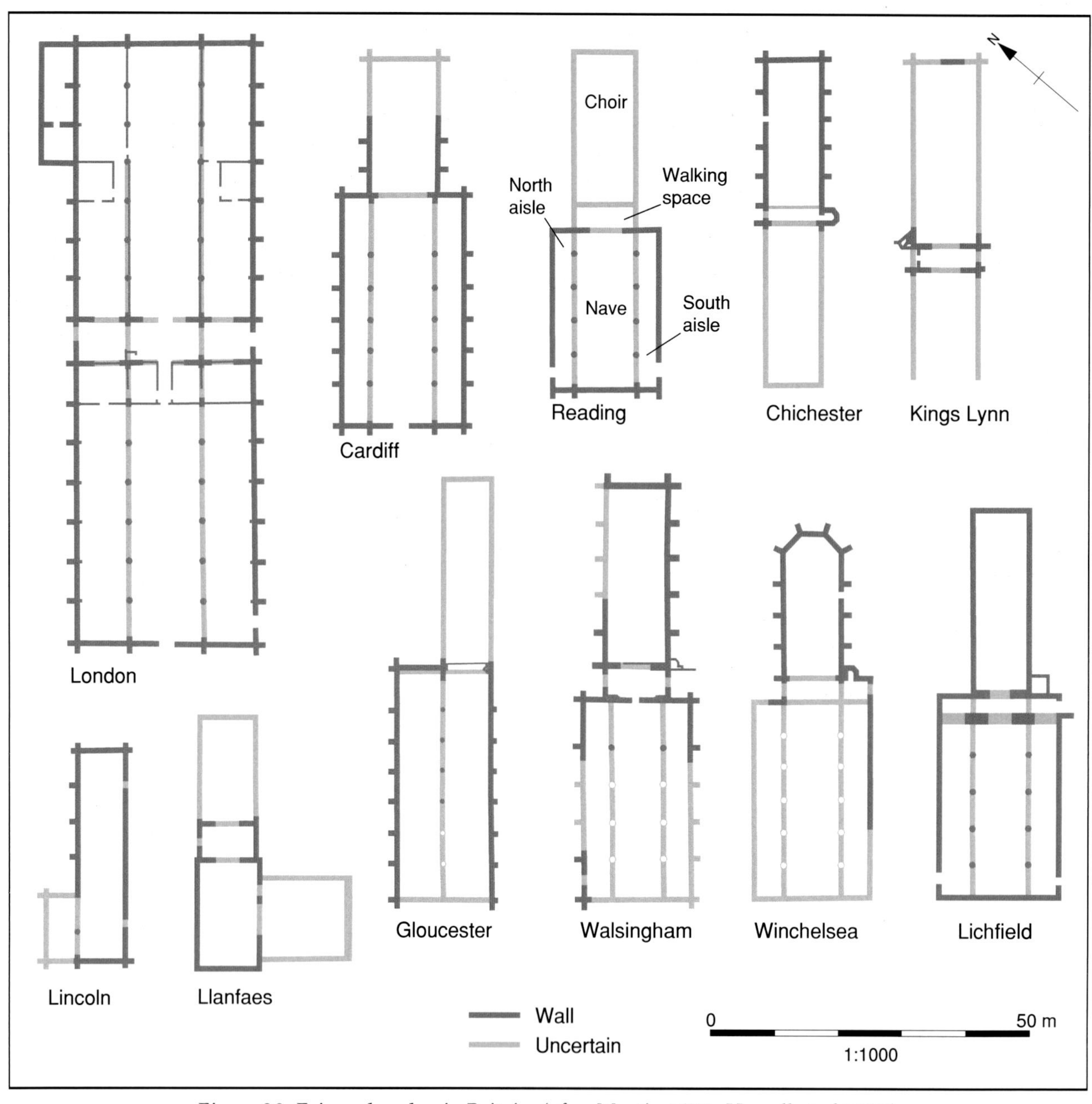

Figure 30: Friary churches in Britain (after Martin 1966; Hassall et al 1989)

simple in plan, and were generally long and narrow (the width of many appears to fall within a range of 8-12 m; Fig 30), being divided almost equally between the choir and the nave (O'Sullivan, 2013b, 19). These were separated by the 'walking space', a characteristic feature of Franciscan friary churches that allowed relatively private access to the choir and any northern chapels from the claustral buildings (Gilchrist and Sloane 2005, 67). Burials could take place at each of those locations, as well as within chapels appended to the nave, but also in the cloister walk and graveyards within open areas immediately adjoining the church.

The most obvious identification of the stone building at Brunel Court is as a truncated remnant of the friary church, albeit that, at first sight, the structural remains do not appear particularly sizable or robust. It can be noted that early churches constructed in accordance with the constraints of the Order were usually built of wood (Röhrkasten 2012), although it was not long after their arrival in England that construction of stone churches was permitted. At Chester, for instance, founded in 1237/8, the church of the Dominican friary had been built in stone by *c* 1245 (Gilchrist and Sloane 2005); the suggested relatively late foundation or refoundation date of Preston Friary (*c* 1260; *Ch 1, p 9*) makes it likely that its church was of stone from the first.

Moreover, the foundations of even quite important medieval buildings were not necessarily substantial or deep. For instance, those at Chester comprised rubble within shallow cuts (Ward 1990), whilst the walls of the Blackfriars at Carlisle stood on a cobble footing (McCarthy 1990), very similar to that marking the west wall at Brunel

Court. The size of the north-western buttress, and the width of the cobble footings for this wall, would suggest that it was up to 1.5 m in width, and presumably the north and east walls would have been similar. This is almost directly comparable to the foundations at Warrington's Austin Friary (Heawood *et al* 2002).

It must also be borne in mind that, since the mid-sixteenth century, the Friary's stonework has been extensively and thoroughly robbed. Historical accounts indicate that much of the building stone was removed for reuse immediately after its dissolution (Fishwick 1900, 200), and the presence of post-medieval pottery amongst the foundations (*Ch 4, p 44*) suggests that, even after the initial demolition, there was continued, if piecemeal, stone-robbing. In addition, the degree of modern truncation, indicated by, amongst other things, the shallowness of the surviving burials, probably means that only the lowest component of the foundations remained.

Whilst its layout and appearance must remain speculative, there are several potential interpretations of this building. What essentially survived was the west wall and north-western corner of a rectangular structure (Fig 31). Although little survived of its east wall, the degree of symmetry between features at the better-preserved north-western corner and fragments at its putative corner to the north-east allow its position to be reconstructed with relative confidence. These suggest that the structure was around 12 m east to west, and 6 m north to south; although it is apparent that other parts of the building lay to the south, their extent is uncertain. Judging by the quantity of extramural burials further to the north-east and north-west, it seems unlikely to have extended in those directions.

It could be argued that this structure was a remnant of the original church, which might, of necessity, have been rather small. Although the original church is generally thought to form the basis for an expanded entity at many friaries (Bruzelius 2012, 369), at some sites it was replaced completely. That was the case at Oxford (one of the first Franciscan churches built in England, *c* 1225), the original chapel being

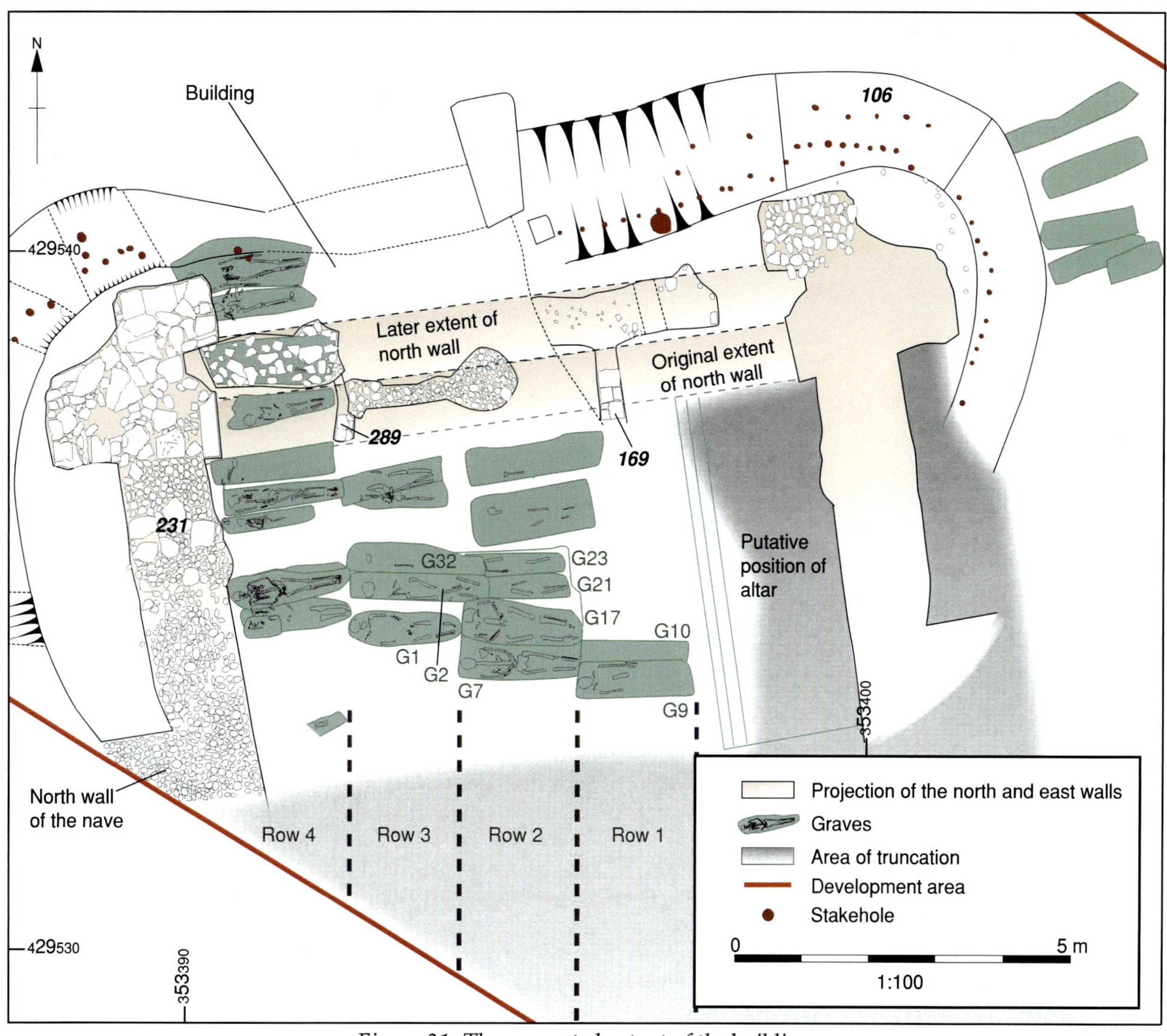

Figure 31: The suggested extent of the building

demolished when a much larger church was built, around 1246 (Hassall *et al* 1989, 184). At others, such as the Cluniac house in Lewes, Sussex, the original church was retained as a chapel after being replaced by a more substantial building elsewhere within the precinct. There, the original church became the infirmary chapel, and continued to be used for burial (Gilchrist and Sloane 2005, 59). If the remains at Brunel Court were to be viewed as a complete structure, its dimensions (12 x 6 m) are not dissimilar to those of chapels at small medieval hospitals and chantries, such as the simple rectangular example at Partney, Lincolnshire (Atkins and Popescu 2010).

There is, however, one small but highly pertinent piece of structural evidence at Brunel Court that argues strongly against the remains being the last vestiges of such a simple building. Although it only survived as a short stretch of cobble foundation, there was, at the southern end of the west wall (*231*), the stump of a westwards return, clearly implying the existence of a second east-west wall, presumably the north wall of either the main body of the nave, or a northern aisle. Thus the building can probably best be seen as a northerly projection from the body of the church. As the mendicant orders became more popular, it was not uncommon for the nave to be enlarged and become more elaborate, sometimes with the addition of a northern aisle (Martin 1966, 13, 16), as was the case at the Franciscan friaries of Hartlepool and Carmarthen (Daniels 1986, 300-1, fig 16; James 1997, 171-2). These were essentially funerary chapels, intended for the interment and memorialising of generous benefactors, a commitment that Franciscans undertook in the pursuit of benefice; such a function can be suggested at Brunel Court, judging by the orderly rows of intramural burials. Moreover, the density of those burials is also very high, a feature that Gilchrist and Sloane (2005, 56-7) correlate with lay burials concentrated around the altars of family chapels.

Rather than an aisle, however, the surviving structure was more likely to have been an addition to the north wall of the church, projecting from the nave or (much less likely) the choir. Although relatively uncommon, this is a recurring feature of English and Irish Mendicant churches (Mersch 2009, 152). It could be a so-called north nave, as at Oxford Greyfriars (Hassall *et al* 1989; Fig 32), or what is described as

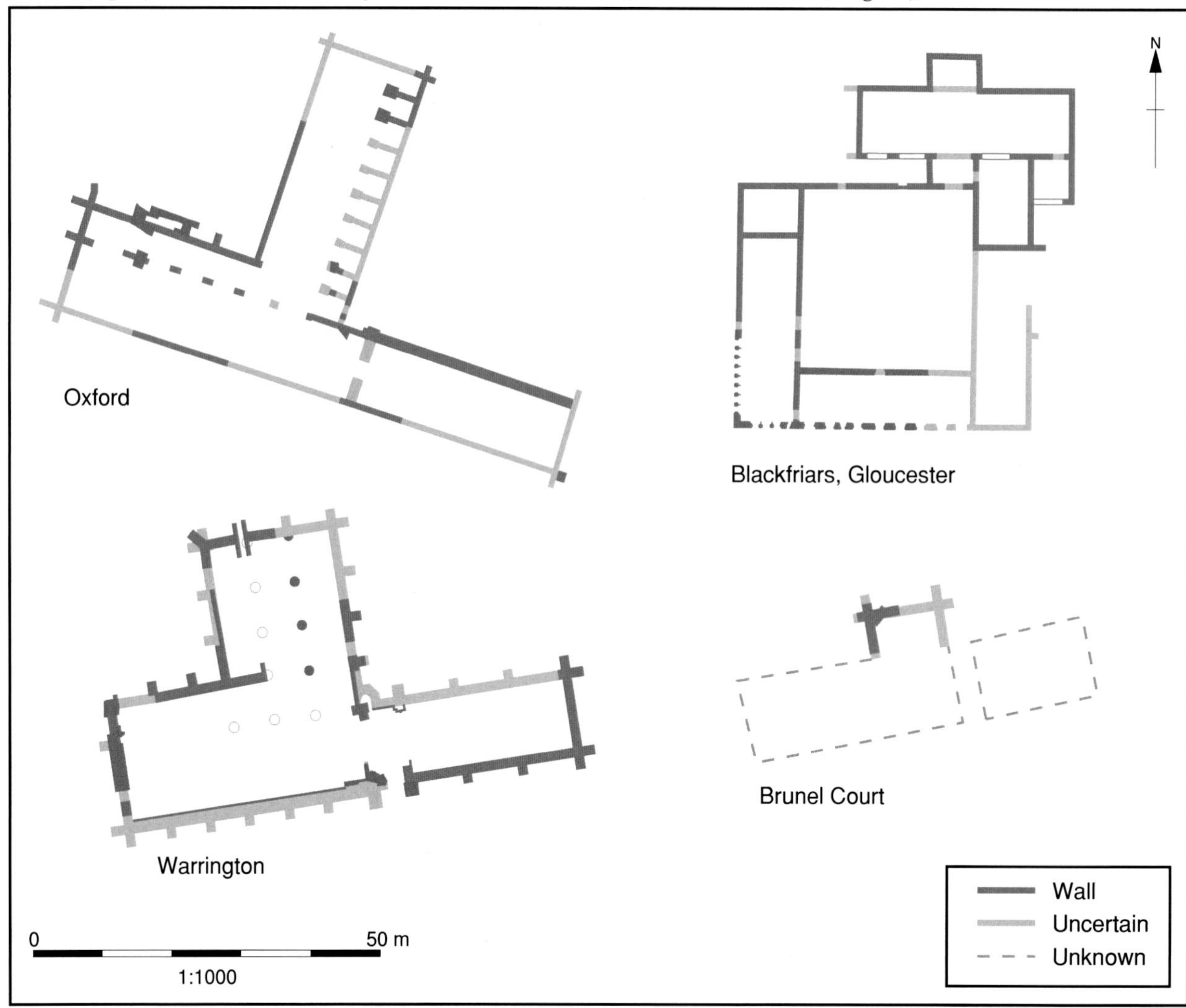

Figure 32: Chapels on the north sides of friary churches (after Hassall et al *1989; O'Sullivan 2013b; Heawood* et al *2002)*

a transeptual chapel at Chester (Ward 1990), and Gloucester Blackfriars (O'Sullivan 2013b, 145), or even the L-shaped arrangement added to Warrington Friary, *c* 1350 (Heawood *et al* 2002). Irish Franciscan churches appear, on occasion, to have had a somewhat more fluid layout, with a northern sacristy and transept at Askeaton (Discovery Programme 2014a) and a southern 'transept' at the Black Abbey, Kilkenny (Fenning nd). In Yorkshire, early reports of the friary church at Doncaster suggest an unusual north porch, although this is now contested (Historic England 2015b). On the Continent, many such extensions were built to accommodate the numerous family chapels and burial places which are a characteristic of Franciscan churches in Europe (Bruzelius 2012). That the remains at Brunel Court formed part of such an extension not only accords well with the position of ditch *106*, dug just outside it in the late fourteenth or fifteenth century (Fig 31; *p 69*) but also, beyond that, with the position of extramural graves to the east and west, which seem to represent the remains of an extensive graveyard on the north side of the church. A similar situation is as seen at Claregalway in Ireland (Discovery Programme 2014b), which also has a northwards extension to the church close to the walking space.

The northern chapels at Warrington Friary and Oxford Greyfriars were demonstrably later additions to the church, with the Warrington example believed to have been erected at some time before 1350 (Heawood *et al* 2002, 181; Greene 1992, 22). The same may have been the case at Llanfaes and Lincoln (Martin 1966), where the continued presence of the north wall of the church suggested that the chapels were not integral to the original structure (Fig 30). At Gloucester Blackfriars, the north transept, so similar in dimensions to those of the structure at Brunel Court, was a fourteenth-century addition, with apparent removal of the intervening section of the thirteenth-century nave wall (O'Sullivan 2013b, 144, fig 3.14). Several monastic churches were substantially altered to accommodate the mausolea of powerful local dynasties, such as the de Roos family of Helmsley, who funded the rebuilding of the east end of the church at Kirkham Priory in North Yorkshire (Greene 1992, 57), or the burial chapel added in a similar position at Norton Priory, Cheshire (Brown and Howard-Davis 2008).

If the structure at Brunel Court represents a chapel, the date of the earliest internal burials (*Ch 2, p 18*) would indicate that it was either an original component of the church, or had been added at an early date, as was the case with the earliest north 'transept' at the Greyfriars, Oxford (*p 66*; Hassall *et al* 1989). There is considerable evidence for the subsequent modification of many friary churches (there is evidence of rebuilding or expansion at 34 English Franciscan churches; Butler 1984, 129), but the presence of an early, or even, given

the dating of the skeletons in Row 1 (*Ch 2*), original side chapel at Preston would be unusual.

There is one other possible identification which remains to be considered, but is much less likely. It could be suggested that the structure was possibly the chapter house, another location used for prestigious burials. At the unusually well-preserved Franciscan friary at Walsingham, this was small and partially detached (at ground level at least) from the surrounding buildings (Dickinson 1961, 147), and a similar arrangement has been postulated for the Greyfriars, Leicester (University of Leicester 2013). At both sites, however, the chapter house is thought to have occupied a traditional position within the eastern claustral range (Dickinson 1961), and thus such an identification would have serious consequences for any speculation on the position of the friary church at Preston, placing it considerably to the north of the surviving building.

Appearance and decoration

Almost nothing can be reconstructed of the appearance of the building, although the Franciscan Order required that it should not be overly ornate, 'every boundlessness concerning length, width, and height of the building should be avoided' (Mersch 2009, 146 (citing the Statutes of Narbonne)). The nature of the foundations has led to the assumption that the building had stone walls, but even this is uncertain, as dwarf walls with a timber superstructure, or even a timber framework set directly on the cobble foundations, is possible. Small amounts of sheet glass hint at glazed windows (perhaps grisaille) and a few line-impressed tiles indicate mosaic-tiled floors, both of which are fairly standard in medieval churches (Friar 1996). The tiles from Brunel Court are a significant group, however, particularly as they illuminate more than just the appearance of parts of the building. A very small amount of glazed roof tile was recovered in 1991, but whether this indicates fully tiled roofs or ceramic ridge tiles capping thatch is not ascertainable. Fairly rough-and-ready sculptural elements recovered in the nineteenth century (*Ch 4*, Pl 15) indicate some decoration, but so little has survived that further speculation is almost impossible.

Whilst the tiles were competently made, and had clearly been used, they gave a workmanlike impression overall, the design stamps being fairly basic and comparatively poorly cut, varying in depth and fineness (Pl 19). Problems were also encountered with the glazes. Nonetheless, the production of shaped tiles, for use in a mosaic floor, suggests high aspirations (Fig 33).

The surviving assemblages of medieval floor tiles from the North West are small but, in the present

Plate 19: Line-impressed medieval floor tiles

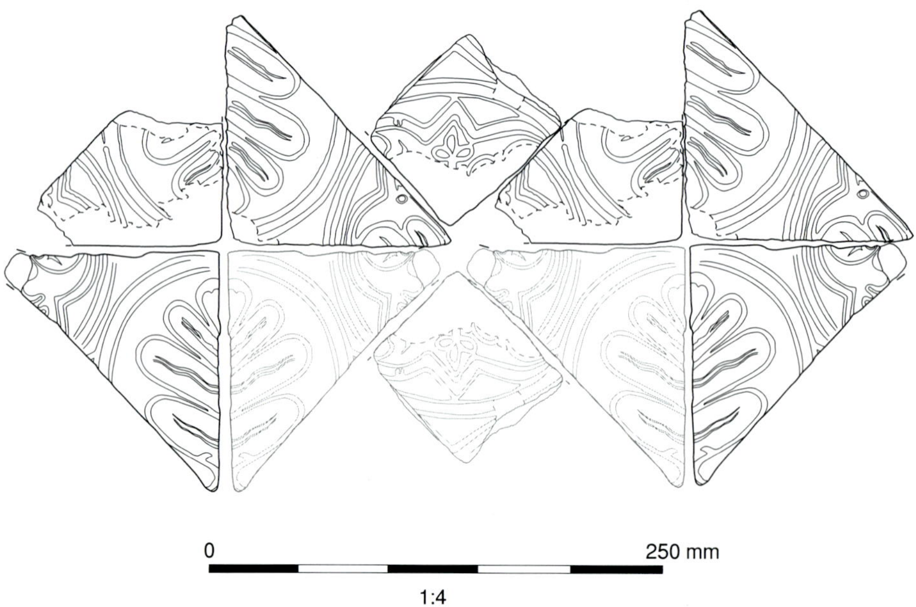

Figure 33: Composite pattern that could be formed by a mosaic of the line-impressed floor tiles

state of knowledge, the Brunel Court tiles suggest a similar pattern of production and distribution to other assemblages from the more remote sites in the region. It appears that tiles found in Lancashire and Cumbria were produced on a smaller scale, and a more idiosyncratic basis, than in other areas of northern England, seemingly involving people with limited technical knowledge, who operated on a fairly localised basis (Stopford 2005). Floor tiles from Shap Abbey, for instance, and some of those from Carlisle Cathedral, both in Cumbria, have crude, hand-incised decoration, and a distinctly homemade character (*op cit*, 255-7; tile groups 32 and 33, figs 25.1-25.2).

More professionally produced tiles are also found in the region, often with line-impressed decoration made using rather crudely carved design stamps. Several of the small assemblages with line-impressed decoration include a few shaped mosaic tiles, for example at the Dominican Friary, Lancaster (*op cit*, 186-8; tile group 11, fig 16.4), at Bolton Priory, North Yorkshire (*op cit*, 184-6; tile group 10, figs 16.1-16.3), and at Holm Cultram Abbey, Cumbria (*op cit*, 192; tile group 14, fig 17.5). The assemblage from Brunel Court is similar in conception to these, with line-impressed decoration on a circular tile (used in a mosaic arrangement), as well as regular-sized line-impressed square tiles and triangles split from the squares.

Designs similar to 14.2 and 14.3 (*Ch 4, pp 46-7*) have been found at sites across the Midlands and in north Wales (British Museum catalogue: BMD 218 and BMD 219; Eames 1980, II). The examples of BMD 219 came from Croxden Abbey, in Staffordshire, and Beauchief Abbey, near Sheffield (BMC 1412, 2053-6), whilst BMD 218 is distributed across Cheshire and north Wales (Lewis 1999, tile group 52, design 744, 195, 90-2). Two fragments from Whalley Abbey, Lancashire, are of a similar design (Stopford 2005, 261; Unassigned/13, fig 25.4). None of these tiles was made with the same design stamp, or are thought to be from the same workshop, as the Brunel Court examples, however. The closest parallel is thus the Holm Cultram tiles, and these may indicate that those used at Brunel Court were also distributed to more than one site.

The use and development of the building

Although the remains of the building are scant, it is still possible to reconstruct something of the sequence of changes that it underwent through time. Assuming that the original church was built soon after the foundation of the friary in, or not long before, 1260, it seems to have been the case that the northern extension was added relatively soon after. Indeed, the dated graves in Rows 1 and 2 indicate that the chapel was in use for burial by the late thirteenth or early fourteenth century (Fig 34), and it is possible that extramural graves 28 and 30, cut by the apparently rebuilt northern wall, were contemporary with these rows. It is reasonable to assume that the internal graves were oriented on a family altar or altars set along the east wall of the building, this being the most usual place for such structures, but the heavy disturbance at its eastern end implies that any structures there would have suffered a similar fate to the adjoining wall. It might be argued that the slight angularity in the central group of burials (represented by Row 1, graves 9 and 10; Row 2, graves 7, 17, 21, and 23; and Row 3, graves 1, 2, and 32; *Ch 2, pp 18-20*) might indicate that their alignment was influenced more by such a feature set at the south-east end of the structure, rather than simply by the surrounding walls.

Burial within the probably unaltered confines of the chapel continued during the mid- to late fourteenth century. The arrangement of these graves in a single discrete row (Row 3) adds to the supposition that this was a private, family, chapel, as there was clearly little pressure on space. There is, however, a broad coincidence between the dating of this row of graves and the repeated outbreaks of plague in the mid-late fourteenth century (Sharpe France 1938, 21-2), when more than 3000 died in Preston alone (*ibid*), which might be of significance. The fact that in several instances the foot of the graves in Row 3 cut the heads of Row 2, and that grave 18 was inserted at an angle, cutting through grave 19, might hint at some disarray or haste, as the Franciscans are widely known for their meticulous recording of the location of burials (Steer 2018, 119).

It is possible that the group of external burials to the east of the structure can also be dated to this point or earlier, as they were cut by flat-bottomed ditch *106*, which encircled the building (Fig 31). Although the ditch and the holly stakes that had been driven into it had a clear spatial and chronological relationship, dating evidence indicates that the former was probably in existence some time before the stakes were added, and remained in use after any structure had gone. The ditch, cleaned periodically, can perhaps be seen as draining water from the surroundings and from the eaves of the building. Certainly, the palaeoenvironmental evidence indicates that the low-lying area in which the church was built was as damp as the name Marsh Lane suggests, and that the ditch itself contained water at most times of the year (*Ch 4, p 61*).

The role of the stakes remains rather enigmatic, and, although they are superficially similar to the timber piles, *c* 100 mm in diameter, that had supported the walls of the Blackfriars' church at Carlisle (McCarthy 1990), their smaller size and alignment suggests that their purpose was different. Given both the dating and the practical considerations of cleaning out the ditch, they are likely to represent only a temporary feature, and evidence from several other sites provides a basis for interpretation. A very similar combination of a ditch and closely spaced stakes was interpreted as a boundary at the Augustinian friary at Leicester (Mellor and Pearce 1981, 11-13), where they formed the northern limit of the site in the thirteenth century, with the ditch also acting as the main drain (*op cit*, 15). However, the position of the features at Brunel Court, so close to the wall of the building, rather negates any such function. Given the depth to which they were sunk, it is also unlikely that the stakes represented the remnants of a wattle lining to the ditch (see Carver 1987, fig 8, 16), although the identification of roundwood in the palaeoenvironmental samples (*Ch 4, p 57*), potentially the vestiges of the otherwise absent wattles, is of interest.

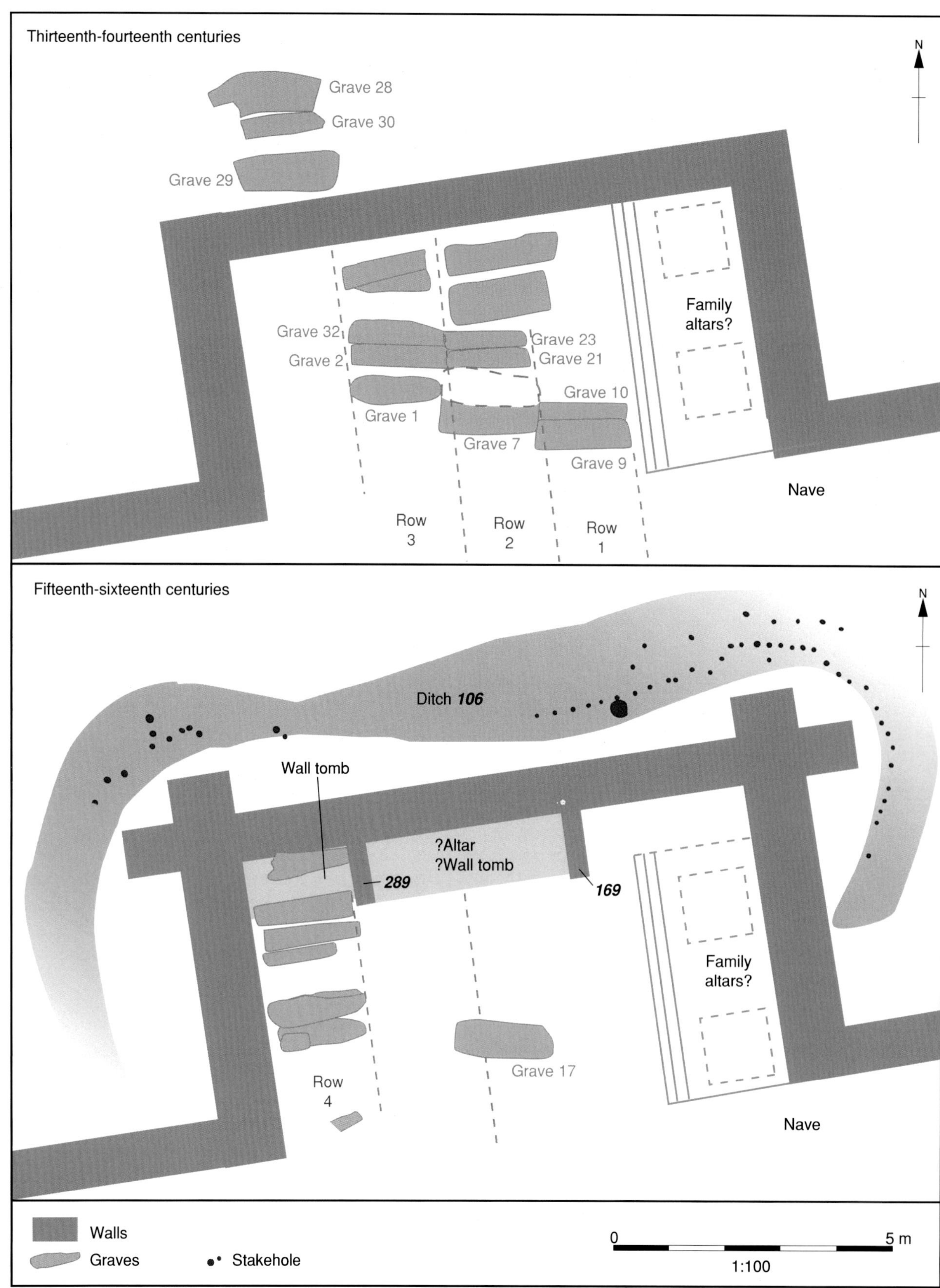

Figure 34: The development of the chapel in the thirteenth-fourteenth and the fifteenth-sixteenth centuries

Two other interpretations are more closely associated with the building. Postholes at Gisborough Priory, Fountains Abbey (both North Yorkshire), and Bordesley Abbey (Worcestershire) have been attributed to scaffolding systems (Greene 1992, 79), but the closely spaced and deeply set stakes at Brunel Court are far from analogous. Contemporary depictions of medieval scaffolding suggest that such temporary structures were not earthfast, but were instead very much like those in use today (albeit with the use of wood), with well-spaced uprights (Salzman 1923, 124; 1952, 318-22). Alternatively, or perhaps additionally, their proximity might suggest that they could have formed a windbreak, perhaps during modifications or repairs.

Notwithstanding that they may be atypical, on balance, the stakes are perhaps most likely to be associated with a scaffold system. Certainly, their later fourteenth- to early fifteenth-century date (*Ch 4, p 48*) precludes their use in either the construction or demolition of the adjacent wall, but it is similar to the dating of graves in Row 4 within the building. As such, they may coincide with the suggested modification to the north wall (*Ch 2, p 23*). These modifications involved a change in structural technique in the north-west buttress, where cobbled foundations were replaced by sandstone slabs, but otherwise were not of enormous scope, apparently moving the wall northwards by approximately its original width at the most, incidentally cutting through two of the closest of the extramural graves (G28, G30), which were immediately outside the original north-west corner of the building.

The motivation behind the alterations is far from clear, although the approximate date is of interest, for it may reflect an upturn in the community's fortunes following the catalogue of miseries brought by the fourteenth century. Substantial alterations, such as the insertion of one or more windows, or perhaps a private door to the chapel, may have necessitated reinforcing the lower elements of the walls. It is also possible that a necessary structural renovation was accompanied somewhat opportunistically by internal modification and beautification. For example, there may have been a structural imperative to dig the ditch and reinforce the wall, perhaps to tackle poor drainage and resultant subsidence (B Sloane *pers comm*). The most obvious change was the creation of a prestigious wall tomb within the fabric of the north wall, but that may not have been the only modification. Short walls *289* and *169* (Fig 31) may well have been added at right-angles to the north wall at that time, and could have been associated with one of several structures, including further wall tombs, or perhaps a family altar. Certainly it is notable that fifteenth-century grave 17 was inserted into Row 2 roughly midway between the two short walls.

It could well have been these changes, and any resulting refurbishment, which necessitated the installation of the decorative tiled floor, as the few floor tiles recovered (*Ch 4*) are stylistically contemporary. They are unlikely to have been the original floor, however, as, aside from the practical difficulties associated with making repairs after each interment, the tiles are stylistically somewhat later than the earliest burials. Indeed, they are perhaps best seen as indicating a continuing process of beautification and adornment funded by patrons. This may also have included modification of the structure's windows, such as the replacement of the plain or grisaille lights with stained glass. It is even possible that a private entrance might have been driven through the north wall, as would appear to have been the case at Warrington (Heawood *et al* 2002). After this, burials continued to be made within the structure (Row 4) well into the fifteenth century.

The nave and chancel

All of the evidence at Brunel Court indicates that the main body of the friary church lay to the south of the remains excavated. Its full size can only be speculated upon, although the historical townscape, antiquarian references, and other comparable friary plans do provide some potential for extrapolation. At its closest, Barracks Street, and its post-medieval precursor, lay *c* 20 m to the west of the remains excavated, and it is thus possible that it skirted the western end of the nave.

With the exception of the friary at London (not unexpectedly the country's largest and, in plan, most complex, Franciscan church; O'Sullivan 2013b, 225-30), existing and reconstructed English friary church plans show that side chapels and additional aisles were added to the nave, rather than to the east of the walking space, which would require modification of the choir (Fig 32). Whilst there appears to have been variation in the position of any side chapel, the combined length of the choir and walking space generally appear to be of a similar size to the nave (*ie* accounting for half the length of the church; Fig 30).

If that rule of thumb is used in the case of Preston Friary, then it might not be unreasonable to suggest that the east end of the church lay *c* 20 m to the east of the chapel, making the friary church about 40-50 m long. Moreover, the alignment of a short stretch of stone wall identified about 20 m to the east, in evaluation Trench 11 (*Ch 2, p 26*), suggests it to have been part of the north wall of the church (Fig 35). Whilst the friary churches at Lincoln, Llanfaes, and Gloucester Blackfriars, were only about 30 m and 40 m long, respectively, at many other friaries, such as at Gloucester Greyfriars, Chichester, Lichfield, and Reading, churches were around 60 m long, and *c* 10 m wide (Martin 1966; O'Sullivan 2013b; Fig 30).

Beyond an educated estimate of the size of the friary church, it might be assumed that other common elements were present, including a tower built over the walking place, and that the choir was hidden from

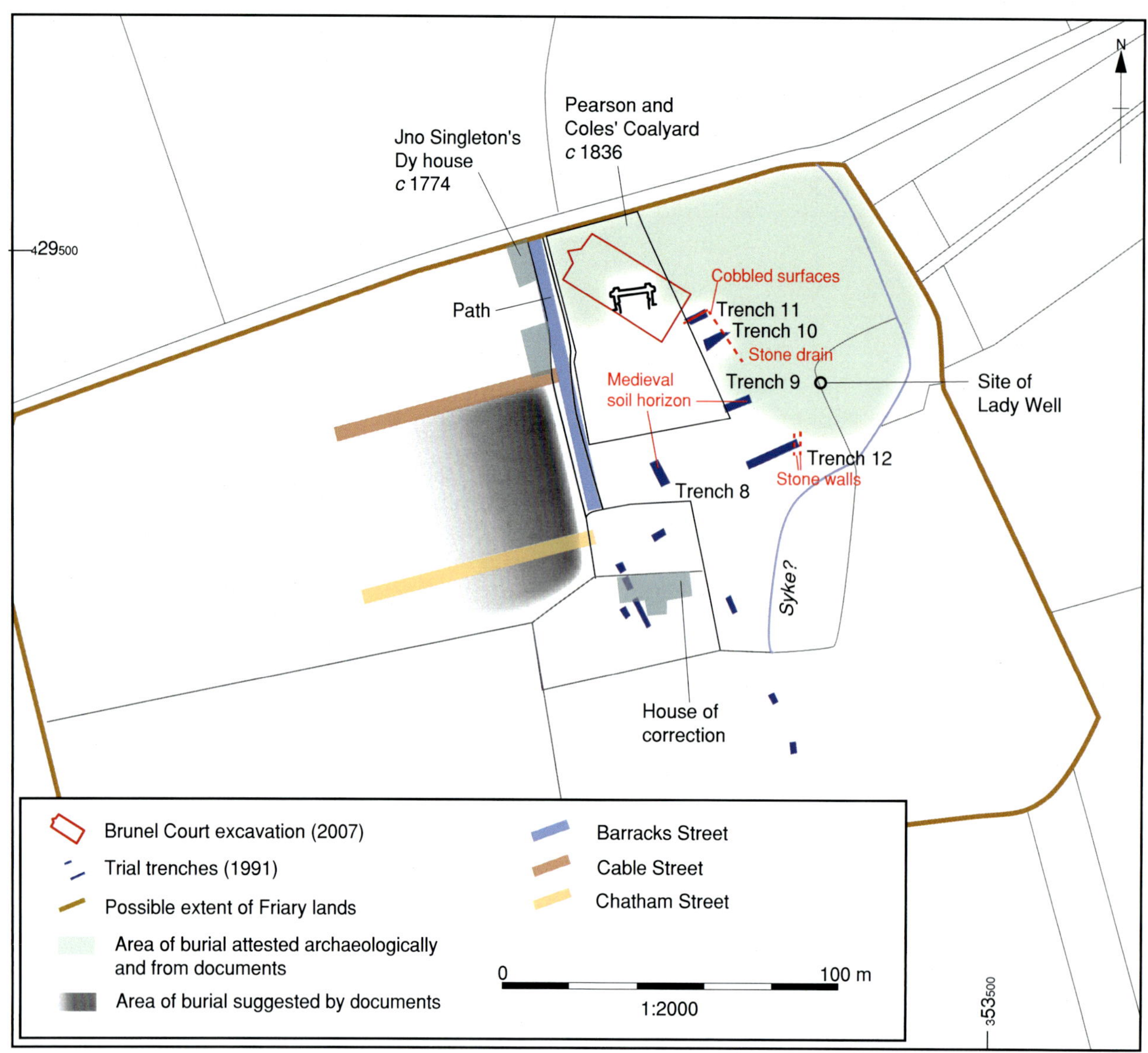

Figure 35: Possible configuration of the friary precinct from the archaeological, cartographical, and documentary evidence

public view by the installation of a pulpitum (choir screen), often, in the Franciscan case, ornately painted with didactic scenes (Bruzelius 2012, 369). Used exclusively by the friars, the choir could be expected to be devoid of aisles and ancillary chapels, although at many sites, and with time, the latter proliferated in the nave. Similarly, the nave could be expanded with one or more additional aisles, although, given the size of Preston, in common with the majority of small town friaries, it could be thought that the nave remained relatively simple.

The Friary Precinct

The claustral ranges

The church was, of course, not the only building within the friary enceinte, which would have comprised a complex of structures and open areas, including the cemetery, and probably gardens to provide food for the friars. However, the positions and nature of other components of the friary complex at Preston are not possible to predict with any precision, not least because Franciscan friaries appear to show a considerable degree of variability in terms of layout (Dickinson 1961, 47; Martin 1966, 29).

Nonetheless, it is possible to give some consideration of the layout of the friary precinct by combining several pieces of evidence. These include various historical references to the discovery of funerary remains from particular locations, and a succession of maps that label friary buildings within the developing townscape (*Ch 1*). To that can be added the findings from the 1991 investigation (*Ch 2*; LUAU 1991a; 1991b), as well as some of those from the latest excavation, including the analysis of palaeoenvironmental remains (*Ch 4*). It is worth noting that map regression indicates that none of the

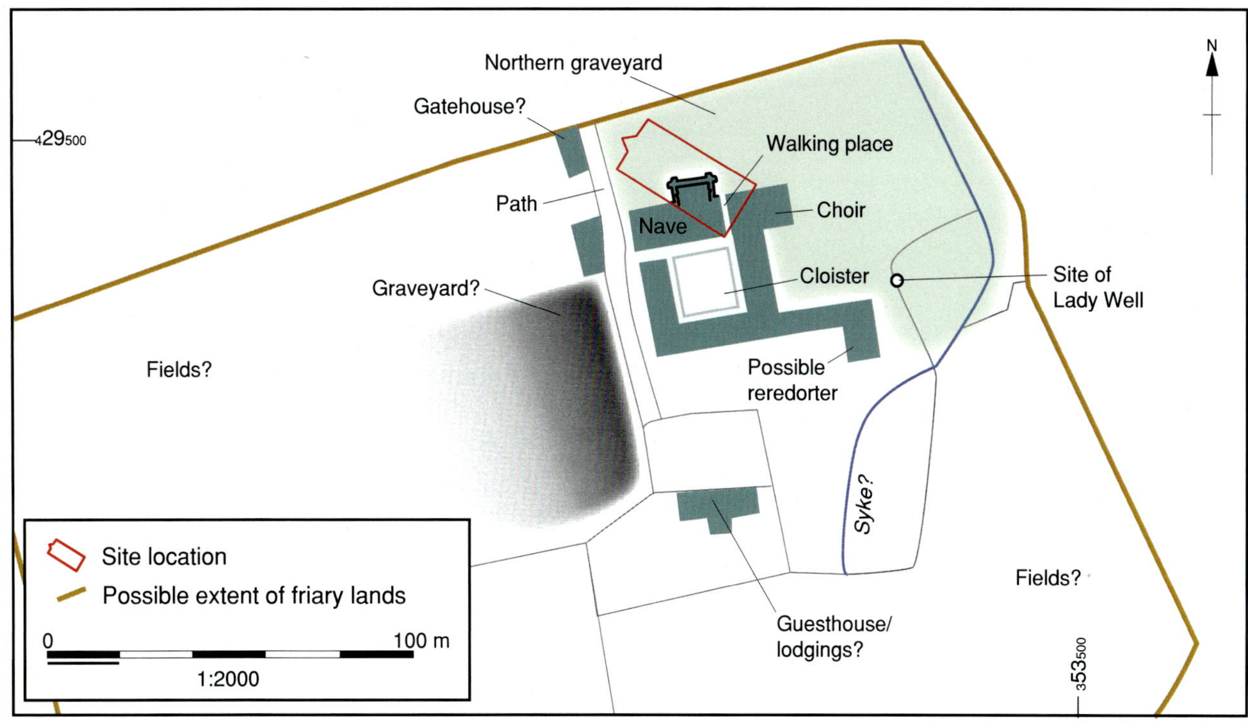

Figure 36: The conjectural layout of the friary precinct

remains identified within the evaluation trenches (LUAU 1991a; 1991b) can be equated with any structures depicted since Lang and Porter's map of 1774 (and arguably, Carpenter and Wills' map of 1715; see also OS 1849; 1893), and it is very tempting to believe that they must be earlier. Other building fragments located by the excavations are too small for certain identification, but are presumably glimpses of the claustral ranges and service buildings (Fig 36). Finally, and notwithstanding a degree of variability, study of comparative friary sites provides a template around which the data can be modelled.

In general terms, the layout of friaries founded by the two most important of the mendicant orders in England (Dominican and Franciscan) seem to have differed little from those of other monastic orders (Forgens and Singman 1999) except that, being in urban areas and dependent on charitable gifts of land, the precise arrangement of claustral and secular buildings was more fluid. It was often adapted to fit the site and finance available, with the construction of a friary tending to be piecemeal and agglomerative, and seldom a single event (Bruzelius 2012, 368). This can be seen for instance in London, where separate individuals paid for the construction of chapels, the nave, dormitories, and the chapter house (Steer 2018). Whilst there was some dispute within the order as to the necessity for cloistered space (Röhrkasten 2012), the majority of English and Welsh friaries appear to have had one (O'Sullivan 2013b). When space was at less of a premium, for instance at Walsingham (Knowles and St Joseph 1952), the monastic plan was

only slightly modified, so that it was 'in accordance with English Franciscan architectural practice' (*op cit*, 252).

The palaeoenvironmental evidence suggests that Preston Friary was founded on a wet site (*Ch 4, p 54*), which map regression suggests was relatively spacious, and lay slightly beyond the edge of the thirteenth-century town (*Ch 1, p 9*). This might well have meant that it was not particularly constrained by extant urban boundaries. In such a situation, it seems likely that the arrangement of the principal structures (the church, the cloister, and the ranges of buildings around it) may, as at Walsingham, have more closely matched the Benedictine model aspired to by most monastic orders (*op cit*, 48, 147), with an enclosed cloister to the south of the church, appended to the nave's south wall (Fig 36). This allowed the church to provide shelter from northerly winds, without blocking the sunlight (*op cit*, 14-15).

Contact with the laity was an important tenet of the Franciscan mission. Thus, the west end of their churches was deliberately placed close to an extant road so that the laity could access the public space of the nave without needing to enter the more enclosed parts of the precinct (Martin 1966, 29). Such a road at Preston would appear to be the course of what in the nineteenth century was known as Barracks Street, but which is also clearly shown on the seventeenth- and eighteenth-century maps of Kuerden, and Lang and Porter, respectively.

The archaeological remains discovered in 2007 lay somewhat to the north of the friary buildings depicted on post-medieval maps (*eg* Carpenter and Wills 1715; Lang and Porter 1774; Baines 1824). This might be taken as evidence to strengthen the identification of the stone building as the conventual church, with the lane allowing good public access, as the church is likely to have been preferentially targeted for destruction at the Dissolution. This would mean that it could well have been lost, despite the survival of service and accommodation ranges, which later became the House of Correction (*Ch 1*).

Thus it would seem reasonable to postulate for Preston a friary church with a northern chapel, claustral buildings adjoining the south wall of the church, and a cemetery to the north. There is further support for the position of the cloister: firstly, where mendicant churches had lateral extensions, such as the sort of side chapel seen at Brunel Court, these tended to be constructed on the side of the church opposite the cloister (Martin 1966, 12, 14). Secondly, there would have been very little room to fit a cloister of any size between the presumed line of the northern wall of the church and Marsh Lane, and such cramping hardly seems necessary given the size of the wider holding; and, thirdly, and perhaps more importantly, a northern position would have placed the cloister undesirably close to the most publicly accessible parts of the precinct.

By convention, the cloister would have been enclosed to the north by the church, and each of the other sides by ranges of buildings (O'Sullivan 2013b). The administrative and domestic buildings, principally the chapter house, and above it, the brethren's accommodation, would usually have formed its eastern range, allowing the brethren direct access to the choir without entering the more public parts of the church, with buildings such as the refectory and other offices to the south and west. Service buildings, for instance the bakery, brew-house, and so-on, could lie beyond the claustral range, as they also had a requirement for contact with the outside world (*ibid*). At Preston, it might be imagined that these were in or near the west range, where they could be accessed from Barracks Street. Perhaps it was the walls of those buildings, and also of the west end of the nave, that were documented on that street in the nineteenth century (*Ch 1, p 12*).

Not all of the friary's structures might have surrounded the main cloister, however. Many friaries appear to have had buildings that were detached or arranged around a little or lesser cloister (O'Sullivan 2013b). In particular, these could include lodgings for guests and the warden of the friary and, typically, the infirmary was usually set at a distance from the cloister, mainly for pragmatic reasons, and thus often had an attached chapel.

It seems highly likely that the walls encountered in evaluation Trench 12 (Fig 35) represent parts of other friary buildings, perhaps a reredorter. To the south was the position of what is thought to be the post-medieval House of Correction (*Ch 1, p 10*), which, by virtue of its survival into the mid-nineteenth century (OS 1849), must be the lancet-windowed structure described by Hardwick as a chapel (1857, 115). Although it is possible that this House of Correction, formerly the Breres' residence (*Ch 1, p 10*), had once been part of one of the claustral ranges, it is more likely, given its distance from the postulated position of the church and cloister, that it had been a better-appointed domestic range or structure, perhaps a guesthouse.

Certainly, such accommodation would have been far easier to convert into a high-status house after the Dissolution than any other part of the friary. Indeed, at many other monastic sites, the Abbot's house or the guesthouse was often adapted for such use: at the Greyfriars, Chester, for example, part of the friary, including the guest accommodation occupying the western side of the main cloister, was leased to a Ralph Wryne, just before the institution's dissolution. At about the same time, another house on that site, this one in a 'Lesser Cloister' between the dorter and the infirmary, was leased to one Thomas Pyllyon (Ward 1990, 199-200, fig 134). If the situation at Preston Friary was similar, as perhaps suggested by the pre-Dissolution sale of at least one parcel of land to Thomas Breres (*Ch 1, p 10*), then a guesthouse seems more suited for such conversion, as, traditionally, the Warden's (the head of a friary) quarters were little better than those of the other brethren (Dickinson 1961, 49).

There is an interesting parallel with the Franciscan friary at Canterbury, where the only surviving structure is the former guesthouse, which lay beyond the cloisters (*ibid*). This small, simple, two-storey rectangular structure is now referred to as a chapel, much as seems to have been the case in the nineteenth century, when referring to the surviving structures of Preston Friary (*Ch 1, p 12*; Eastbridge Hospital 2017; Fishwick 1900, 202). It is possible that the medieval glazed roof tiles recovered in 1991 from Evaluation Trench 8 (*Ch 4, p 46*) possibly originated from that building. Indeed, it might be argued that the presence of such items supports the idea that the building was constructed to rather higher specifications than might have been expected of the more humble accommodation for the friars.

Beyond the cloister

Whilst the area covered by the conventual buildings seems to have been quite compact at most friaries (O'Sullivan 2013b), most had additional land, its extent varying in accordance with availability and the generosity of grants. The longest axes of some urban friary precincts were about 100-120 m, as at the Franciscan friaries at Beverley (Foreman 1996, 5, fig 2), Carmarthen (James 1997, 173, fig 34), and Chester (Ward 1990, 199, fig 134), and the Austin friary at Leicester (Mellor and Pearce 1981, 7, fig 1). If the House of Correction marked the southern extent of the friary precinct at Preston, then its dimensions would be in keeping with those elsewhere.

An examination of cartographic sources suggests that Preston Friary may have had rather more land than just the tract occupied by its buildings. Lang and Porter's map of 1774 (Fig 37) is particularly useful in this context, because not only does this show all the fields around Preston, but it gives their names as well. Of some interest is the fairly regular rectangle formed by four distinctive fields, the shapes of which contrast with the narrow plots in the surrounding area, which often have aratral (S-shaped) edges indicative of having been ploughed as strips (Aston 2002, 120). It is possible that two of these peculiar fields, *Nearer House of Correction Field* and *Further House of Correction Field*, are so named because they were under the ownership of the gaol and thus, presumably, were former friary lands. Together with *Little Syke* and *Great Syke*, they surround the enclosure around what was probably then the House of Correction.

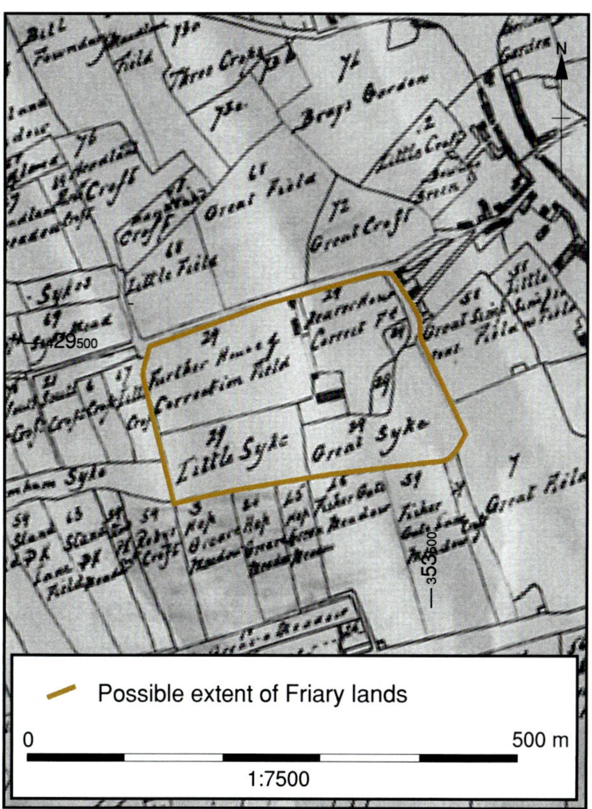

Figure 37: The wider friary precinct, from Lang and Porter's map of 1774

Arguably, the distinctive pattern of fields shown by Lang and Porter, and their influence on the developing townscape, means that it is still possible to trace the putative friary curtilage on early nineteenth-century maps, and, to a lesser extent, the subsequent OS depictions. This interpretation is aided by the longevity of Marsh Lane as the area's northern boundary. For example, it seems highly likely that modern Ladywell Street (Mount Pleasant in 1824 (on Baines' map); St Ann's Square in 1836 (on Myers)) passed along the eastern edge of *Nearer House of Correction Field*, whilst the western edges of *Further House of Correction Field* and *Little Syke* are likely to have corresponded to the line of Kay Street. The southern edge might be tentatively correlated with Ribble Street (no longer extant) on Myers' map and on the OS Town Plan of 1849.

If these fields preserve the friary's curtilage, then it seems that the establishment occupied some 15 acres (6 ha). Whilst that area is similar to those of the majority of urban friaries, such as the 16 acres of Derby Blackfriars (O'Sullivan 2013a, 128-9; 2013b), it is far smaller than the Franciscan friaries at Llanfaes (30 acres/12 ha) and Babwell (Suffolk; 43 acres/17.5 ha; Dickinson 1961, 9). It is probable that the friary buildings occupied the north-east quadrant of the area, placing them closer to the town, and thus to the townsfolk with whom they would have interacted. The buildings might thus have occupied the drier parts of the plot, with the land becoming increasingly wet as it dipped south-westward in the direction of the river Ribble.

Such additional land was important to the friars, as, by the 1240s, Franciscans were expected to provide their own sustenance (Röhrkasten 2012). A good water supply and drainage was important to monastic houses of all types (Greene 1992, 168), and it may be no coincidence that the friary's eastern curtilage probably bounded the Lady Well. This well, which is thought to have had medieval (or earlier) origins, is described as a holy well in later sources (Hardwick 1857, 116), and lent its name to the street bounding Brunel Court to the east. Indeed, it is likely to have been in that area, as there are nineteenth-century accounts of a 'lead conduit' supplying water to the friary (*ibid*). Holy wells were a focus of popular devotion, and were often associated with hospitals, hospices, and hermitages (Hardwick 1857, 116; Taylor 1906; Farrer and Brownbill 1912, 91; Tostevin and Iles 1992; Gilchrist 1995, 3, 43). The name 'Lady Well' suggests an association with the Virgin Mary, or perhaps a female saint, although it is not possible to determine whether the well's holiness pre-dated the friary, or derived from an association with that institution. If the latter, then the 'Lady' might be a reference to St Clare, the friary's patron saint.

Further evidence for the water supply is possibly provided by the curious hourglass arrangement of two small plots shown by Lang and Porter (1774) between *Nearer House of Correction Field* and *Great Syke*. 'Syke' is an Old English term for a stream (Mills 1991, 383), and it is quite possible that these field boundaries followed a brook. The closest archaeological remains to that field boundary was a wall identified in Trench 12 (*Ch 2, pp 25-6*), which, it might be postulated, could have pertained to the reredorter (Fig 36). Associated with privacy and hygiene, such installations were generally built close to running water and away from more public areas.

A wall bounding the precinct was also a feature of many friaries (O'Sullivan 2013b), although, given the friars' requirement for interaction with the laity, it was sometimes contested as a necessity (Röhrkasten 2012). There is no evidence for a wall at Preston, although a building shown by Kuerden, in *c* 1685 (Smith nd), at the corner of Marsh Lane and the route of what was later known as Barracks Street, stands in the position that might be expected of a gatehouse, another common feature of the monastic enceinte (O'Sullivan 2013b).

The Burials

The graves formed distinct spatial groups, even though the burials themselves present a mixed demographic profile. Men, women, and children were all present, with people buried both inside and outside the building. Some were seemingly of sufficient wealth to have afforded wooden coffins, and one may even have been interred within a stone tomb (*Ch 2, p 21*). No evidence survives to show how they were marked at ground level, but floor-set slabs or brasses might have been the most likely memorials.

Where human remains survived to illustrate the position of the body within the grave, all had been laid on their backs, with their heads to the west, and generally with their hands either folded in their laps (Pl 20), or placed at their sides. These are common postures for medieval Christian burials (Gilchrist and Sloane 2005, 152), deriving from the core belief in corporeal resurrection on the Day of Judgement, and the need to face in the direction of Christ, who would appear from the east.

*Plate 20: Skeleton **178** in grave 7 (Row 2), with hands placed across the waist: the most common posture at Brunel Court*

More than any other form of evidence, the scientific dating of both the skeletons and their coffins emphasises the length of time over which burials continued, spanning several hundred years from the second half of the thirteenth century to perhaps the mid-fifteenth century (*Ch 3*, Table 1). This, coupled with the few dated artefacts (*Ch 4*), suggests that burial, and perhaps other religious activity, had ceased, within this chapel at least, somewhat before the formal dissolution of the friary in 1539.

Extramural burial

The putative reconstruction of the relative positions of church and cloister at Preston fits with the excavated and documentary evidence for burials in the locale, which, in antiquarian accounts, are most commonly associated with the friary (*Ch 1, p 13*). Burials observed in the nineteenth century were assigned to a fairly broad area, although the core was attributed to Pearson and Cole's Coalyard (Hewitson 1883, 280; Fig 35). The latter area may well have encompassed much of the church, the part of the graveyard excavated to its north, and at least part of the cloister to its south. Indeed, as elsewhere, the cloister walk would have been a popular location for the burials of 'rank and file' friars (Steer 2018).

Most of the putative external graves excavated were shallow and apparently empty and, whilst such features are common in the North West, mostly as a result of soil conditions inimical to bone preservation (Newman and Leech forthcoming; Paterson *et al* 2014), it is entirely possible that some of the human remains reported by antiquarians actually originated in the now-empty graves revealed next to Marsh Lane. These suggest that there may once have been an extensive cemetery there and, indeed, the area to the north of a friary church was often used for lay burials (Steer 2018). The easternmost extent of that graveyard may be represented by fragments of human bone encountered somewhere in the region of the Lady Well during works on the canal in 1861 (Fishwick 1900, 201),

There are also hints of other areas of burial, although it is unclear how far beyond the coalyard inhumations, some with timber and lead coffins, were identified in the nineteenth century (Hewitson 1883). Certainly the southern limit (*ie*, the former line of Chatham Street) lies well beyond what is reasonable to consider as part of the church's footprint or even the cloister, whilst, technically, the description of between Cable Street and Chatham Street places the extent of burial activity well to the west of the putative church and cloister. If burials were indeed found in that locale, then they may represent another graveyard associated with the institution.

Intramural burial

Notwithstanding the existence of external cemeteries, the church was the most sought-after location for burial (Robson 2006, 166-7), and evidence from excavations at other friaries, including those at Carmarthen and Hartlepool (James 1997; Daniels 1986), confirms this view. The church and graveyard were clearly not the sole foci for such activity, however, and, excavations at the Franciscan friary in Lewes, Sussex, have shown that interment in the cloisters could be equally intense (Gardiner *et al* 1996, 97-9, fig 21). Other locations might include the chapter house, as at the Greyfriars in Carmarthen (James 1997, 134, 137, fig 16), and in side chapels, often financed by donor families (Robson 2006, 166-7).

Indeed, given the mixed demography represented by the skeletons from Brunel Court (*Ch 3, p 29*), it is of interest to note that it was common for mendicant friaries to accept for burial women and children from high-status families (Gilchrist and Sloane 2005, 67), in the church, the chapter house, and the cloister. For example, at the Chester Blackfriars, most of the women, and children below the age of approximately 11 years, had been buried at the west end of the north aisle of the nave. At the Franciscan friary at Hartlepool, large numbers of women and children were found at the eastern end of the presbytery (the easternmost and holiest part of the church, where the high altar stood; *ibid*), whilst at the Oxford Blackfriars, five of the eight burials in the chapter house were children aged six to ten years (*op cit*, 67-8).

It is thought that the Franciscans' pastoral role, which included visiting the homes of the dying, brought them into closer contact with family life, making them particularly popular with women (Röhrkasten 2012, 43). In addition, excavations at several friary sites have demonstrated a tendency for infants to be buried in the western part of the church (*op cit*, 67). Attitudes clearly varied, however, as, at the Carmarthen Greyfriars, burials within the chapter house and cloister were considered to be those of the friars (James 1997, 176), and certainly the chapter house would be expected to be the preserve of senior churchmen or founding benefactors for many of the monastic orders, as was the case among the Cistercians (Tobin 1995, 102).

Thus, there is substantial evidence to indicate that a person's position in life was reflected in their place of burial within the friary. Shortly before the Reformation, a record was made of all the marked burials within the church of the Greyfriars, London, and this shows a distinct hierarchy, with the most important people, royalty among them, buried in front of the high altar at the eastern end of the church, gentry and nobles in chapels, and citizens and merchants in the nave. Friars were buried within the walking place (between the nave and the choir), and within the cloister alley, used as an expression of humility (O'Sullivan 2013a, 272-4, fig 15.8; Daniell 1997; Tarlow and Stutz 2013)). The record does not appear to include the graveyard, perhaps suggesting that it contained few, or no, marked burials.

Even spiritual welfare came at a price; for the Franciscans, the provision of family side-chapels within, or appended to, the nave of the church was almost inescapable, given that much of their income came from donations in return for prayer on behalf of the deceased and their families (Bruzelius 2012; Jupp and Gittings 1999, 109-10). Thus, encouraging close links with influential families in the locality would guarantee future funding, as families continued, often over extended periods, to bury their relatives within personal chapels. The position and form of chapels reflect this function: equipped with an altar or altars, they were a place where private masses could be said for the souls of patrons and benefactors buried within or nearby. Whilst chapels had an essentially spiritual function, their role in perpetuating the theatre of competition and conspicuous consumption among noble and aspirant families associated with the town was probably not insignificant.

John Leland mentions 'divers of the Sherburns and Daltuns, gentilmen (*sic*)' (Hardwick 1857, 115) being interred at Preston Friary, amongst whom, presumably, was Sir Richard Sherburne, knight of Stonyhurst. Recorded in 1437, he was one of several benefactors known to have bequeathed money to the friary (Hewitson 1883, 280; Fishwick 1900, 199). Other wealthy patrons known to have been buried within the precinct include Robert Holland, and members of the Preston family (Farrer and Brownbill 1908, 162). It may be no coincidence that the latter were later associated with the foundation of the friary (*Ch 1, p 9*).

At Brunel Court, the influence of the patrons may also be indicated by the tantalising glimpses of decorative embellishment. It is most likely that the fourteenth- to fifteenth-century decorative tiles (*Ch 4, p 46*) derive from a mosaic floor laid within the building. Although they saw little wear, these tiles would, despite their rather unaccomplished manufacture (*Ch 4, p 46*), have formed a colourful and impressive floor (*p 84; Pl 19; Fig 33*).

The people
Arguably, the seemingly structured process of burial within the building has a chronological progression from south-east to north-west, at the rate of approximately one row per century. Indeed, they are all likely to have been associated in some way, perhaps by family ties, and were focused on a specific altar of relevance to them all, with perhaps just a few interments being made in each generation. This rather infrequent use of what may well have been prime burial space could imply a certain degree of exclusivity. The late insertion of a fifteenth-century burial within grave 17 into a row of otherwise late

thirteenth- to earlier fourteenth-century interments (*Ch 2, p 18*; Fig 34) would not be incongruous within this context. Rather, it could be seen as reinforcing the familial basis of the burials, as might the apparently repeated use of several of the graves. It did not, however, prove possible to test for family relationships using DNA, or by using genetically influenced non-metric traits on any of the burials inside the building (*Ch 3, pp 31-2*), so that this must remain speculation.

Coffins
A significant proportion (45%) of the burials within the building contained evidence of coffins or other forms of grave furniture (Pl 21). Well-preserved examples are not frequent finds (Daniell 1997), being reliant on exceptional circumstances for survival. In this case, the graves in which they were deposited were cut through wet sandy clay deposits, which allowed varying levels of preservation. Occasional well-preserved wooden coffins are, however, known from several medieval sites, perhaps the closest to Preston being the Augustinian Priory at Norton, near Warrington (Brown and Howard-Davis 2008), and the Augustinian Friary within Warrington (Heawood *et al* 2002, 164). Although some thirteenth-century coffin wood survived in the burials at the latter, showing them to have been simple rectangular oak coffins similar to the Brunel Court examples, the fragmentary remains were not lifted or conserved. There have, however, been larger assemblages of oak coffin boards excavated, at sites as diverse as St Peter's, Barton-upon-Humber (Rodwell with Atkins 2011), dated to the eleventh and twelfth centuries (Tyers 2001), Hull Magistrates Court, dated to the fourteenth century (Tyers 1998), and London Guildhall, dated to the eleventh and twelfth centuries (Tyers 2008), with smaller assemblages from London Vintry House, dated to the tenth century, Merton Priory, dated to the twelfth century, York Swinegate, dated to the tenth and eleventh centuries, and Beverley Minster, dated to the eleventh century (I Tyers *pers obs*). The Preston material is thus one of a rare group.

Most of the wood used was oak (*Quercus*), which dendrochronology has shown to be from the North West (*Ch 4, p 50*). The use of locally sourced oaks for coffins at this period in Preston tallies with the evidence from most of the sites studied, the exception being all but one of the coffins from the Augustinian Friary at Hull, situated within a port, and of roughly the same period. Those coffins used riven oak boards imported from the eastern Baltic, and are part of a wide range of tree-ring and documentary evidence for the use of imported oak boards along much of the eastern and southern seaboards of England from the thirteenth century onward (Childs 2002; Tyers 2003; 2010). Elsewhere, for instance in York (Lilley *et al* 1994), Perth (Boyd 1989), and Kebister in the Shetlands (Owen and Lowe 1999), Scots pine was occasionally used for lids, or

Plate 21: Lifting the base plate of the coffin from grave 18

for the entire coffin. This raises the possibility that the fragment of ash found amongst the wood from coffin **161** (grave 8; *Ch 2, p 20*) could have been from the lid.

The availability of old, slow-growing, and straight-grained oaks, sourced from somewhere in the vicinity of Preston at this period (*p 78*), suggests that the timber market was still relatively self-contained, that the woodland resources were primarily self-sufficient, or perhaps that the trade links of the North West were not focused towards northern Europe. It may be no coincidence that the Forest of Fulwood, which lay to the north of Preston and at one time formed part of the extensive Royal Forest of Lancaster, was undergoing various assarts (clearances) in the thirteenth century (Cunliffe Shaw 1956), and may have been the source of much of the town's timber.

Several wooden coffins, seemingly of oak, were recovered from the monastic cemetery at Norton Priory, and that on display appears to have been constructed from tangentially sawn planks, with the base board and lid made from single timbers, whilst the surviving side is made from two overlapping boards. The ends, again single boards, are much thinner, at *c* 5 mm, than the side boards, which are around 20 mm thick (Brown and Howard-Davis 2008, 414, pl 218). A series of large holes at the end of each side board suggested that they were joined with hazel rods (Greene 1989, 56). This is a substantially different method of manufacture from that seen at Brunel Court,

where what evidence there is shows that the side boards of the coffin were nailed in place with little finesse, as might be expected if the coffin was intended, during any burial ceremony, to be concealed by a pall or other covering until it was finally placed in the ground. Some of the large group of wooden coffins from the site of the Augustinian Friary at Hull were also roughly nailed together, but others were carefully pegged or dowelled (Evans 2000), the roughly made examples there being interpreted as having been hurriedly constructed during the plague years of the fourteenth century (*ibid*). A plain fourteenth-century oak plank coffin from the Carmelite Friary in Norwich (Litten 1991, 89) probably resembles the Brunel Court material quite closely.

In other places, for instance York (Dawes and Magilton 1980), wooden coffins have been inferred from the presence of nails within the grave, although, on occasion, there have been as few as six recovered, despite careful excavation. This could accord quite well with the evidence from Brunel Court, where the most complete coffin could easily have been held together with as few as eight nails. Further, it is possible that the body of the coffin was held together with wooden dowels, whilst only the lid was nailed on (R M Newman *pers comm*). At York (Dawes and Magilton 1980), it has been suggested, on the evidence of the nails, that the boards were *c* 20 mm thick, again similar to the thickness of boards from Brunel Court. In addition, several of the coffins from within the Jewish cemetery at Jewbury, York (Lilley *et al* 1994), had iron reinforcing straps.

There, it was suggested that the reinforced coffins were those of members of the Jewish community in Lincoln, which, in order to survive the journey to York, needed reinforcement. The same necessity could have been faced by those bringing a deceased member of a patron's family to the friary from afar.

The presence of coffins in the graves at Preston might suggest that those people had enjoyed a degree of wealth (Litten 1991, 85; Jupp and Gittings 1999, 102-4). Placing the coffin within the grave (rather than using it simply as a container for carrying the corpse to its place of burial; *ibid*) must indicate a level of conspicuous display and by extension wealth, a supposition which might be borne out by the presence of only two coffins among 106 burials at Warrington Friary (Heawood *et al* 2002), and the small numbers from monastic cemeteries, such as at the Greyfriars in Norwich (Gilchrist and Sloane 2005, 244).

However, a direct association of coffins with wealth may be too simplistic. Large numbers of coffin nails from the Blackfriars in Carlisle might suggest that a proportion of both intra- and extramural burials had once included coffins (McCarthy 1990, 77), as was also clearly the case at the Guildford Blackfriars (Surrey; Poulton and Woods 1984). The use of coffins by a wider social spectrum might have been influenced by changing social and cultural conditions, with many towns apparently insisting on coffined burial during the Black Death, in the mid-fourteenth century (Jupp and Gittings 1999, 104). Some attempt to conform to such an ideal might be seen at the Augustinian Friary in Hull, where coffins were at their most common in the plague years of the mid-fourteenth century, when corpses, plague-ridden or otherwise, may have been considered particularly unclean, and in need of containment.

From the late fourteenth century, however, shrouded burials, often tightly packed within the increasingly limited space of Hull's friary church, seem to have been the norm (Evans 2000; Gilchrist and Sloane 2005). Arguably, there was no such chronological trend among the burials at Brunel Court, nor could any demographic influence be discerned. Moreover, there is a possibility that some of the planks encountered might actually represent grave linings or the remains of biers, rather than coffins *per se*, and thus the bodies would not have been fully enclosed. Although rare, such structures have been noted in association with lay burials in the presbytery of the Carmelite friary at Perth, and in the south transept of the Benedictine priory church of St Mary Sandwell, Staffordshire (Gilchrist and Sloane 2005, 145). Perhaps the clearest indication of wealth is provided by the possibility that child *209* within grave 22 had been laid within a wooden coffin (*Ch 2, p 21*), probably inside some sort of wall tomb (Pl 22). Such treatment, at a young age, implies inherited, rather than acquired, status.

Plate 22: The base of the tomb recess for grave 22

Although friars may, in the main, have been buried in the choir, where they had worshipped (Daniell 1997), they may not necessarily have all been segregated from the lay population, as extensive excavations of the Ipswich Blackfriars have shown (Mays 1991a). It cannot be determined, therefore, whether friars and laity were buried together at Brunel Court. It might perhaps be expected that the poor friars and the wealthy lay people would have had different diets, although religious doctrine dictated that meat should not be consumed on Fridays, during Lent, and on the eves of feast days, but the truly observant might also avoid flesh on Wednesdays and Saturdays (Hammond 1995, 18). The association of meat with carnal desires, perhaps even more of an issue for the urban friars than it was for their secluded brethren in enclosed, rural monastic establishments, meant that the monastic diet, when maintained in accordance with the Benedictine Rules, only allowed meat for invalids (Tobin 1995). Isotope analysis of several of the skeletons from Brunel Court suggest that marine and freshwater foods had played a part in what was otherwise a predominantly terrestrial diet (*Ch 4; p 53*). Whilst the consumption of fish and other seafood, rather than flesh, may be evidence of piety, it is not necessarily an indication of a religious life. Indeed, the availability of resources, with the tidal reaches of the Ribble nearby and the sea only a few miles distant, must have had some influence.

Skeleton *235* (grave 30; *Ch 2, pp 21-2*), buried outside the building, had been laid to rest with his hands placed on his chest. This posture is unique among the Brunel Court skeletons, and is generally less common at other monastic sites, where the hands, as with most of the Brunel Court burials, tended to be placed across the midriff (Pl 20), or below (Gilchrist and Sloane 2005, 156). It is possible that the position of his hands may represent an attitude of prayer (as displayed on many medieval tomb-top effigies) and, from the location and demography of similarly posed burials, particularly at the Augustinian friaries at Leicester and Hull, he may well have been a member of the religious community (*ibid*). This raises interesting questions about his relationship with skeleton *260* in neighbouring grave 28 (*Ch 2, pp 21-2*). Their proximity and their shared genetically influenced non-metric cranial traits (*Ch 3, pp 31-2*) suggest that they could have been family members, but their origins, whether one or both were friars, and the exact nature of their relationship, can only be a matter of speculation.

It is difficult to be certain just how representative the assemblage is in terms of the demographic and mortality profiles of the friary's religious and lay communities. None of the adults was particularly young, or especially elderly, with most appearing to have died between the ages of 35 and 45 years. It is, however, widely recognised that current osteological age-estimation techniques have a tendency to under-age the old and over-age the young (Cox 2000). In addition, infants are often under-represented, to an unpredictable degree, in burial assemblages, since their bones are especially prone to taphonomic damage and destruction (Scheuer and Black 2000), and it is apparent that these processes have been particularly severe at Brunel Court. However, these caveats aside, the demographic profile would seem to be broadly in keeping with those noted for assemblages from other contemporary friaries, namely a mixed population, with fewer adult women and children than adult men, and few or no infants and neonates (see, for example, Gilchrist and Sloane 2005; Mays 1991a, 11; *Ch 3, p 29*).

This demographic distribution may have been affected by changing attitudes over time, for the more diverse demographic profile of those buried in the later, more westerly, rows within the building seems to contrast with the predominance of males to the east. This is typified by grave 2, where two women and a child were interred (*Ch 2, p 19*). An increase in female burials throughout the medieval period, and particularly in the fourteenth and fifteenth centuries, is a trend seen at other monastic sites. The period saw a 50% increase in such burials at the Augustinian Priory of St Mary, Merton (Surrey), where these burials had a marked concentration within the north transept (Gilchrist and Sloane 2005, 205). The Hospitaller preceptory of St John, Clerkenwell, London, also showed a distinct increase in female burials from the late fifteenth century onwards (*op cit*, 66). This apparent trend towards what Gilchrist and Sloane refer to as 'the social permeability of monastic cemeteries', allowing for greater inclusion of women and children, may have been a result of the urban location of the house (*op cit*, 65).

Comparison with skeletons from other sites may provide further clues to the social status of many of those buried at Brunel Court. For example, and preservation notwithstanding, osteoarthritis was not that common, and was mostly restricted to the older individuals. This might suggest age-, rather than accelerated occupation-related, degeneration. Conversely, osteoarthritis was frequent among the skeletons buried to the south of the church of the Austin Friars, Leicester (Stirland 1981). Those affected were predominantly young adults, a finding which, combined with evidence for Schmorl's nodes and traumatic lesions in the neck and lower back, led Stirland to conclude that those individuals were 'strong hard-working males, engaged in continued hard manual labour...' (*op cit*, 169). In contrast, skeletons excavated from within the Austin Friary church were more gracile. These observations suggest that there was a marked social divide in the use of the two areas excavated at that site.

In a similar vein, at the Carmarthen Greyfriars, skeletons recovered from the cloister alley and chapter house showed evidence of poorer dental hygiene, a higher rate of osteoarthritis, and 'strong' muscle development, when compared with skeletons from the church (James 1997, 176). The latter group was interpreted as the 'well-to-do' and the former as the poorer friars (*ibid*). Within such a context, it is interesting to note that skeleton *235*, despite only living into his early twenties, had suffered a range of dental and vertebral arthritic conditions similar to the much older individuals buried within the building (*Ch 3, p 33, pp 38-9*). He was also the only skeleton from the site to display evidence of both childhood iron deficiency and developmental physiological stress, although such conditions appeared individually common at the site.

The rates of caries and ante-mortem tooth loss at Brunel Court are high when compared with other sites, although, unlike at the Greyfriars, Carmarthen (James 1997), it was not possible to undertake any meaningful comparison between intra- and extramural burials. Whilst these traits might highlight poor oral hygiene to a certain degree, they could also suggest that the diet was somewhat more cariogenic (cavity-causing), with a greater component of expensive sugary foodstuffs. Certainly, the carbon and nitrogen isotopes would imply that these people had a relatively mixed diet from a range of sources (*Ch 3, p 42*). Further, individuals with caries tended to be among the oldest in the group, and to have lost teeth ante-mortem, suggesting that most

dental disease related to longer-term degradation rather than poor hygiene *per se*.

The small size of the assemblage means that a degree of caution needs to be exercised when interpreting other conditions observed on several skeletons, particularly in terms of the socio-economic status of the group. None of the Brunel Court skeletons showed any evidence for DISH (diffuse idiopathic skeletal hyperostosis), a disease common among high-status monastic groups, and more specifically well-nourished males with a tendency to develop late-onset type two diabetes (Rogers and Waldron 1995). Rather, conditions such as cribra orbitalia and periostitis were observed, all of which indicate that the individuals experienced periods of poor health that were sufficiently severe to affect their bones, and were active at the time of their death (*Ch 3, pp 36-7*).

Dental enamel hypoplasia, an indicator of childhood health, was relatively infrequent, and this might imply that the individuals enjoyed low levels of childhood health stress. However, the opposite might be inferred if the presence of these defects is considered to reflect recovery from a stress episode during childhood (Lewis and Roberts 1997). Given the high frequency of cribra orbitalia and periostitis, it might be argued that the lack of enamel hypoplasia could mean continued health stress, from which the individuals did not recover during their childhood. In addition, there was evidence of mechanical stress (*ie*, injury, and wear and tear) to the spines of many of the skeletons.

It is interesting that at least one individual buried within the building (possible male skeleton *203*, grave 6; *Ch 2, p 20*; Pl 23) had cortical defects (*Ch 3, p 40*). Although there is limited clinical evidence to

Plate 23: Skeleton **203**, *in grave 6*

substantiate an association between these defects and specific activities (Jurmain 1999), it has been linked in the palaeopathological literature to powerful arm movements (*eg* Knüsel 2000), and high frequencies have been observed on the skeletons of martial and specialist (but not necessarily high-status) groups, for example battle victims from Towton and men from the Mary Rose (*ibid*; Stirland 2000). The high prevalence of cortical defects seen on elite burials from Pontecagano, Italy, was thought to relate to these individuals being members of a class which regularly engaged in aristocratic sports and martial exercise (Robb *et al* 2001). It might be argued, therefore, that their presence on an individual whose family had sufficient wealth to secure a burial place within the friary buildings suggests a member of the knightly class. Interesting though these associations may be, it is important to remember that cortical defects may be seen among 'non-professional' groups as well, and therefore are not very useful when employed at an individual level.

Several other observations can be made about the health and lives of the group based on the palaeopathology. Perhaps most notable of them all is the evidence for neoplastic disease in older child *189* (*Ch 3, p 40*; Pl 13). Despite the fact that this diagnosis, whether of an aneurysmal bone cyst or Langerhans' cell histiocytosis (*Ch 3, pp 40-1*), remains unconfirmed, impaired vision, eyeball deviation, headaches, conjunctivitis, and a bulging eye are among the clinical features that one might expect from such a defect, regardless of the cause (Resnick 1995d). Whether the non-specific bone inflammation identified on the skeleton's forearm was related to this condition or not, it nonetheless contributes further to the overall impression of an individual who had suffered long-standing poor health during their life. Other than benign osteomas (smooth ivory roundels of bone that tend to affect the flat bones of the skull), neoplasms such as these are rarely diagnosed in archaeological populations. Indeed, Roberts and Cox (2003, 280) cite only 19 examples (excluding benign tumours) in their review of over 3000 skeletons from various medieval sites in Britain.

Post-Dissolution Activity

There was only limited archaeological evidence for the nature of post-medieval activity on the site, and an absence of sixteenth- and earlier seventeenth-century pottery correlates with what might be expected of an abrupt cessation associated with the dissolution of the house in 1539 (*Ch 1, p 10*). Although it has been argued that the dearth of early post-medieval pottery from sites in the North West reflects its limited use among most social strata (Lewis 2002), documentary evidence suggests that there is every reason to attribute its absence from Brunel Court to abandonment and demolition, and to the site's position away from the core of the town. Just as significant, perhaps, is the possibility that any post-Dissolution domestic activity was focused on the building that would become the residence of Oliver Breres, well to the south of Brunel Court (*Ch 1, p 10*).

At several friary sites, including those at Warrington (Heawood *et al* 2002) and Perth (Gilchrist and Sloane 2005), there is good evidence for the continuation of burial within the former friary church. None of the burials from Brunel Court could be demonstrated to belong to the post-Dissolution period, however.

The palaeoenvironmental evidence would suggest that, following abandonment and demolition, the area of Brunel Court (and, quite possibly, other parts of the precinct) was turned over to agriculture, effectively returning it to its pre-friary use. Given the concentrations of dung beetles in ditch *106* (*Ch 2, pp 24-5*), it might be imagined that some parts of the complex were used as animal folds, much as was the case in the ruins of Dolforwyn Castle, Powys (L Butler *pers comm*), until the point that they were completely robbed out and overgrown. The hiatus in concentrated activity is reflected both in the historical mapping (Carpenter and Wills 1715; Lang and Porter 1774), and in the pottery, with the documented reoccupation and intensive development of the site matched by the increasing appearance of later eighteenth- and nineteenth-century vessels (*Ch 4, pp 43-4*).

Conclusion

The combined weight of evidence: archaeological; historical; anecdotal; and cartographic, indicates that the remains found at, and around, Brunel Court, relate to Preston's Franciscan friary. The findings are highly significant, particularly within the context of the North West, since only two other Franciscan friaries, at Chester and Carlisle, are known from the region, and neither has been extensively excavated (*cf* O'Sullivan 2013b). As such, the findings substantially augment a very limited corpus of mendicant institutions investigated that otherwise comprises in any substantive form only Warrington's Austin Friary (Heawood *et al* 2002), and the Dominican friaries of Chester (Ward 1990) and Carlisle (McCarthy 1990).

Although the remains of Preston Friary were truncated, incomplete, limited in their scope, and poorly preserved, analysis has shown that they are likely to have been those of a chapel, perhaps an original component of, or a very early addition to, the north side of the friary church. Most, if not all, of the men, women, and children buried within were likely to have been members of patronal families, people of substance and status, who were buried close together, and sometimes in the same grave. This latter practice may have been aided by timber-lined graves or by the use of coffins, and it is possible that these same families funded the installation of an ornate tiled mosaic floor and decorative stained glass windows. Many suffered dietary deficiency and physiological stress during childhood, as well as various infections as adults, but equally, many had survived into, and probably beyond, middle age. In contrast, the skeleton of what may have been a young friar, buried just outside the building (*Ch 2, p 21*), showed just as many pathological lesions, but these had been acquired in a very much shorter lifespan.

The outline of the wider friary precinct can be interpolated from historical maps (Fig 37) and may have encompassed an area of *c* 6 ha, which in turn can be equated with the, very different, modern townscape (Fig 38). It seems probable that the majority of that land was used for horticulture and other means of supplementing the diet of the friars, whilst the friary buildings occupied the north-eastern quadrant. Whilst the configuration of those buildings can only be a matter for speculation, it is probable that the church lay close to Marsh Lane, and that the cloister was to the south. The building that became the Breres' residence, and then the House of Correction, may have originally been the guesthouse, or possibly the infirmary, placed to the south of the main claustral range, perhaps associated with a second, smaller cloister, although without direct evidence this cannot be confirmed.

Thus these excavations, especially the detailed analysis and dating of the burials, have together made an important contribution to an understanding of Preston's medieval past. They have served both to confirm the site of the friary, which had been totally lost, and illustrate the appearance, lives, and health, not only of the brethren, but also of significant lay people. As such, they have contributed to the relatively understudied archaeology of mendicant houses, and particularly those in provincial towns.

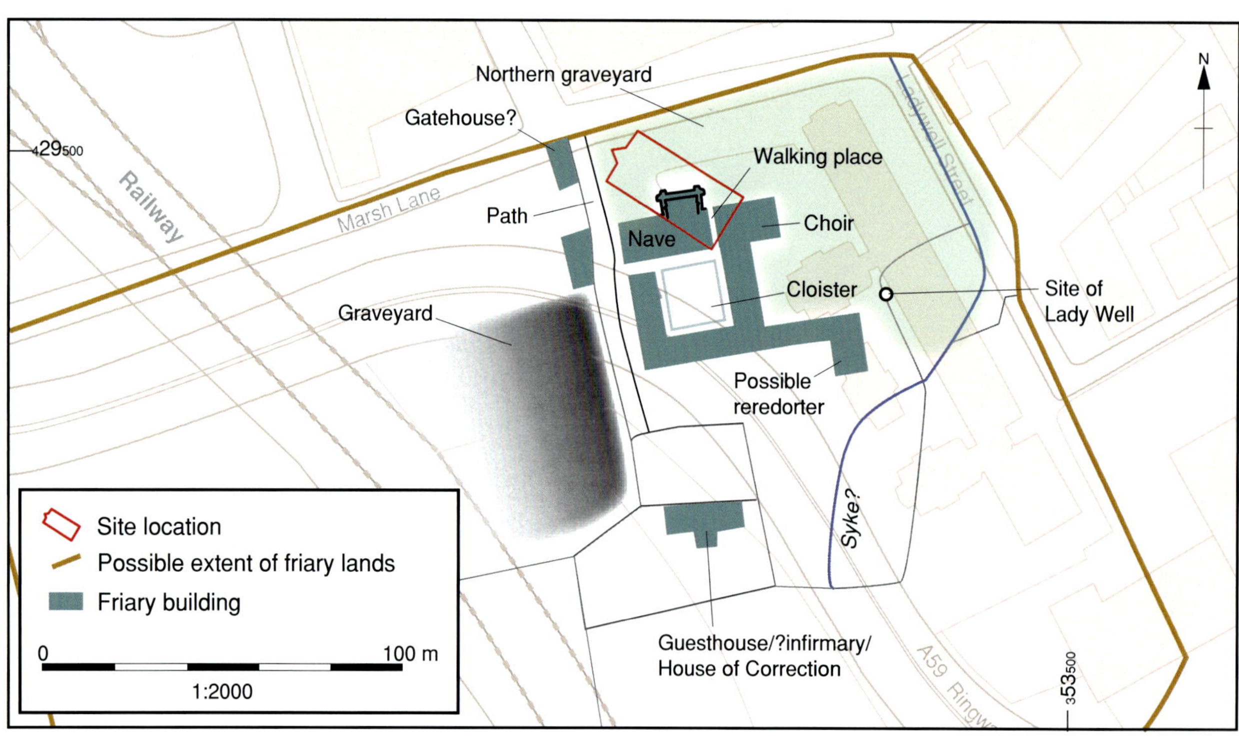

Figure 38: Conjectural layout of the friary precinct overlain onto modern Ordnance Survey mapping

BIBLIOGRAPHY

Cartographic Sources

Baines, E, 1824 *Preston*, LA DDX 177/31/5

British Geological Survey (BGS), 1979 *British regional geology: Northern England*, 4th edn, London

British Geological Survey (BGS), 2008 *DiGMapGB-625 (digital geological maps of Great Britain* [Online] Available at: https://www.bgs.ac.uk/products/digitalmaps/digmapgb.html (Accessed 11 January 2017)

Buck, S, and Buck, N, *c* 1728 *The south prospect of Preston in the County Palatine of Lancaster*

Carpenter, Lt-Gen, and Wills, Maj-Gen, 1715 *An exact plan of ye town of Preston with the barricades and canon of the rebells (sic) and disposition of the King's forces*, 1715, LA DDPR 141/1

Kuerden, R, *c* 1680 *Plan of Preston*, LA DDX/194/9

Lang, G, and Porter, R, 1774 *Survey of Preston*, LA DDK/1549/6a

Lawes Agricultural Trust (Soil Survey of England and Wales), 1983 *Soils of Northern England*, Sheet 1, Southampton

Myers, J J, 1836 *Map of the town of Preston*, LA SRL/MC

Ordnance Survey, 1849 First Edition 6″ to 1 mile, Sheet 61

Ordnance Survey, 1893 First Edition 25″ to 1 mile, Sheet LXI.10

Shakeshaft, W, 1809 *Plan of the Township of Preston*, LA DX 2044/147

Secondary Sources

Anderson, S, 2010 Human skeletal remains, in Atkins and Popescu 2010, 242–9

Anderson, T, and Andrews, J, 2001 The human remains, in M Hicks and A Hicks, *St Gregory's Priory, Northgate, Canterbury: excavations 1988-1991*, Archaeol Canterbury, n ser, **2**, Canterbury, 338-70

Angel, J L, 1964 The reaction area of the femoral neck, *Clinical Orthopaedics*, **32**, 130-42

Archibald, M M, 1992 Dating Cuerdale: the evidence of the coins, in J Graham-Campbell (ed), *Viking treasure from the North-West: the Cuerdale hoard in its context*, Nat Mus Gall Merseyside, Occ Pap, **5**, Liverpool, 15-20

Armstrong, A M, Mawer, A, Stenton, F M, and Dickens, B, 1952 *The place-names of Cumberland, Part 3*, Eng Place-name Soc, **22**, Cambridge

Armstrong, A, and Tomlinson, D, 1987 *Excavations at the Dominican Priory, Beverley, 1960-1983*, Hull

Aston, M, 2002 *Interpreting the landscape: landscape archaeology and local history*, London

Atkins, R, and Popescu, E, 2010 Excavations at the Hospital of St Mary Magdalen, Partney, Lincolnshire, 2003, *Medieval Archaeol*, **54**, 204-70

Aufderheide, A C, and Rodriguez-Martin, C, 1998 *The Cambridge encyclopaedia of human palaeopathology*, Cambridge

Bailey, R N, 2010 *The British Academy corpus of Anglo-Saxon stone sculpture*, **9**, *Cheshire and Lancashire*, Oxford

Baines, E, 1870 *The history of the county palataine and duchy of Lancaster: a new improved and revised edition*, J Harland (ed), London

Bantock, T, and Botting, J, 2012 *British Heteroptera checklist* [Online] Available at: http://www.britishbugs.org.uk/systematic_het.html (Accessed 12 January 2017)

Barker, D, 2008 Post-medieval pottery, *Medieval Pottery Research Group and English Heritage continued professional training for ceramic archaeologists: course notes*, unpubl doc

Barlow, F, 1999 *The feudal kingdom of England 1042-1216*, 5th edn, Harlow

Bass, W M, 1987 *Human osteology: a laboratory and field manual*, 2nd edn, Spec Publ, **2**, Missouri Archaeol Soc, Columbia

Batey, C E, 1995 Aspects of rural settlement in northern Britain, in D Hooke and S Burnell (eds), *Landscape and settlement in Britain AD 400-1066*, Exeter, 69-94

Bayley, J, 1975 *Chelmsford Dominican priory: human bone report*, Engl Heritage Ancient Monuments Lab Rep, **1890**, unpubl rep

Bayliss, A, and Marshall, P, forthcoming *Guidelines on the use of radiocarbon dating and chronological modelling in archaeology*

Beresford, M, 1967 *New towns of the Middle Ages: town plantation in England, Wales and Gascony*, Cambridge

Berry, A C, and Berry, A J, 1967 Epigenetic variation in the human cranium, *J Anat*, **101**, 361-79

Boocock, P, Roberts, C, and Manchester, K, 1995 Maxillary sinusitis in medieval Chichester, England, *Amer J Phys Anthropol*, **98**, 483-96

Bowler, D P, Cox, A, and Smith, C (eds), 1995 Four excavations in Perth 1979-1984, *Proc Soc Antiq Scot*, **125**, 919-99

Boyd, W E, 1989 Perth: the coffins and other wood samples, in J A Stones, *Three Scottish Carmelite friaries: excavations at Aberdeen, Linlithgow, and Perth 1980-1986*, Soc Antiq Scot Monog Ser, **6**, Edinburgh, 117-18

Boyle A, 1998 *The human skeletal assemblage from Eynsham Abbey*, Oxford Archaeol, unpubl rep

Boyle, A, and Rowlandson, I, 2009 A Midlands Purple and Cistercian ware kiln at Church Lane, Ticknall, South Derbyshire, *Medieval Ceram*, **30**, 49-60

Boylston, A, and Weston, D, 2001 *The human remains from Warrington Friary*, Univ Bradford, unpubl rep

Boylston, A, and Weston, D, 2002 The human bone, in Heawood *et al* 2002, 173-7

Brickell, C (ed), 1992 *The Royal Horticultural Society encyclopedia of gardening*, London

Brickley, M, 2000 The diagnosis of metabolic disease in archaeological bone, in M Cox and S Mays (eds), *Human osteology in archaeology and forensic science*, London, 183-98

Brickley, M, 2004 Determination of sex from archaeological skeletal material and assessment of parturition, in Brickley and McKinley 2004, 23-5

Brickley, M, Berry, H, and Western, G, 2006 The people: physical anthropology, in M Brickley, S Buteux, J Adams, and R Cherrington, *St Martin's uncovered: investigations in the churchyard of St Martin's-in-the-Bull Ring, Birmingham, 2001*, Oxford, 91-151

Brickley, M, and McKinley, J, 2004 *Guidelines to the standards for recording human remains*, IfA Pap, **7**, Oxford

Brooks, S T, and Suchey, J M, 1990 Skeletal age determination based on the *os pubis*: a comparison of the Acsádi-Nemeskéri and Suchey-Brooks methods, *Human Evolution*, **5**, 227-38

Brothwell, D R, 1981 *Digging up bones*, Oxford

Brown, F A, and Howard-Davis, C, 2008 *Monastery to museum: excavations at Norton Priory 1970-87*, Lancaster Imprints, **16**, Lancaster

Brown, R, and Hardy, A, 2011 *Trade and prosperity, war and poverty: an archaeological and historical investigation into Southampton's French Quarter*, Oxford Archaeol Monog Ser, **15**, Oxford

Bruzelius, C, 2012 The architecture of the mendicant orders in the Middle Ages: an overview of recent literature, *Antiquité/Moyen Âge*, **2/2012**, 365-85, *Perspective: actualité en histoire de l'art* [Online] Available at: https://perspective.revues.org/195 (Accessed 11 January 2017)

Buchmann, S, and Repplier, B, 2005 *Letters from the hive: an intimate history of bees, honey, and humankind*, New York

Buckberry, J, and Chamberlain, A, 2002 Age estimation from the auricular surface of the ilium: a revised method, *Amer J Phys Anthropol*, **119**, 231-9

Bufkin, W J, 1971 The avulsive cortical irregularity, *Amer J Roentgenol*, **112**(3), 487-92

Buikstra, J E, and Ubelaker, D H, 1994 *Standards for data collection from human skeletal remains*, Arkansas

Butler, L, 1984 The houses of the mendicant orders in Britain: recent archaeological work, in P V Addyman and V E Black (eds), *Archaeological papers from York presented to M W Barley*, York, 123-36

Cappers, R T J, Bekker, R M, and Jans, J E A, 2006 *Digital seed atlas of the Netherlands*, Groningen

Carrott, J, and Kenward, H, 2001 Species associations among insect remains from urban archaeological deposits and their significance in reconstructing the past human environment, *J Archaeol Sci*, **28**, 887-905

Carver, M, 1987 *Underneath English towns: interpreting urban archaeology*, London

Cassady, R F, 1986 *The Norman achievement*, London

Charles-Edwards, T M, 2013 *Wales and the Britons, 350-1064*, Oxford

Chartered Institute for Archaeologists (CIfA), 2014 *Standards and guidance for the collection, documentation, conservation and research of archaeological materials*, Reading

Childs, W R, 2002 Timber for cloth: changing commodities in Anglo-Baltic trade in the fourteenth century, in L Berggren, N Hybel, and A Landen (eds), *Cogs, cargoes and commerce: maritime bulk trade in Northern Europe 1150-1400*, Toronto, 181-211

Clemesha, H W, 1912 *A history of Preston in Amounderness*, Manchester

Colgrave, B (ed and trans), 1927 *The life of Bishop Wilfrid by Eddius Stephanus*, Cambridge

Colgrave, B, and Mynors, R A B (eds), 1969 *Bede's ecclesiastical history of the English people*, Oxford

Conzen, M R G, 1968 The use of town plans in the study of urban history, in H J Dyos (ed), *The study of urban history*, London, 113-30

Cox, M, 1996 *Life and death in Spitalfields 1700-1850*, York

Cox, M, 2000 Ageing adults from the skeleton, in M Cox and S Mays (eds), *Human osteology in archaeology and forensic science*, London, 61-81

Cunliffe Shaw, R, 1956 *The royal forest of Lancashire*, Preston

Daniell, C, 1997 *Death and burial in medieval England 1066-1550*, London

Daniels, R, 1986 The excavations of the church of the Franciscans, Hartlepool, *Archaeol J*, **143**, 260-304

Davis, B N K, 1983 *Insects on nettles*, Naturalists' Handbooks, **1**, Slough

Dawes, J D, and Magilton, J R, 1980 *The cemetery of St Helen-on-the-Walls, Aldwark*, Archaeology of York: the medieval cemeteries, **12** (1), York

Dickinson, J C, 1961 *Monastic life in medieval England*, London

Discovery Programme, 2014a *Askeaton Franciscan Friary* [Online] Available at: http://www.monastic.ie/tour/askeaton-franciscan-friary/ (Accessed 11 January 2017)

Discovery Programme, 2014b *Claregalway Franciscan Friary* [Online] Available at: http://www.monastic.ie/history/claregalway-franciscan-friary/ (Accessed 11 January 2017)

Duff, A G (ed), 2012a *Checklist of beetles of the British Isles*, 2nd edn, Iver

Duff, A G, 2012b *Beetles of Britain and Ireland, Volume 1: Sphaeriusidae to Silphidae*, West Runton, Norfolk

Duray, S M, 1996 Dental indicators of stress and reduced age at death in prehistoric Native Americans, *Amer J Phys Anthropol*, **99**, 275-86

Eames, E S, 1980 *Catalogue of medieval lead-glazed earthenware tiles in the Department of Medieval and Later Antiquities, British Museum*, London

Eastbridge Hospital, 2017 *Greyfriars Chapel* [Online] Available at: http://www.eastbridgehospital.org.uk/explore/greyfriars-chapel/ (Accessed 11 January 2017)

Edmonds, F, 2009 History and names, in J Graham-Campbell and R Philpott (eds), *The Huxley Viking hoard: Scandinavian settlement in the North West*, Liverpool, 3-12

Ekwall, E, 1922 *The place-names of Lancashire*, Manchester

English Heritage, 1991 *Management of archaeological projects*, 2nd edn, London

English Heritage, 1998 *Dendrochronology: guidelines on producing and interpreting dendrochronological dates*, London

English Heritage, 2003 *Implementation plan for Exploring Our Past 1998, external version*, London

English Heritage, 2005 *Discovering the past, shaping the future* [Online] Available at: http://webarchive.nationalarchives.gov.uk/20060213205517/http://english-heritage.org.uk/upload/pdf/Research_Strategy.pdf (Accessed: 11 January 2017)

Evans, D, 2000 Buried with the friars, *Brit Archaeol*, **53**, 18-23

Eyre, S R, 1955 The curving plough-strip and its historical implications, *Agricult Hist Rev*, **3**, 80-94

Farrer, W, and Brownbill, J (eds), 1908 *The Victoria history of the County of Lancaster*, **2**, London

Farrer, W, and Brownbill, J (eds), 1912 *The Victoria history of the County of Lancaster*, **7**, London

Faull, M L, and Stinson, M (eds), *Yorkshire*, in J Morris (ed), Domesday Book, **30**, Chichester

Fenning, H, nd *The Black Abbey, 1225-1996*, Kilkenny

Ferris, I M, 2001 Excavations at Greyfriars, Gloucester, in 1967 and 1974-5, *Trans Bristol Gloucestershire Archaeol Soc*, **119**, 95-146

Finnegan, M, 1978 Non-metric variation of the infracranial skeleton, *J Anat*, **125**, 23-37

Fishwick, H, 1900 *The history of the parish of Preston in Amounderness in the County of Lancaster*, Rochdale

Foreman, M, 1996 *Further excavations at the Dominican Friary, Beverley, 1986-1989*, Sheffield Excav Rep, **4**, Sheffield

Forgens, J L, and Singman, J L, 1999 *Daily life in medieval Europe*, Westport, Connecticut, and London

Friar, S, 1996 *The companion to the English parish church*, Stroud

Galloway, A, 1999 *Broken bones: anthropological analysis of blunt force trauma*, Springfield, Illinois

Gardiner, M, Russell, M, and Gregory, D, 1996 Excavations at Lewes Friary 1985-6 and 1988-9, *Sussex Archaeol Collect*, **134**, 71-123

Gibbons, P, Howard-Davis, C, and Olivier, A, in prep *Excavations at Walton-le-Dale, Lancashire*

Gibson, M, 2002 *Extramasticatory wear on Royal Navy personnel from Greenwich Naval Infirmary: a comparative study*, unpubl MSc diss, Univ Bournemouth

Gilbanks, G E, and Oldfield, F H, 1900 *Some records of a Cistercian abbey: Holm Cultram, Cumberland*, London

Gilchrist, R, 1995 *Contemplation and action: the other monasticism*, London

Gilchrist, R, and Sloane, B, 2005 *Requiem: the medieval monastic cemetery in Britain, London*, Mus London Archaeol Serv, London

Graham-Campbell, J, 1992 The Cuerdale hoard: comparisons and context, in J Graham-Campbell (ed), *Viking treasure from the North-West: the Cuerdale hoard in its context*, Nat Mus Gall Merseyside, Occ Pap, **5**, Liverpool, 107-15

Graham-Campbell, J, 2011 *The Cuerdale hoard and related Viking-age silver and gold from Britain and Ireland in the British Museum*, London

Greene, J P, 1989 *Norton Priory: the archaeology of a medieval religious house*, Cambridge

Greene, J P, 1992 *Medieval monasteries*, Leicester

Greenwood, M, and Bolton, C, 1955 *Bowland Forest and the Hodder Valley*, privately publ

Grieve, M, 1971 *A modern herbal*, New York

Hall, A R, and Kenward, H K, 1990 *Environmental evidence from the Colonia: General Accident and Rougier Street*, Archaeology of York, **14** (6), London

Hammond, P W, 1995 *Food and feast in medieval England*, Stroud

Hansen, M, 1987 The Hydrophiloidea (Coleoptera) of Fennoscandia and Denmark, *Fauna Entomologica Scandinavica*, **18**, Leiden

Harbottle, B, 1968 Excavations at the Carmelite friary, Newcastle upon Tyne, 1965 and 1967, *Archaeol Aeliana*, 4 ser, **46**, 163-224

Harbottle, B, 1976 Black Friars, Newcastle upon Tyne, in Anon 1976, Report of the summer meeting of the Royal Archaeological Institute at Newcastle upon Tyne in 1976, *Archaeol J*, **133**, 242-44

Harde, K W, 1984 *A field guide in colour to beetles, edited and with additional introductory material by P M Hammond*, London

Hardwick, C, 1857 *History of the borough of Preston and its environs in the County of Lancaster*, Preston

Harkness, D D, 1983 The extent of the natural ^{14}C deficiency in the coastal environment of the United Kingdom, *PACT*, **8**, 351–64

Harrison, S, 2008 Medieval carved stonework from the priory buildings, in Brown and Howard-Davis 2008, 282-315

Harrison, S, Wood, J, and Newman, R M, 1998 *Furness Abbey*, London

Hassall, T G, Halpin, C E, and Mellor, M, 1989 Excavations in St Ebbe's Oxford, 1967-1976: part 1: late Saxon and medieval domestic occupation and tenements, and the medieval Greyfriars, *Oxoniensia*, **54**, 71-278

Hather, J G, 2000 *The identification of the Northern European woods*, London

Hawkey, D E, and Merbs, C F, 1995 Activity-induced musculoskeletal stress markers (MSM) and subsistence strategy changes among ancient Hudson Bay Eskimos, *Int J Osteoarchaeol*, **5**(4), 324-38

Heawood, R, Howard-Davis, C L E, Boylston, A, and Weston, D, 2002 Excavations at Warrington Friary, 2000, *J Chester Archaeol Soc*, **77**, 131-85

Helms, C A, 1989 *Fundaments of skeletal radiology*, Philadelphia

Henderson, J D, 1984 *The human skeletal remains from Guildford Friary, Surrey*, Engl Heritage Ancient Monuments Lab Rep, **3234**, unpubl rep

Hewitson, A, 1883 *History of Preston*, Preston

Higham, N J, 1992 Northumbria, Mercia and the Irish Sea Norse, 893-926, in J Graham-Campbell (ed), *Viking Treasure from the North-West: the Cuerdale hoard in its context*, Nat Mus Gall Merseyside Occ Pap, **5**, Liverpool, 21-30

Higham, N J, 2004 *A frontier landscape: the North-West in the Middle Ages*, Macclesfield

Hillson, S, 1986 *Teeth*, Cambridge

Hillson, S, 1996 *Dental anthropology*, Cambridge

Hinton, D, 1987 Archaeology and the Middle Ages -recommendations by the Society for Medieval Archaeology to the Historic Buildings and Monuments Commission for England, *Medieval Archaeol*, **31**, 1-12

Hinton, H E, 1941 The Ptinidae of economic importance, *Bull Entomol Res*, **31**, 331-81

Hinton, H E, 1945 *A monograph of the beetles associated with stored products*, London

Historic England, 2015a *Management of research projects in the historic environment: the MoRPHE project managers' guide*, London

Historic England, 2015b *Doncaster Greyfriars* [Online] Available at: http://www.pastscape.org.uk/hob. aspx?hob_id=55888 (Accessed 11 January 2017)

Hunt, D, 2009 *A history of Preston*, 2nd edn, Lancaster

Huntley, J, and Hillam, J, 2000 Environmental evidence, in K Buxton and C Howard-Davis, *Bremetenacum: excavations at Roman Ribchester 1980, 1989-1990*, Lancaster Imprints, **9**, Lancaster, 356-7

James, T, 1997 Excavations at Carmarthen Greyfriars, 1983-1990, *Medieval Archaeol*, **41**, 100-94

Jessop, L, 1986 *Dung beetles and chafers*, Coleoptera: Scarabaeoidea, Handbooks for the identification of British insects, **5**(11), Roy Entomol Soc London, London

Jupp, P C, and Gittings, C, 1999 *Death in England, an illustrated history*, Manchester

Jurmain, R, 1977 Stress and the etiology of osteoarthritis, *Amer J Phys Anthropol*, **46**, 353-66

Jurmain, R D, 1999 *Stories from the skeleton – behavioural reconstruction in human osteology*, Amsterdam

Kahl, K, and Smith, M, 2000 The pattern of spondylosis deformans in prehistoric samples from west-central New Mexico, *Int J Osteoarchaeol*, **10**, 432-46

Katz, N J, Katz, S V, and Kipani, M G, 1965 *Atlas and keys of fruits and seeds occurring in Quaternary deposits of the USSR*, Moscow

Keaveney, E M, and Reimer, P J, 2012 Understanding the variability in freshwater radiocarbon reservoir offsets: a cautionary tale, *J Archaeol Sci*, **39**, 1306-16

Kenward, H, 1997 Synanthropic decomposer insects and the size, remoteness and longevity of archaeological occupation sites: applying concepts from biogeography to past 'islands' of human occupation, in A C Ashworth, P C Buckland, and J T Sadler (eds), Studies in Quaternary entomology: an inordinate fondness for insects, *Quaternary Proc*, **5**, 135-52

Kenward, H, 2009 *Northern regional review of environmental archaeology: invertebrates in archaeology in the north of England*, Engl Heritage Res Dept Rep Ser, **12-2009**, unpubl rep

Kenward, H K, and Hall, A R, 1995 *Biological evidence from 16-22 Coppergate*, Archaeology of York, **14**(7), York

Kenward, H K, Hall, A R, and Jones, A K G, 1986 *Environmental evidence from a Roman well and Anglian pits in the legionary fortress*, Archaeology of York, **14**(5), London

Kenward, H, and Large, F, 1998 Recording the preservational condition of archaeological insect fossils, *Environmental Archaeol*, **2**, 49-60

Kenyon, D, 1991 *The origins of Lancashire*, Manchester

Kerr, N W, Bruce, M F, and Cross, J F, 1988 Caries experience in the permanent dentition of late medieval Scots (1300-1600 AD), *Archives Oral Biol*, **33**(3), 143-8

Kershaw, J, 2014 Viking-Age silver in north-west England: hoards and single finds, in S E Harding, D Griffiths, and E Royles, *In search of Vikings: interdisciplinary approaches to the Scandinavian heritage of north-west England*, London, 149-64

Knowles, D, and Hadcock, R N, 1953 *Mediaeval religious houses: England and Wales*, London

Knowles, D, and St Joseph, J K S, 1952 *Monastic sites from the air*, Cambridge

Knüsel, C J, 2000 Activity-related skeletal change, in V Fiorato, A Boylston, and C Knüsel (eds), *Blood red roses: the archaeology of a mass grave from the Battle of Towton, AD 1461*, Oxford, 103-18

Knüsel, C J, Batt, C M, Cook, G, Montgomery, J, Müldner, G, Ogden, A R, Palmer, C, Stern, B, Todd, J, and Wilson, A S, 2010 The identity of the St Bees Lady, Cumbria: an osteobiographical approach, *Medieval Archaeol*, **54**, 271–311

LCC (Lancashire County Council), and Egerton Lea Consultancy, 2006 *Lancashire historic town survey programme: Preston with Walton-le-Dale and Penwortham historic town assessment report*, Preston

Lancaster University Archaeological Unit (LUAU), 1991a *Preston Friary archaeological evaluation, Phase I*, unpubl rep

Lancaster University Archaeological Unit (LUAU), 1991b *Preston Friary archaeological evaluation, Phase II*, unpubl rep

Lanting, J N, and van der Plicht, J, 1998 Reservoir effects and apparent ^{14}C ages, *J Irish Archaeol*, **9**, 151-65

Lewis, J M, 1999 *The medieval tiles of Wales*, Cardiff

Lewis, J, 2002 Sefton rural fringes, in J Lewis and R Cowell (eds), The archaeology of a changing landscape: the last thousand years in Merseyside, *J Merseyside Archaeol Soc*, **11**, 5-88

Lewis, M E, 2004 Endocranial lesions in non-adult skeletons: understanding their aetiology, *Int J Osteoarchaeol*, **14**, 82-97

Lewis, M, and Roberts, C, 1997 Growing pains: the interpretation of stress indicators, *Int J Osteoarchaeol*, **7**, 581-6

Lilley, J M, Stroud, G, Brothwell, D R, and Williamson, M H, 1994 *The Jewish burial ground at Jewbury*, Archaeology of York: the medieval cemeteries, **12** (3), York

Linsley, E G, 1944 Natural sources, habitats and reservoirs of insects associated with stored food products, *Hilgardia*, **16**(4), 187-222

Litten, J, 1991 *The English way of death: the common funeral since 1450*, London

Little, A G, 1917 *Studies in English Franciscan history*, Manchester

Lott, D A, 2009 *The* Staphylinidae *(rove beetles) of Britain and Ireland, Part 5*: Scaphidiinae, Piestinae, Oxytelinae, Handbooks for the identification of British insects, **12** (5), Shrewsbury

Lovejoy, C O, Meindl, R S, Pryzbeck, T R, and Mensforth, R P, 1985 Chronological metamorphosis of the auricular surface of the ilium: a new method for the determination of adult skeletal age at death, *Amer J Phys Anthropol*, **68**, 15-28

Lovell, N, 1994 Spinal arthritis and physical stress at Bronze Age Harappa, *Amer J Phys Anthropol*, **93**, 149-64

Lovell, N, 1997 Trauma analysis in palaeopathology, *Yearbook Physical Anthropol*, **40**, 139-70

Lukacs, J R, 1989 Dental palaeopathology: methods of reconstructing dietary patterns, in M Y Iscan and K A Kennedy (eds), *Reconstruction of life from the skeleton*, New York, 261-86

McCarthy, M R, 1990 *A Roman, Anglian and medieval site at Blackfriars Street, Carlisle*, Cumberland Westmorland Antiq Archaeol Soc, Res Ser, **4**, Kendal

McCarthy, M R, and Brooks, C M, 1988 *Medieval pottery in Britain AD 900-1600*, Leicester

McCarthy, M R, and Brooks, C M, 1992 The establishment of a medieval pottery sequence in Cumbria, England, in D Gaimster and M Redknap (eds), *Everyday and exotic pottery from Europe, c 650-1900*, Oxford, 21-37

McGrayne, S B, 2011 *The theory that would not die: how Bayes' Rule cracked the Enigma Code, hunted Russian submarines, and emerged triumphant from two centuries of controversy*, New Haven

MacGregor, N, and Langmuir, E, 2000 *Seeing salvation: images of Christ in art*, London

McKinley, J I, 1995 *The human remains from Mottisfont Abbey*, Wessex Archaeol, unpubl rep

McKinley, J I, 2004 Compiling a skeletal inventory: disarticulated and co-mingled remains, in Brickley and McKinley 2004, 14-17

McNeil, R, and Newman, R, 2006 The post-medieval resource assessment, in M Brennand (ed), *The archaeology of North West England; an archaeological research framework for North West England: volume 1, resource assessment*, Archaeol North West, **8**, Manchester, 145-64

Margary, I D, 1957 *Roman roads in Britain*, London

Marshall, P D, and Beavan N, 2012 *Furness Abbey-radiocarbon dating and source proportional diet modelling*, unpubl rep

Marshall, P, Bronk Ramsey, C, Cook, G, and Tyers, I, 2015 *Brunel Court, Preston, Lancashire: radiocarbon dating and chronological modelling*, Hist Engl Res Rep Ser, **18/2015**, unpubl rep

Martin, A R, 1966 *Franciscan architecture in England*, Farnborough

Martini, F, Timmons, M J, and Tallitsch, R B, 2003 *Human anatomy*, London

Mays, S, 1991a *The medieval burials from the Blackfriars Friary, School Street, Ipswich, Suffolk*, Engl Heritage Ancient Monuments Lab Rep, **16/91**, Part 1, unpubl rep

Mays, S, 1991b *The burials from the Whitefriars Friary site, Buttermarket, Ipswich, Suffolk*, Engl Heritage Ancient Monuments Lab Rep, **17/91**, unpubl rep

Mays, S, 1998 The archaeology of human bones, London

Medieval Pottery Research Group (MPRG), 1994 *A research strategy and agenda for post-Roman ceramic studies in Britain* [Online] Available at: http://mprg.wikispaces.com/ (Accessed 10 September 2016)

Meier, E, 2019 *English holly* [Online] Available at: www.wood-database.com/lumber-identification/hardwoods/English-holly (Accessed 1 November 2016)

Meindl, R S, and Lovejoy, C O, 1985 Ectocranial suture closure: a revised method for the determination of skeletal age at death based on the lateral-anterior sutures, *Amer J Phys Anthropol*, **68**, 29-45

Mellor, J E, and Pearce, T, 1981 *The Austin Friars, Leicester*, CBA Res Rep, **35**, London

Mersch, M, 2009 Program, pragmatism and symbolism in mendicant architecture, in A Muller and K Stobner (eds), *Self-representation of medieval religious communities: the British Isles in context*, Berlin, 143-66

Middleton, R, Tooley, M J, and Innes J B, 2013 *The wetlands of South West Lancashire*, North West Wetland Survey, **7**, Lancaster Imprints, **20**, Lancaster

Middleton, R, Wells, C E, and Huckerby, E, 1995 *The wetlands of North Lancashire*, North West Wetland Survey **3**, Lancaster Imprints, **4**, Lancaster

Miller, I, and White, A, forthcoming The post-Roman pottery, in C Howard-Davis, I Miller, N Hair, and R M Newman, *Excavations at Mitchell's Brewery and 39, Church Street, Lancaster, 1988-2000*

Mills, A D, 1991 *A dictionary of English place-names*, Oxford

Millward, R, 1955 *Lancashire: an illustrated essay on the history of the landscape*, London

Moorees, C F A, Fanning, E A, and Hunt, E E, 1963 Age variation of formation stages for ten permanent teeth, *J Dental Res*, **42**, 1490-502

Morris, M G, 1997 *Broad-nosed weevils*: Coleoptera Curculionidae (Entiminae), Handbooks for the identification of British insects, Roy Entomol Soc, **5** (17a), London

Morris, M G, 2002 *True weevils (Part 1)*, Coleoptera Curculionoidae (*Subfamilies* Raymondionyminae *to* Smicronychinae), Handbooks for the identification of British insects, Roy Entomol Soc, **5** (17b), London

Morris, M G, 2008 *True weevils (Part 2)*, (Coleoptera: Curculionoidae, Ceutorhynchinae), Handbooks for the identification of British insects, Roy Entomol Soc/Field Studies Council, **5** (17c), Shrewsbury

Müldner, G, Montgomery, J, Cook, G, Ellam, R, Gledhill, A, and Lowe, C, 2009 Isotopes and individual: diet and mobility among the medieval Bishops of Whithorn, *Antiquity*, **83**, 1119-33

Müldner, G, and Richards, M P, 2007 Diet and diversity at later medieval Fishergate: the isotopic evidence, *Amer J Phys Anthropol*, **133**, 162-74

Newman, C, 2006 The medieval period resource assessment, in M Brennand (ed), *The archaeology of North West England; an archaeological research framework for North West England: volume 1, resource assessment*, Archaeol North West, **8**, Manchester, 115-44

Newman, C, and Newman, R, 2007 The medieval period research agenda, in M Brennand (ed), *Research and archaeology in North West England; an archaeological research framework for North West England: volume 2, research agenda and strategy*, Archaeol North West, **9**, Manchester, 95-114

Newman, R, and McNeil, R, 2007 The post-medieval research agenda, in M Brennand (ed), 2007 *Research and archaeology in North West England; an archaeological research framework for North West England: volume 2, research agenda and strategy*, Archaeol North West, **9**, Manchester, 115-32

Newman, R M, 1996 The Dark Ages, in R Newman (ed), *The archaeology of Lancashire, present state and future priorities*, Lancaster, 93-108

Newman, R M, and Leech, R H, forthcoming *An early Christian monastic site at Dacre, Cumbria*

O'Donnabhain, B, 1991 *The human remains of Tintern Abbey, County Wexford*, Dept Anthropol, Univ Chicago, unpubl rep

Ogden, A, 2008 Advances in the palaeopathology of teeth and jaws, in R Pinhasi and S Mays (eds), *Advances in human palaeopathology*, Chichester, 283-307

Oliger, L, 1910 Mendicant friars, in C G Herbermann (ed), *The Catholic encyclopaedia*, **10**, New York, 183-5

Ortner, D, 2003 *Identification of pathological conditions in human skeletal remains*, 2nd edn, San Diego

O'Sullivan, D, 2013a Burial of the Christian dead in the later Middle Ages, in S Tarlow and L Nilssen-Stutz (eds), *The Oxford handbook of the archaeology of death and burial*, Oxford, 259-80

O'Sullivan, D, 2013b *In the company of the preachers: the archaeology of medieval friaries in England and Wales*, Leicester Archaeol Monog, **23**, Leicester

Owen, O, and Lowe, C, 1999 *Kebister: the four thousand-year-old story of one Shetland township*, Soc Antiq Scot Monog Ser, **14**, Edinburgh

OA North, 2007 *Brunel Court, Marsh Lane/Ladywell Street, Preston, Lancashire, archaeological excavation: project design*, unpubl doc

OA North, 2008 *Brunel Court, Marsh Lane/Ladywell Street, Preston, Lancashire: proposal for post-excavation assessment*, unpubl doc

OA North, 2010 *Brunel Court, Marsh Lane/Ladywell Street, Preston, Lancashire, project design for Execution Stage 1: processing of the fieldwork archive*, unpubl doc

OA North, 2011 *Brunel Court, Marsh Lane/Ladywell Street, Preston, Lancashire, project design for Execution Stage 2: archaeological post-excavation assessment*, unpubl doc

Oyler, C R, 2001 The human remains, in Ferris 2001, 139

Palm, T, 1959 *Die Holz- und Rinden-käfer der Sud- und Mittelschwedischen aubbaume*, Opuscula Entomologica Supplementum, **16**, Lund

Paterson, C, Parsons, A J, Newman, R M, Johnson, N, and Howard-Davis, C, 2014 *Shadows in the sand: excavations of a Viking-age cemetery at Cumwhitton, Cumbria*, Lancaster Imprints, **22**, Lancaster

Pfitzner, M, Thatcher, T, Pettifor, J, Zoakah, A, Lawson, J, Isichei, C, and Fisher, P, 1998 Absence of vitamin deficiency in young Nigerian children, *J Paediatrics*, **133**, 1-4

Phenice, T W, 1969 A newly developed visual method of sexing the *os pubis*, *Amer J Phys Anthropol*, **30**, 297-301

Platt, C, 1979 *The English medieval town*, St Albans

Potts, S, 1996 The brick, in Foreman 1996, 104-10

Poulton, R, and Woods, H, 1984 *Excavations on the site of the Dominican friary at Guildford in 1974 and 1978*, Surrey Archaeol Soc Res Vol, **9**, Guildford

Raw, F, 1951 The ecology of the garden chafer *Phyllopertha horticola* (L), with preliminary observations on control measures, *Bull Entomol Res*, **42**, 605-46

Reimer, P J, Baillie, M G L, Bard, E, Bayliss, A, Beck, J W, Blackwell, P G, Bronk Ramsey, C, Buck, C E, Burr, G S, Edwards, R L, Friedrich, M, Grootes, P M, Guilderson, T P, Hajdas, I, Heaton, T J, Hogg, A G, Hughen, K A, Kaiser, K F, Kromer, B, McCormac, G, Manning, S, Reimer, R W, Remmele, S, Richards, D A, Southon, J R, Talamo, S, Taylor, F W, Turney, C S M, van der Plicht, J, and Weyhenmeyer, C E, 2009 INTCAL09 and MARINE09 radiocarbon age calibration curves, 0–50,000 years cal BP, *Radiocarbon*, **51**, 1111–50

Resnick, D (ed), 1995a *Diagnosis of bone and joint disorders*, 3rd edn, London

Resnick, D, 1995b Tumours and tumour-like diseases, in Resnick 1995a, 3611-4063

Resnick, D, 1995c Lipidoses, histiocytoses, and hyperlipoproteinemias, in Resnick 1995a, 2190-246

Resnick, D, 1995d Diseases of the hematopoietic system, in Resnick 1995a, 2105-321

Resnick, D, and Niwayama, G, 1995 Osteomyelitis, septic arthritis and soft tissue infection: mechanisms and situations, in Resnick 1995a, 2325-418

Robb, J, Bigazzi, R, Lazzarini, L, Scarsini, C, and Sonego, F, 2001 Social 'status' and biological 'status': a comparison of grave goods and skeletal indicators from Pontecagnano, *Amer J Phys Anthropol*, **115**, 213-22

Roberts, C, and Cox, M, 2003 *Health and disease in Britain from prehistory to the present day*, Stroud

Roberts, C, and Manchester, K, 1995 *The archaeology of disease*, Stroud

Robinson, D, 1998 Vale Royal, in D Robinson (ed), *The Cistercian abbeys of Britain: far from the concourse of men*, London, 192-4

Robinson, P, 1913a Francis of Assisi, in C G Herbermann (ed), *The Catholic encyclopaedia*, **6**, New York, 221-30

Robinson, P, 1913b Friars Minor, in C G Herbermann (ed), *The Catholic encyclopaedia*, **6**, New York, 281-302

Robson, R, 2006 *The Franciscans in the Middle Ages*, Woodbridge

Rodwell, W, with Atkins, C, 2011 *St Peter's, Barton-upon-Humber, Lincolnshire: 1, history, archaeology and architecture*, Oxford

Rogers, J, 2000 The palaeopathology of joint disease, in M Cox and S Mays (eds), *Human osteology in archaeology and forensic science*, Cambridge, 163-82

Rogers, J, and Waldron, T, 1995 *A field guide to joint disease in archaeology*, Chichester

Röhrkasten, J, 2012 The convents of the Franciscan province of Anglia and their role in the development of English and Welsh towns in the thirteenth and fourteenth centuries, *Espaces monastiques et espaces urbains de l'Antiquité tardive à la fin du Moyen Âge - Varia*, **124-1**, Melanges de l'Ecole française de Rome-Moyen Âge [Online] Available at: http://mefrm.revues.org/230 (Accessed 11 January 2017)

Salzman, L F, 1923 *Medieval English industries*, Oxford

Salzman, L F, 1952 *Building in England down to 1540*, Oxford

Scheuer, L, and Black, S, 2000 *Developmental juvenile osteology*, Oxford

Schweingruber, F H, 1990 *Microscopic wood anatomy*, 3rd edn, Swiss Federal Inst for Forest, Snow and Landscape Res, Birmensdorf

Sharpe-France, R, 1938 A history of plague in Lancashire, part 1, *Trans Hist Soc Lancashire Cheshire*, **90**, 1-49

Sjøvold, T, 1984 A report on the heritability of some cranial measurements and non-metric traits, in G N van Vark (ed), *Multivariate statistical methods in physical anthropology*, Groningen, 223-46

Skidmore, P, 1991 *Insects of the British cow-dung community*, Field Studies Counc Occ Publ, **21**, Slough

Slowikowski, A, Nenk, B, and Pearce, J, 2001 *Minimum standards for the processing, recording, analysis, and publication of post-Roman ceramics*, London

Smith, D, Whitehouse, N, Bunting, M J, and Chapman, H, 2010 Can we characterize 'openness' in the Holocene palaeoenvironmental record? Modern analogue studies of insect faunas and pollen spectra from Dunham Massey deer park and Epping Forest, England, *Holocene* **20**(2), 215-29

Smith, P, nd *The 1685 survey of Preston* [Online] Available at: https://prestonhistory.com/maps-and-plans/the-1685-survey-of-preston/#_ftn2 (accessed 15 August 2019)

Southwood, T R E, and Leston, D, 1959 *Land and water bugs of the British Isles*, London

Stace, C, 2010 *New flora of the British Isles*, 3rd edn, Cambridge

Steer, C, 2018 The Franciscans and their graves in medieval London, in M Robson and P Zutshi, *The Franciscan Order in the medieval English province and beyond*, Amsterdam, 118-38

Stirland A J, 1981 The human bones, in Mellor and Pearce 1981, 168

Stirland A J, 2000 *Raising the dead: the skeleton crew of King Henry VIII's great ship, the Mary Rose*, Chichester

Stopford, J, 1990 *Recording medieval floor tile*, CBA Practical Handbook, **10**, York

Stopford, J, 2005 *Medieval floor tiles of northern England*, Oxford

Stuart-Macadam, P, 1982 *A correlative study of palaeopathology of the skull*, unpubl PhD thesis, Univ Cambridge

Stuart-Macadam, P, 1991 Anaemia in Roman Britain: Poundbury Camp, in H Bush and M Zvelebil, *Health in past societies: biocultural interpretations of human skeletal remains in archaeological contexts*, BAR Int Ser, **567**, Oxford, 101-13

Stuiver, M, and Kra, R S, 1986 Editorial comment, *Radiocarbon*, **28**(2B), ii

Stuiver, M, and Polach, H A, 1977 Reporting of 14C data, *Radiocarbon*, **19**, 355–63

Stuiver, M, and Reimer, P J, 1993 Extended 14C data base and revised CALIB 3.0 14C age calibration program, *Radiocarbon*, **35**, 215–30

Swanton, M J, 2000 *The Anglo-Saxon chronicles*, London

Tarlow, S, and Stutz, L N, 2013 *The Oxford handbook of the archaeology of death and burial*, Oxford

Taylor, H, 1906 *The ancient crosses and holy wells of Lancashire*, Manchester

Tobin, S, 1995 *The Cistercians: monks and monasteries of Europe*, London

Torgersen, J H, 1951a The developmental genetics and evolutionary meaning of the metopic suture, *Amer J Phys Anthropol*, **9**, 193-205

Torgersen, J H, 1951b Hereditary factors in the sutural patterns of the skull, *Acta Radiologica*, **36**, 374-82

Tostevin, P, and Iles, P, 1992 Preston Friary: an archaeological evaluation, *Contrebis*, **17**, 62-7

Trotter, M, 1970 Estimation of stature from intact long limb bones, in T D Stewart (ed), *Personal identification in mass disasters*, Nat Mus Natur Hist Smithsonian Inst, Washington DC, 71-83

Tyers, I, 1998 *Tree-ring analysis and wood identification of timbers excavated on the Magistrates Court site, Kingston upon Hull, East Yorkshire*, ARCUS, unpubl rep

Tyers, I, 2001 *The tree-ring analysis of coffin timbers excavated at the Church of St Peter, Barton on Humber, North Lincolnshire*, Centre for Archaeol Rep, **48/2001**, unpubl rep

Tyers, I, 2003 The eastern Baltic timber trade, in A Massing (ed), *The Thornham Parva retable: technique, conservation and context of an English medieval painting*, London, 219-21

Tyers, I, 2008 Tree-ring analysis of medieval timbers, in D Bowsher, T Dyson, N Holder, and I Howell, *The London Guildhall: an archaeological history of a neighbourhood from early medieval to modern times*, MoLAS Monog Ser, **36**, London, 501-4

Tyers, I, 2010 Aspects of the European trade in oak boards to England 1200-1700, in J Kirby, S Nash, and J Cannon (eds), *Trade in artists' materials: markets and commerce in Europe to 1700*, London, 42-9

University of Leicester, 2013 *New understanding of old Leicester* [Online] Available at: http://www.le.ac. uk/richardiii/archaeology/newunderstanding.html (Accessed 11 January 2017)

Waldron, T, 1998 A note on the estimation of height from long-bone measurements, *Int J Osteoarchaeol*, **8**, 75-7

Waldron, T, 2009 *Palaeopathology*, Cambridge

Walker, I W, 1997 *Harold, the last Anglo-Saxon king*, Stroud

Ward, S W, 1990 *Excavations at Chester: the lesser medieval religious houses*, Grosvenor Mus Archaeol Excav Surv Rep, **6**, Chester

Watkin, J, 1987 Objects of stone, fired clay, jet and mica, in P Armstrong and B Ayers, *Excavations in High Street and Blackfriargate*, Hull Old Town Rep Ser, **5**, East Riding Archaeologist, **8**, 191

White, A, 1996 Medieval towns, in R Newman (ed), *The archaeology of Lancashire: present state and future priorities*, Lancaster, 125-38

White, A, 2000 Pottery making in Silverdale and Arnside, *Trans Cumberland Westmorland Antiq Archaeol Soc*, n ser, **100**, 285-91

Whittle, P, 1837 *The history of the borough of Preston, in the County palatine of Lancaster*, **2**, Preston

Williams, A, and Martin, G H, 2002 *Domesday Book: a complete translation*, London

Willis-Bund, J W, and Page, W (eds), 1971 *The Victoria history of the county of Worcester*, **2**, London

Wise, P J, 1985 Hulton Abbey: a century of excavations, *Staffordshire Archaeol Stud*, **2**, 1-19

Wood, P N, Bradley, J E, and Miller, I, 2008 A pottery production site at Samlesbury, near Preston, Lancashire, *Medieval Ceram*, **30**, 21-48

Young, J, Vince, A, and Nailor, V, 2005 *A corpus of Anglo-Saxon and medieval pottery from Lincoln*, Lincoln Archaeol Stud, **7**, Lincoln

INDEX